BRAND MEDICINE

Other books by Interbrand:

Nicholas Kochan *The World's Greatest Brands*
Paul Stobart *Brand Power*
Rita Clifton and Esther Maughan *The Future of Brands*
Susannah Hart and John Murphy *Brands: The New Wealth Creators*
Tom Blackett *Trademarks*
Tom Blackett and Bob Boad *Co-Branding: The Science of Alliance*

Brand Medicine

THE ROLE OF BRANDING IN THE PHARMACEUTICAL INDUSTRY

Edited by

Tom Blackett

and

Rebecca Robins

palgrave

First published 2001 by
PALGRAVE
Houndmills, Basingstoke, Hampshire RG21 6XS and
175 Fifth Avenue, New York, N.Y. 10010
Companies and representatives throughout the world

PALGRAVE is the new global academic imprint of
St. Martin's Press LLC Scholarly and Reference Division and
Palgrave Publishers Ltd (formerly Macmillan Press Ltd).

ISBN 0–333–93098–3 hardcover

This book is printed on paper suitable for recycling and
made from fully managed and sustained forest sources.

A catalogue record for this book is available
from the British Library.

Cataloging-in-Publication Data is available from the Library
of Congress

Editing and origination by
Aardvark Editorial, Mendham, Suffolk

10 9 8 7 6 5 4 3 2 1
10 09 08 07 06 05 04 03 02 01

Printed and bound in Great Britain by
Creative Print & Design (Wales), Ebbw Vale

Contents

Part II
Rx to OTC Switching

3   The Rx to OTC switch – creating the climate
for change GARY LYON *Evidence Based Marketing*   **47**

4   Successful switch strategies
HUGH FERRIER *Sudler & Hennessey*   **60**

Part III
The Rise of Patient Power

5   Direct-to-consumer branding – the US perspective
ANNE DEVEREUX *Merkley Newman Harty Healthworks*   **85**

6   Direct-to-consumer branding – Europe and Asia
ROB BENSON *Bates Health World*   **95**

7   The role of advertising in branding pharmaceuticals
MICHAEL PALING *Paling Walters Targis*   **113**

Part IV
Brand Development

Part V
Trade Mark and Regulatory Issues

Part VI
The Expanding Healthcare Market

17 Complementary and alternative medicines

Part VII
Conclusion

18 The future of branding in the pharmaceutical industry

List of figures

List of tables

List of plates

Acknowledgements

Every successful book is the product not only of the commitment and dedication of each individual author, but also of the valuable contributions of those people who are involved 'behind the scenes'. We would like to thank Tom Harrison, for his advice on the scope of the book, John Murphy, whose brand evangelism sparked the idea for this book, Jan Lindemann, for his good advice on the intricacies of pharmaceutical industry economics and Chris Coke, Tom Blackett's co-editor of *Branding in the Pharmaceutical Industry*, published by FT Management Reports in 1998.

We would also like to thank Alex Zürcher, Catherine Jackson, Emma Baptist and Catriona Crombie for their support throughout the writing and publication of this book. Thanks go to Julian Thomas and Sheila Kelly for their contribution to Jeremy Scholfield's chapter, to Teo Hee Chai, regional manager of Haw Par Healthcare Ltd for providing Patricia Tan with information on Tiger Balm, to Ralph Jackson from the British Museum and to Ruth Oliver for her advice on name research in Rebecca Robins' chapter. Nick Liddell would like to thank Jan Lindemann, Alex Batchelor, Jane Yates, and Stephanie Adams for their helpful comments. Alison Azulay would like to thank her former colleagues at Glaxo Wellcome, Maury Tepper and Tejinder Soor, for their contributions to her chapters on trade mark law and regulatory issues. Special thanks go to Ged Equi and Grant Perry for the cover design.

TOM BLACKETT AND REBECCA ROBINS

The authors and publisher wish to thank the following for their permission to use images:

McNeil Consumer Products Company for Plates 12.3, 12.4 and 12.6a; J&J Merck Consumer Pharmaceuticals for Figure 12.2; Whitehall-Robins Health-care for Figure 12.1 and Plate 12.7; Le Nigen N for Plate 12.6b.

Every effort has been made to trace all the copyright holders but if any have been inadvertently overlooked the publishers will be pleased to make the necessary arrangements at the first opportunity.

Authors' note

Please note that, for ease of reading, trade mark (™) and registered trade mark (®) symbols have been omitted throughout the book.

Notes on contributors

Alison Azulay, a qualified solicitor and trade mark attorney, joined Markforce Associates in January 2000, from Glaxo Wellcome plc. At Glaxo Wellcome, Alison was responsible for intellectual property issues relating to the anti virals and HIV portfolio, with involvement in regulatory and commercial issues. She previously specialized in the intellectual property and sports departments at Bird & Bird. Alison has co-edited *Trade Marks: World Law and Practice* (a *Financial Times* law and tax publication) and has also co-edited *The European Trade Mark Reports*.

Rob Benson is executive vice president and joint head of the Global Business Group of Bates Healthworld. His 23-year marketing career started in consumer brand management at Bristol-Myers Clairol, from which he stepped into the world of advertising at NCK, later part of FCB, and then at The CM Partnership to handle the Sterling Health account. Involvement in the pharmaceutical industry progressed at Milton Healthcare where Rob initiated and managed prescription to OTC switches of brands such as Nicorette, Clarityn and Imodium. From the mid-1990s, now with the Healthworld international network of healthcare agencies, Rob concentrated on the development of international and global brands, especially in the strategic advancement of direct-to-consumer communication of prescription brands in Europe.

Tom Blackett is deputy chairman of the Interbrand Group. Interbrand was founded in London in 1974 and now has 22 offices in 20 countries and employs over 700 people. The company specializes in all aspects relating to the development and management of brands, including name creation, graphic design, trade mark legal services and brand valuation.

Tom joined Interbrand in 1983. He was managing director of the company's London business from 1985 to 1989 and was appointed group deputy chairman in 1996. Experienced in all areas of Interbrand's work, he has handled projects for major international brand owners such as Heineken, British Telecom, Unilever, Glaxo Wellcome, BP Amoco and Volvo.

Before joining Interbrand, Tom worked for five years with Inbucon Management Consultants as research director in their marketing division. This followed five years with Research International, then Unilever's market research subsidiary, and three years with Attwood Statistics, another leading market research firm.

In addition to many articles and papers on issues relating to branding, Tom has published *Trademarks* (1998) and, as co-editor, *Co-Branding* (1999).

David Catlett is a partner and global healthcare director at Ketchum, New York. Prior to joining Ketchum in 1990, David had amassed 25 years of communications experience, 12 of which were in the pharmaceutical industry. He has worked for Abbott Laboratories, G.D. Searle & Co., and Ciba-Geigy Pharmaceuticals, where he was director of public relations. Holding a BA(Hons) degree in journalism from the University of Illinois, David began his career as a journalist, and entered the healthcare field when he joined the Chicago Lung Association.

Stuart Cooper is chief executive officer of Adelphi Group, a premier global healthcare company specializing in Medical Communications and Intelligence. As CEO he has responsibility for its six healthcare divisions in Europe and the USA. Stuart currently takes a specific interest in and management responsibility for the group's communications division. Prior to this Stuart was founder and managing director of the marketing research group Adelphi International Research, and created Adelphi's Health Outcomes joint venture, Mapi Values.

Stuart graduated in economics and politics from the University of London. His career prior to Adelphi encompassed economics, product management, marketing planning and research in the consumer and pharmaceutical industries. He has previously worked for WHSmith, Milk Marketing Board, and ICI Pharmaceuticals (now AstraZeneca) in both UK and international divisions.

Adelphi has worked with virtually all the pharmaceutical global headquarters, preparing and positioning brands for their successful market launch.

Anne Devereux is president and chief operating officer of MNH Healthworks. She is a pioneer in the dynamic environment of consumer healthcare advertising (DTC) and founded Consumer Healthworks for the Omnicom Group of Companies in 1995. Anne directed the firm's rapid growth and thriving corporate culture, providing strategic marketing expertise and creative advertising support in the growth of such brands as Glucophage, Zantac 75, Taxol, Clarityn and Copaxone.

In January 2000, Anne merged Consumer Healthworks with Merkley Newman Harty, the fastest growing, and one of the most innovative consumer agencies in the USA, so Healthworks' clients such as Mercedes, Forbes (and Forbes.com) and Oxford could benefit from Merkley Newman Harty's planning and creative prowess.

Anne harnesses ten years of experience in DTC and professional health-care marketing and education in categories such as metabolics, upper respiratory, oncology, CNS, GI and herbal supplements, with a deep personal commitment to delivering innovative strategic initiatives and creative solutions that generate business results.

Hugo S. Ehrnreich is the research and analysis manager for Datamonitor's Consumer Business Unit. His experience at Datamonitor and with Reuters Business Insight has primarily focused on strategic analysis of the European and global food and drinks industry, with a special focus on change, future trends and innovation. Hugo holds a degree in business administration from Nijenrode University (the Netherlands) and an MSc(Econ) degree from the London School of Economics.

Gareth Evans senior consultant, joined Government Policy Consultants (GPC) in January 2000. He advises a number of key, blue-chip clients within the healthcare industry at UK, European and international levels. He previously worked for the Association of British Pharmaceutical Industries (ABPI) as international affairs manager monitoring both European and international pharmaco-political environments, reporting on and advising member companies and their subsidiaries on any potential implications and forthcoming challenges for industry. Before joining the UK public affairs political arena, Gareth worked in Europe for many years in pharmaceutical/chemical sales and marketing, which provided him with a far-reaching knowledge and understanding of industry and its workings. Having lived and worked abroad, his appreciation for different business cultures is underpinned by his fluency in French and Italian.

Hugh Ferrier is business development director of Sudler & Hennessey Consumer Care – Europe. He joined Sudler & Hennessey from TBWA Worldwide in Brussels, where he handled Novartis Consumer Health pan-European businesses in cough–cold, skincare and analgesics, and directed TBWA Düsseldorf as launch market agency for the diclofenac (Voltaren) Rx to OTC switch.

Previously Hugh managed professional audience communications on Nurofen for Boots Healthcare International, and on Total for Colgate, at Omnicom's healthcare agency, Paling Walters, as well as managing a pharmacist advisory panel, Counterview.

In his career, Hugh has followed a specialization in new product development; first, in brand management at CPC (Best Foods), then at Lintas and Reeves Robertshaw Needham. In healthcare, he has handled brand line extension work for Reckitts, Boots Healthcare International, and Novartis Consumer Health.

Hugh is a graduate of Selwyn College, Cambridge, and a postgraduate of King's College, London.

Tom Harrison was named chairman and chief executive officer of Omnicom Group's Diversified Agency Services (DAS) division in 1998, after serving as president and chief operating officer of the division since 1997. DAS, the world leader in providing marketing services and specialty communications, is the largest and fastest growing unit of Omnicom, the world's largest advertising and marketing services organization.

While president of DAS, Thomas also served as chairman of the Harrison & Star Group, a healthcare advertising and communications group he founded in 1987 and sold to Omnicom in 1992, and chairman of Diversified Healthcare Communications, a group of eight healthcare agencies within Omnicom. The Harrison & Star Group was acknowledged in 1990 as the most successful and rapidly growing agency in the healthcare industry. During his five years running the independent firm, Thomas started a medical education company, a direct-to-consumer healthcare company and a medical PR group and acquired a managed care consultancy.

Prior to starting his own business in 1987, he spent six years with an advertising firm, having began his business career in 1974 as a sales representative for Pfizer Laboratories, where he held positions of increasing authority before being named a marketing director.

Thomas holds an advanced graduate degree in cell biology and physiology from West Virginia University, where he worked on cancer research until moving into the business world.

Nick Liddell is brand valuation consultant with Interbrand Newell & Sorrell. He graduated from Lincoln College at the University of Oxford in 1999 with a BA(Hons) degree in philosophy, politics and economics. Nick began as a consultant with Interbrand in September 1999 and since joining the brand valuation team he has worked on projects with diverse and international clients in various sectors, including financial services, energy, fashion and entertainment. His clients have included major global financial institutions such as Nationwide Bank and American Express, luxury brands, including Prada and Consolidated Gold Bullion, and other international brands including BP and Heineken. Nick was also extensively involved in carrying out an analysis of the top 75 global brands for publication in the *Financial Times* and *Marketing Week*.

Gary Lyon is a director of Evidence Based Marketing, a specialized business planning consultancy, based in the UK. Gary's business experience in the consumer healthcare sector spans 20 years, in international management roles with blue-chip players such as Procter & Gamble, Schering-Plough and Merck & Co. Most recently, he was general manager of Glaxo Wellcome's global OTC operations. He is a 1979 graduate of the Ivey Business School (Ontario, Canada) and completed his MBA/DIC at Imperial College (University of London) in 2000. Comments on his chapter are welcome at lyonmail@aol.com.

Richard Marsh is a director of Government Policy Consultants (GPC) and has worked for the company since April 1996. He advises a number of clients, mainly in the field of pharmaceuticals but has worked across the sphere of the company's activities. He is also the editor of GPC's public affairs journal *Access Politics*. Richard is a former special adviser at the Department of Health, Department of National Heritage and the Department of the Environment. He has worked for Rt Hon. Virginia Bottomley MP, Rt Hon. William Waldegrave, Rt Hon. Michael Portillo MP and Rt Hon. Chris Patten, among others. Immediately before joining GPC he was working in the then Prime Minister's Political Office in Downing Street.

Herbert M. Meyers is the retired founding partner of Gerstman+Meyers. Born in Germany, he served as interpreter in the US Army Air Corps in Europe during the Second World War. Upon his return to the USA Meyers studied design and has a Bachelor of Fine Arts degree from Pratt Institute.

In 1970, after several years' experience as corporate art director and design agency account manager, Herb Meyers joined with Richard Gerstman to found Gerstman+Meyers, a leading brand identity and design consultancy, servicing over a hundred 'Fortune 500' clients worldwide. In 1996, the firm joined Interbrand.

A past president of Package Design Council International and recipient of numerous design awards, Herb Meyers was the first ever to receive the organization's PDC Award for Lifetime Packaging Excellence and Leadership.

A frequent lecturer, Meyers co-authored the book *The Marketer's Guide to Successful Package Design* and contributed chapters to several other professional books. At present he is co-editing *Branding @ the Digital Age* for Interbrand/Palgrave.

Michael Paling is the chairman and managing director of Paling Walters Targis, the UK's largest healthcare advertising agency. He also coordinates the Targis group of agencies. Michael studied zoology at Nottingham University before joining his first pharmaceutical company in 1971, the then Burroughs Wellcome. After amassing sales and marketing experience with Burroughs Wellcome and Winthrop, Michael joined Michael Bungey and Partners to set up a healthcare agency within their group. In 1980 Michael started his own agency, which has since been responsible for many important Rx launches, with over 200 brands and line extensions in total. These include Zantac and Zofran for Glaxo Wellcome, Innovace and Pepcid for Merck Sharp and Dohme, Opren and Zyprexa for Lilly and Viagra for Pfizer, to name but a few.

Rebecca Robins is a senior consultant of Interbrand Healthcare in New York. Prior to joining the New York office, she worked in the London office of Interbrand for four years.

Rebecca has managed brand name development projects for a diverse range of clients, including Glaxo Wellcome, AstraZeneca, Oxford Glyco-Sciences, Ford, Philips, Boots, Sony, Reuters and British Airways. She has also worked on a number of brand identity and packaging projects. One of her specialist areas of interest is branding in the pharmaceutical industry and she has worked with many of the major pharmaceutical companies.

Rebecca graduated from Cambridge University with a First Class degree in French and German and an M Phil in European Literature. Rebecca has a passion for languages and is currently learning Italian.

Jeremy Scholfield heads up a specialist brand identity team at Interbrand Newell and Sorrell. Jeremy graduated in graphic design from the London College of Printing in 1980. After heading up the design unit at the advertising agency LansdownEuro he joined Interbrand Newell and Sorrell in 1980, becoming a board director in 1990. Jeremy has directed projects for Schweppes, Coca-Cola, Procter & Gamble, Seagram, Universal Music and AstraZeneca. His work has won many awards including a DBA Design Effectiveness Award, two Clios and an International Global Award. Most recently he has worked extensively with Boots the Chemist in the development of a distinct visual language for their own brand medicines ranges.

Patricia Tan joined Interbrand in October 2000. After spending her first three months in London learning the ropes, she returned to Singapore in early 2001. Interbrand is Patricia's first foray into the private sector. Previously, she has worked in the Singapore Embassy in Washington and the Asia-Europe Foundation, and taught at Stanford University in Palo Alto, CA. Diplomacy and academia may not be the usual inroads into branding, but they share common ground in the mantra: persuade, convince, enthral.

Patricia received her BA and MA from Stanford University, and completed her doctorate this year at Oxford University. Her thesis was entitled Idea Factories: American Efforts in Denazification and Democratisation in the Germany after the Second World War – in fact, effecting ideological and behavioural change at the national level could be seen as an ultimate challenge for good branding, if there ever was one!

Julian Thomas is a project and marketing consultant in the branding and packaging team of Interbrand Newell and Sorrell, working with clients such as Dillons, Seagram, Bass and Laura Ashley. He became an associate director of Interbrand in 2000.

Julian has a degree in history from Edinburgh University and upon graduating, he joined John Swire & Sons in their management programme. He was posted to Australia, Taiwan and Hong Kong in various marketing positions. Much of his time was spent developing Cathay Pacific's International Rugby Sevens and Cricket Sixes events and in launching new destinations for the airline. His interest in brands took him to Leo Burnett Advertising in London where he worked on accounts as diverse as Procter & Gamble's Daz, McDonald's, Tropicana and United Airlines. He was instrumental in setting up their Innovations Unit which encouraged clients to widen their brands' horizons.

List of abbreviations

ABPI	Association of the British Pharmaceutical Industry
ACE	angiotensin-converting enzyme
AoA	Administration on Aging (US)
BAN	British Approved Name
BMA	British Medical Association
CTM	Community Trade Mark
DCF	Dénomination Commune Français
DCIt	Denominazione Comune Italiana
DTC	direct to consumer
EFPIA	European Federation of Pharmaceutical Industries and Associations
EMEA	European Agency for the Evaluation of Medicinal Products
EU	European Union
FDA	Food and Drug Administration (USA)
FMCG	fast-moving consumer goods
FSAB	Financial Accounting Standards Bureau (USA)
HMO	health maintenance organization
INN	International Non-proprietary Name
JAN	Japanese Approved Name
NICE	National Institute for Clinical Excellence (England and Wales)
NSAID	non-steroidal anti-inflammatory drug
OTC	over the counter
POMs	prescription-only medicines
PPRS	Pharmaceutical Price Regulation Scheme (UK)
PTO	Patent and Trade Mark Office (USA)
R&D	research and development

ROI	return on investment
RPM	retail price maintenance
Rx	prescription-only medicine
USAN	United States Approved Name
VMS	vitamin and mineral supplements
WTO	World Trade Organization

Introduction

TOM BLACKETT Interbrand

It seems extraordinary that one of the world's largest consumer good markets – pharmaceuticals – should for so long have flourished with little help from brands. In most other industries, manufacturers, suppliers of services and retailers use branding techniques to help secure competitive advantage. Indeed, increasingly these days, it is the brand which provides the sole means of differentiation, as *Fortune* magazine famously said:

> In the 21st century, branding ultimately will be the only unique differentiator between companies. Brand equity is now a key asset.

What *Fortune* is asserting is that sooner or later, given the increasing ubiquity of capital, technology and skilled workforces, most companies in most industries will be competing on a level playing field. In these circumstances the reputation encapsulated in their brands will become the chief determinant of customer choice.

It has often been said that brands are the true expression of democracy because they thrive in situations where choice is unrestricted and perfect competition exists. This is not so in the pharmaceutical industry, where the relationship between the consumer and the manufacturer is heavily mediated. Regulatory bodies sanction and control the availability of medicines; governments and insurance companies determine what the consumer must pay; and the drug manufacturers themselves are severely constrained in what they can say directly to consumers about their products and their properties. As Rob Benson, who writes in his chapter 'Direct-to-consumer branding – Europe and Asia', says of the industry:

I

[it is] still heavily dependent worldwide on government health expenditure for reimbursement-sourced revenue and product licence approvals, all controlled by powerful regulatory forces resistant to anything that they perceive might upset the public balance sheet.

In most mature economies, therefore, the pharmaceutical industry has been sucked into the maw of public policy, and its well-being is subject to the reforming whim of political parties to a much greater extent than it is to the requirements of the consumer.

These conditions are inimical to brands. Brands thrive where the relationship between buyer and seller is direct and open, where choice is transparent and availability unrestricted. Few of these requirements exist within the prescription pharmaceuticals market. Yet the industry is huge and has great value; it has learned to cope with the extraordinary degree of regulation placed upon it and would seemingly have no need for brands. Why is this?

Quite simply, it is because the power of invention has been paramount in creating the industry's wealth. The pharmaceutical industry is science based and its huge success has been due largely to its ability to invent great new products for the benefit of mankind. My friend and former colleague John Murphy, who founded Interbrand in 1974, often used to chide drugs companies by saying that the Coca-Cola Corporation, without a patent to its name but with one of the world's oldest and most valuable trade marks, is a hugely successful business – while the pharmaceutical industry, flush with patents but bereft largely of meaningful brands, expends huge amounts of cash and energy in the development of intellectual property of a comparatively evanescent quality.

In June 2000 Interbrand published its list of the world's 75 most valuable brands (this may be found in the Appendix at the end of the book). Not one pharmaceutical brand or company name featured in this list. The majority of the brands featured have been in existence at least since the Second World War, although it was notable that, compared to the same league table published in 1999, several new economy brands, such as Yahoo!, Amazon.com and AOL had entered the reckoning. Perhaps this is not surprising – but for the pharmaceutical industry it should be a matter of some concern.

Most analyses of the source of company value nowadays point to intangible rather than tangible assets as the chief wealth creators within a business. Investors place a high premium on knowledge-based companies and on companies that own distinct and defensible assets such as brands. Thus proprietary skills and reputation will be the basis on which successful companies compete in the future. How true will this be of the pharmaceutical industry? If ever there was an industry where the biggest and most successful companies depended upon proprietary skills and the mantle of patents to create value, then this was it. The present round of mergers and acquisitions taking place within the industry testifies to the very high value placed on innovation, and the sheer cost of achieving this. There is a never-ending need for new and more effective products; patent law exists to protect the interests of innovative companies and virtually guarantees that, if the product works and the marketing is good, then the company will more than recoup its investment and make a handsome profit. But the rights conferred in a patent rarely last more than 20 years, and as it can take up to 10 years to get a new product to the marketplace, the patent owner has only a limited period of exclusivity. The rights conferred in a trade mark, however, can last indefinitely, subject to the regular renewal of the registration and other rules of maintenance which are far from onerous.

While it is almost certain that patents will remain the chief source of corporate economic value added for many leading pharmaceutical companies, there are a series of important and irreversible developments taking place which militate in favour of brands.

Governments everywhere are seeking to mitigate the cost of state-subsidized healthcare. This is already huge, and with the forecast increase in the elderly population is likely to grow to an unmanageable size. Transferring the cost of medicine from the public to the private purse will help partially to alleviate this, and encouraging the pharmaceutical manufacturers to make more products available over the counter (OTC) will be an important part of this strategy. But in order for this to be effective, major changes will be required in consumer behaviour based on wider understanding of the nature of the medicines becoming available.

This will necessitate a revolution in communication, more widespread channels of distribution (including the Internet) and regulatory changes. Many of these things are already happening, such as the dramatic growth in direct-to-consumer (DTC) advertising in the United States, and some are still years away. Nevertheless there is an irresistible force in the market, driven largely by government will, that means that consumers must be encouraged to take much greater responsibility for their well-being. For them to do so they will require unfettered access to information, freedom of choice, first class products and good value for money. It is in situations like these that brands thrive – yet the pharmaceutical industry at large has little experience in creating and managing brands.

Interestingly, these circumstances could well bring about a transformation in the way the industry creates value for its shareholders. The pharmaceutical industry is a highly successful and wealthy one; the leading players have for many years been the stars of the world's stock markets through ever-expanding sales and profits. Sales growth to a large extent has come about through huge economic improvements in the Third World, increasing longevity and the demands of the elderly, and success in the development of drugs for the treatment of hitherto intractable diseases. These factors will continue to drive the growth of the industry, but there are signs that it is becoming increasingly difficult to sustain the levels of innovation necessary to deliver the successful new products of the future. Without these products profit margins will fall and returns to investors will suffer.

The industry is of course alert to this threat and during the last few years we have seen several major mergers (for example Glaxo Wellcome with SmithKline Beecham, Astra with Zeneca, Pharmacia with Upjohn) as companies have sought to improve the productivity of research and development, widen product portfolios and optimize sales and marketing costs. Many companies are now actively pursuing the sale of OTC brands as a way of building sales, recognizing that in these brands they have potentially a new source of business value. Many companies too are seeking ways to exploit established Rx (prescription-only medicine) brand names in the OTC world, with a view to leveraging the reputations of these names with pharmacists and consumers. Others are seeking to introduce entirely new brands to the wider OTC market and are faced with the formidable task of building consumer awareness and confidence. Whatever the strategy, brands have a central role to play in the future of the industry.

All this is happening at a time of growing awareness of and interest in well-being. Functional foods (or nutraceuticals as they are sometimes called) and alternative (natural) medicines have become immensely popular with consumers who attach a high importance to maintaining healthy lifestyles. A few years ago, interest in such products would have been regarded as faddish. Nowadays their use is considered perfectly normal – and indeed a very sensible alternative to a visit to the doctor's surgery. Both functional foods and alternative medicines are unrestricted in their availability, and the power of choice lies entirely with the consumer. Conventional medicine still dominates in the West, but such is the interest in natural remedies that it is not inconceivable that in many therapeutic areas they may come to dominate.

This book endeavours to comment on all these major trends and provide some advice on how brands and the branding process can be made integral to future business strategy. We examine the chief drivers of change, in particular the Internet and the growth of DTC advertising; government policy; the ageing population; the Rx to OTC switch; and trends in communication and brand building, together with the complex regulatory frameworks that circumscribe these.

Throughout we have tried to focus on the value-adding contribution that strong brands can make to corporate performance. The pharmaceutical industry possesses some strong, well-established brands, a large number of which enjoy little or no patent protection. Brands such as Ventolin, Clarityn and Canesten continue to be valuable to their owners because during their years of exclusivity they created a momentum in demand. This momentum helped to cushion them against the effects of generic competition. Each brand has now become so well known that it stands for a set of distinctive characteristics and benefits, the net impact of which is the belief on the part of prescribers, pharmacists and consumers that the brand is superior to imitations. In a competitive situation this belief may not be strong enough to justify paying more, but given parity – or near parity – in price then the tried and trusted brand will usually enjoy an advantage. A strong brand, therefore, has the ability to command reliable cash flows.

A patent also has an ability to secure strong cash flows which, over its useful life, will be superior to that of the brand. But once the patent lapses, so its economic value to its owner evaporates. It seems to us, therefore, that the role of the brand manager is to ensure that the strong reputation a successful patented drug achieves during its period of exclusivity should, through appropriate marketing and development, be absorbed by the brand name. Then, when the time comes, decisions can be taken on whether to continue to market aggressively the branded generic, exploit the brand's equity in the OTC arena or, as is increasingly the case, implement both strategies.

Successful pharmaceutical companies are rich in intellectual property. Historically this property has taken the form of patents. Now brands can add layers of sustainable value to these hard-won assets, and the skill in prolonging a good product's life lies in managing the branding process. This we believe will be the future of value creation in the pharmaceutical industry.

PART I

The Pharmaceutical Industry: Science meets Business

1 Branding and its potential within the pharmaceutical industry

TOM BLACKETT Interbrand

A short history of brands

The word brand comes from the Old Norse *brandr*, meaning 'to burn', and it was by this means that early man stamped ownership on his livestock. With the development of trade, buyers would use brands as a means of distinguishing between the cattle of one farmer and another, and brands quickly became associated with quality and reliability. Thus brands provided buyers with a guide to choice, a role that has remained unchanged to the present day.

Some of the earliest manufactured goods in mass production were clay pots, the remains of which can be found in great abundance around the Mediterranean region. There is considerable evidence among them of the use of brands, which in their earliest form were the potter's mark (Plate 1.1), but these gradually became more sophisticated through the use of the maker's name or devices such as a cross or star. Under the civilizing influence of the Romans, and with the growth of towns and cities, shopkeepers – including apothecaries, the earliest dealers in medicines – would use signs to advertise their trade (Plate 1.2). In Rome, principles of commercial law developed which acknowledged the origin and title of potters' marks but this did not deter makers of inferior quality pots from imitating the marks of well-known manufacturers in order to dupe the public. Examples of fake Roman pottery, manufactured by crafty Belgian potters and exported to Britain for sale to the gullible natives, can be found today in the British Museum.

With the decline and fall of the Roman Empire, the elaborate and highly sophisticated system of trade that had bound together the Mediterranean and Northern European peoples gradually crumbled. Brands continued to be used but mainly on a local scale, a situation which remained for almost 1000 years until the Renaissance. This period of stunning artistic and scientific advancement brought with it huge increases in international trade. And as trade expanded so did recognition of brands, typically on such desirable items as high quality furniture, porcelain and tapestries.

The widespread use of brands, however, is essentially a phenomenon of the late 19th and 20th centuries. The Industrial Revolution, with its improvements in manufacturing and communications, opened up the civilized world and allowed the mass marketing of consumer products. Indeed, many of today's best-known brands date from that period. Singer sewing machines, Coca-Cola soft drinks, Bass beer, Quaker Oats, Cook's tours, Sunlight soap, Shredded Wheat, Kodak film, American Express travellers cheques, Heinz baked beans and Prudential Insurance are just a few examples.

Hand in hand with the introduction of these brands came early trade mark legislation. This allowed the owners of these names to protect them in law (indeed, the Bass 'Red Triangle' trade mark was the very first registered in the United Kingdom, in 1876, and the beaming Quaker man is now well into his second century). The birth of advertising agencies such as J Walter Thompson and NW Ayer in the late 19th century gave further impetus to the development of brands.

However, it is the period since the end of the Second World War, during which profound improvements to the well-being of much of the world's population have taken place, that has seen the real explosion in the use of brands. Propelled by the collapse of Communism, the arrival of the Internet and mass broadcasting systems, and greatly improved transportation and communications, brands have come to symbolize the convergence of the world's economies on the demand- rather than command-led model. But brands have not escaped criticism. The anti-capitalism protests that took place at the World Trade Organization (WTO) meeting in Seattle in 1999, and London's Carnival of Capitalism, were significant events. They provided a timely reminder to the big brand owners that in the conduct of their affairs they have a duty to society, as well as to customers and shareholders. This said, however, brands have become the ultimate expression of democracy.

Brands as business assets

A glance at the following table shows to what a large extent the stock market value of such major companies as Coca-Cola, Nokia and General Electric depends upon the quality of their intangible assets (Table 1.1).

The stock market value of the Coca-Cola Corporation, for example, is around $140 billion; yet the book value (the net asset value) of the business is only $10 billion. Therefore a vast proportion of the value of the business is dependent

TABLE 1.1

The world's most valuable brands

Company	Stock market value $bn	Net book value $bn	Intangibles as a % of market value	Brand value $bn
Coca-Cola	142	10	93	73
Microsoft	421	28	93	70
IBM	194	21	89	53
intel	448	33	93	39
NOKIA	240	8	97	39
GE	524	43	92	38
Ford	49	28	44	36
Disney	81	44	46	34
McDonald's	44	10	78	28
AT&T	119	71	40	26

Source: Interbrand/Citibank League table, 2000

upon shareholders' confidence in the *intangible* assets. In the case of Coca-Cola, the company has few intangibles other than the contracts it holds with its global network of bottlers and distributors – and its brand name. An independent analysis conducted by Interbrand estimated that the value of the Coca-Cola brand name in mid-2000 was $73 billion, over half of its intangible value. Similarly, high-profile consumer brands Disney and McDonald's can attribute a huge proportion (80–90%) of their intangible value to their brands. At the other end of the scale, for two of the world's largest companies, General Electric and Intel, the ratio of brand value to intangible value is one tenth of Disney and

McDonald's. Both General Electric and Intel are rich in intangibles, but as these are linked to the technology in which these companies excel, they probably take the form of patents and know-how agreements. In this sense General Electric and Intel must be very similar to successful pharmaceutical companies, whose absence from the Interbrand brand league table is conspicuous.

It is not surprising that much of the merger and acquisition activity of the last 15 years or so has involved brand-owning businesses. The durability of brands and their earning power (unlike relatively short-lived technology assets such as patents) and their widespread appeal make them highly desirable properties. The globalization of trade is driving consolidation in many industries and a recent example has been the purchase, for $21 billion, of Bestfoods by Unilever. Bestfoods owns many famous food brands, notably Knorr stock cubes and Hellmann's mayonnaise. These brands have truly global potential, which is more likely to be tapped by a company of the size and scale of Unilever than by Bestfoods, which is large but lacks Unilever's global resources. Equally, in 1998 Volkswagen concluded a deal to acquire Rolls-Royce Motor Cars from Vickers, the UK engineering group, for around £400 million. VW's interest was not in acquiring a pile of venerable manufacturing plant in Derby, the home of Rolls-Royce, but in the famous Rolls-Royce and Bentley brand names, the crown jewels of the global automobile industry. But in an interesting twist to this tale, Rolls-Royce Aero Engines, the owners of the Roll-Royce brand name, refused to grant a licence in perpetuity to VW, handing this instead to BMW, VW's ancient rival. There can be little doubt these brands will thrive under new ownership, as both VW and BMW have state-of-the-art manufacturing and truly global resources far exceeding those of the former owner.

Branding in the pharmaceutical industry

In view of the widespread acceptance nowadays of brands as valuable strategic assets, it seems strange that little evidence exists that the pharmaceutical industry takes long-term brand building very seriously. Perhaps this is because of the characteristics of the industry which, apart from the over-the-counter (OTC) sector (which functions in much the same way as other retail markets), is completely unlike any other. The prescription-only medicine (Rx) sector – which contributes around 90% of global pharmaceuticals revenue – is highly regulated and subject to government and political intervention. Access to information about products has hitherto been restricted to doctors and health-care professionals only. Direct-to-consumer (DTC) advertising is a very recent development and available, largely, only in the USA. And buyers and consumers of products remain in effect separate parties. For manufacturers, the traditional sources of value creation have lain in successful research and development (R&D) – an increasingly difficult and elusive goal – and in agile sales and marketing. The industry retains many old-fashioned, supply-driven characteristics, overlain with government paternalism. The 'Nanny knows best' syndrome still thrives.

The emphasis on product development as the key to commercial success is, of course, no bad thing. Any attempt to eradicate the world's diseases must be applauded and we should not begrudge the profits that might flow from this. Equally we should not criticize the very high level of competitiveness that exists in the industry. Speed to market with new, patented products can bear rich rewards – and manufacturers would argue that the prices they set are not just to reward investment in one successful new product line, but in the many other, unsuccessful, products that never see light of day.

Unlike other consumer goods industries, therefore, the chief motivating force in mergers and acquisitions within the pharmaceutical industry is not the desire of one company to acquire and exploit more successfully the brands of another. Rather it is the R&D and sales and marketing assets that provide the attraction. This would explain all the major mergers and planned mergers of recent years – Pharmacia & Upjohn with American Home Products, Ciba with Sandoz, Astra with Zeneca, Glaxo Wellcome with SmithKline Beecham, Pfizer with Warner-Lambert. Yet despite all this merger activity the biggest grouping – GlaxoSmithKline – will still have only 8% value share of the global pharmaceuticals market. (A word of caution. A recent article in the *Financial Times* (October 2000), commenting on the Pfizer–Warner-Lambert merger, said: 'The deal is going well. Cost savings, at $400 million this year and $1.6 billion by 2002, are ahead of schedule, allowing Pfizer to predict earnings growth of at least 25% a year for the next three.' Yet investors should not be that easily mollified. Drug mergers usually produce an early boost from one-off savings. Few, if any, have delivered a higher long-term growth rate for the enlarged company.)

Yet, for all the emphasis on R&D and the acquisition of patents, the pharmaceutical industry is not wholly agnostic towards brands as a source of potential value. Transactions have in the past taken place, and continue to take place, involving brands, albeit OTC brands. SmithKline Beecham acquired Sterling's OTC operations (famous for Andrews Liver Salts) in 1994; Warner-Lambert and Warner-Wellcome, two marketing operations rather than research-based companies, merged in 1996. Most recently Boots, the UK healthcare and chemists company, announced that it was buying the acne treatment brand Clearasil from Procter & Gamble, paying the company £230 million.

Indeed, over 100 years ago, Thomas Beecham recognized the importance of branding his safe and effective new laxative 'Beechams Pills'. This started a new trend in the marketing of medicines by attaching a personal guarantee of the product's effectiveness, enabling it to stand out from the plethora of other products on the pharmacist's shelves which were likely to cause as much harm as good. As knowledge grew and medicines began to become effective for a whole range of previously untreatable symptoms and conditions, so the pharmaceutical industry prospered. However, as the market expanded, so too did restrictions on product claims and the communication of information, as cautious governments, no doubt for the very best of motives, sought to control consumer demand.

Thus, in reaction to government restrictions and the host of other non-conducive factors mentioned above, the cultivation of brands and the practice of branding has been confined to relatively safe OTC products. The disciplines of branding in the pharmaceutical industry have therefore not developed as the market as a whole has developed. Originators of new medicines have spent increasing amounts to develop new compounds, but relatively little on the brand once it has been registered successfully for use by the medical authorities.

Nor, with very few exceptions, is the pharmaceutical industry noted for building on those brands which *have* become successful. Brands such as Penbritin (ampicillin), Valium (diazepam) and Terramycin (oxytetracycline) were all launched within the last 40 years and became huge successes. All, however, now languish, overtaken by newer and more successful compounds: a sad waste of once-powerful brands.

A major problem with the industry appears to lie in the constant cycle of product improvement; hence new brands are constantly being introduced at the expense of existing products. Thus, when more effective cancer treatments and a novel molecule for the treatment of schizophrenia arrive through the pipeline, existing brands become demoted in importance and transferred to cash cow status. It is hardly surprising then that, with support being withdrawn, brands that were carefully nurtured and polished in their youth become old and decay with alarming rapidity.

Why branding is important

With the cost of R&D rising and the success rate static at best, the need to exploit fully those new products that come to market has never been so crucial. A way in which such success can be enhanced is by branding. This is because when values other than sheer technical excellence are cultivated in the brand name it is possible to create benefits for health authorities, prescribers and patients alike, which in time will come to strengthen the bond between buyer and seller. Drawing upon established branding practice, mainly in the non-prescription drugs world, some of the potential advantages for the brand owner are as follows.

■ A powerful brand provides the platform to build a *relationship with customers* on an individual basis, and for the manufacturer to 'reach over the shoulder of the middle man', as HG Wells famously wrote, 'direct to the consumer'. The strength of the Nike brand with consumers has made the Nike range a 'must have' for any shoe retailer, and no retailer worth his (or her) salt can afford not to stock the brand. Pharmaceutical manufacturers whose brands enjoy 'must have' status with health authorities, prescribers and healthcare professionals can enjoy similar advantages. The rise of DTC advertising and the ubiquity of the Internet can help brand owners create such a relationship – and there is little that those government and regulatory bodies who, Canute-like, wish to resist the encroaching tide of information can do about it.

■ A powerful brand provides significant *competitive differentiation*, of a type that is extremely difficult for rivals to copy. Recognition is gradually being given to the role that branding can play in the post-patent stage of a product's life, as strong branding may confer additional time for the owner to maximize return on its original investment. For a major brand with sales of $1 billion a year, the extension of its primacy by only 100 days would be sufficient to recover the total cost of its R&D. The patent to Glaxo Wellcome's aciclovir has now expired. As a result, topical Zovirax, Glaxo Wellcome's OTC variant for the treatment of cold sores, is starting to feel the effect of generic competition. Bayer launched Soothelip (topical aciclovir) in December 1997 but Glaxo Wellcome, by managing the heritage and established recognition of Zovirax as the prescribed product, made it significantly more difficult for Bayer to compete in this sector.

■ A powerful brand can *cross the borders of countries and markets*. Virgin is a classic example of a brand that has successfully translated into a number of sectors – air travel, record shops, financial services, mobile telephony – often on an international basis. Brands with broad-based appeal can provide a cost-effective way of leveraging value for their owners, and a guarantee of consistency of satisfaction for their customers. In the pharmaceutical market, the opportunity to carry brand value over into new market sectors is becoming increasingly attractive with the growth of the OTC sector. Examples of brands that have managed the transition are Diflucan, Canesten and Zovirax. The jury is perhaps out with Zantac and Tagamet.

▥ A powerful brand can *influence behaviour and attitudes*. As consumer attitudes towards personal computers have changed radically since the advent
of Microsoft, so attitudes towards depression have undergone a transformation since the introduction of Prozac in the late 1980s. Books have been
written about the Prozac generation and this immensely successful brand
has acquired almost iconic status, which should help it to withstand some
of the worst ravages of the post-patent era.

▥ A powerful brand which attracts *customer loyalty* can provide one of the
greatest sources of wealth for a business, by its ability to secure, through
customer commitment, more predictable cash flows ('quality earnings' as
the financial community lip-smackingly refers to it). Branding has now
become a management tool, and through financial evaluation techniques
(described later in Chapter 2) it is now possible to measure the value
creation performance of brands within a given portfolio, and to plan
marketing investment accordingly. As has been demonstrated in so many
other industries, successful brands can deliver enhanced shareholder value
and add significantly to the worth of the business.

Building brand values

At the heart of all brands lies a set of values. Values, quite simply, are beliefs
that customers have about a brand that they find intuitively attractive, and
which are likely to influence their purchase decision. As such they represent
the foundation stones of the buyer–seller relationship. These beliefs can sometimes be entirely rational in character and based on the functionality of the
product per se. 'I buy Coke because it tastes better than Pepsi.' 'I always use
Tide because it washes whiter.' 'Nurofen seems to work best for me because
it gets rid of my headache quickly and doesn't make me feel drowsy.'

These beliefs can also be non-rational in character and based on emotions.
'Coke is a truly international brand – it doesn't recognize boundaries in race,
colour or geography – those are the sort of ideals I can identify with.' 'Tide
makes me feel I'm doing a good job as a mum.' 'Nurofen is a really modern
brand, not just another aspirin variant.'

A host of different influences drives the development of consumers' belief
systems: personal experience, advertising, the purchasing environment, packaging design, brand name and logo, other buyers and their experiences, and so
on. The art of good brand management lies in controlling, as far as possible,
the influences that shape these beliefs, so that at the moment of truth – the
point when the brand is purchased and consumed – the customer is satisfied.

Values can be categorized as follows:

■ *Functional values:* 'what the brand *does* for me'. For Nurofen these values might be 'fast', 'effective' and 'no side effects'.

■ *Expressive values:* 'what the brand *says about* me'. For Tide these might be 'a caring housewife and mother'.

■ *Central values:* 'what the brand and I *share at a fundamental level*'. For Coke these might be 'citizen of the world'.

By their very nature functional values are innate to the product; expressive values are built through the brand's communications, environments and employees; and central values lie at the very heart of the brand's aspirations. When Groucho Marx said that he wouldn't want to belong to a club that would have him as a member, he was employing a complex mixture of expressive and central value judgements.

The best brands of course will have a combination of these values – and there is an excellent example to be found in pharmaceuticals. Renitec (enalapril), a Merck brand known as Innovace in the UK, is an angiotensin-converting enzyme (ACE) inhibitor for the treatment of hypertension. Its values might be classified as follows:

■ *Functional values* (for the GP and the patient): lowers blood pressure with a single daily dose; proven protection from heart attack; for all types of patient with high blood pressure.

■ *Expressive values* (for the GP): possibly a discerning prescriber.

■ *Central values* (for the GP and the patient): low risk.

Renitec/Innovace competes in a crowded marketplace with, literally, dozens of other compounds. All these products have proven effectiveness. Indeed, if any of the leading pharmaceutical sectors are examined, it will be found that there is an abundance of choice in terms of products and types of treatment. In the treatment of hypertension there is also a range of calcium antagonists, including amlodipine, felodipine, isradipine, lacidipine, nicardipine, nifedipine and nisoldipine. However, the degree to which any of these can claim to have developed competitive differentiation is questionable; their advantages have been relatively short lived and have relied mainly on patents.

Given the fundamental importance of demonstrating that a newly discovered substance will work and is safe, it is not surprising that the main emphasis of the industry has been in promoting *functional* brand values; particularly:

■ *Efficacy:* does the product work in its chosen therapeutic area? Will patients get better as a result of taking this product?

■ *Safety:* is the product safe to take, and without side effects? In fact, many of the advances recently have been for drugs that are more specific so that they have minimal incidence of side effects.

■ *Convenience:* if the product has a complicated dosage requirement, or unpleasant way of being taken (injection, nasty taste) it is much more difficult to get patients to comply with necessary treatment.

■ *Cost-effectiveness:* the cost of new drugs is often seen as a barrier since there is an automatic belief that any new product will be more expensive than the previous therapy, although this is not always the case.

It is rare for pharmaceutical companies to explore, develop and promote *expressive* values with which patients might identify. This might be undertaken for such lifestyle products as contraceptive pills, and to a lesser extent for hormone replacement therapy, but nearly always the expressive values – such as they are – will be directed at the physician and not the end-user.

A notable exception, in terms of actively developing expressive values, is Zestril (lisinopril), by the then-named Zeneca. The compound was first launched in 1991 in the UK where it competed with the Merck product Carace (lisinopril) for the treatment of hypertension. Management at Zeneca chose a promotional campaign based on the promise that patients would regain a 'zest for life'. The expressive values were illustrated with humorous visuals illustrating the lifestyle benefits ('become a new person') that would accrue from use of Zestril. By contrast, Carace focused on functional values. There was a serious purpose behind the Zestril approach since the principal way of maintaining blood pressure levels before the introduction of ACE inhibitors such as Zestril had been beta blockers. While these compounds were effective in lowering blood pressure, they were also known to have a low incidence of causing mild depressive-like symptoms. The Zestril campaign was able to combine the functional value of effectiveness without side effects, and this translated into the expressive value of lifestyle enhancement, emphasized in advertising and promotion.

Because lisinopril was one of the earlier ACE inhibitors, many primary care doctors waited for hospital doctor endorsement before prescribing the drug. The culture in hospitals is such that the use of generic prescribing is encouraged at all times, with the result that patients go back to their family doctor with a short-term prescription for the generic name. Within a short space of time general practitioners were writing the same term – lisinopril – but prescriptions were being filled by pharmacists as Zestril. This was attributed to the greater effect of the advertising campaign on the pharmacists and the company's tactic of treating this important group with as much importance as primary care doctors. (Mike Paling has more to say about Zestril and Carace in Chapter 7.)

Building brand strategy

The classic approach to developing brand strategy involves a series of stages in which the following are defined:

- Brand positioning
- Brand personality
- Brand values
- Unique values of the brand that support the values
- How the brand appears to its audience.

Brand positioning

To be competitive, brands must be distinctive. They must possess defining characteristics that are perceived by customers to be unique, attractive and relevant to their needs. These characteristics may be functional – based on product attributes and performance – or emotional – based on perceived benefits or pleasures which flow from the brand experience. Positioning is the analytical process that helps to define the competitive space available to the brand and then states, as the foundation of all subsequent branding activity, how this will be filled. The most successful brands occupy positions in the minds of their customers that are unique and defensible; the branding process is to do with putting the brands in place and keeping them there.

Developing a powerful and distinctive brand positioning involves a series of activities:

- Understanding the product and its area of competence (effectiveness)

- Understanding the needs of different segments of the market

- Identifying the most attractive segment

- Developing the brand so that it can with full justification claim to own a benefit that is relevant to the needs of the target audience

- Evaluating the uniqueness and value of the benefit(s) to the target market

- Depending on the fit between the intended and perceived positioning (blend of benefits), refining the brand according to customer response.

The majority of the world's most successful brands started life with a functional point of difference that was admired by customers and prompted their choice. But as competitors crowded in, the trailblazers were driven to seek alternative ways of maintaining their appeal. Coca-Cola, as ever, is a great example. When it first appeared in Dr Pemberton's drug store, back in the 1880s, its formula was unique. Then, as competition arrived in the shape of other cola drinks, it was driven to seek, and annex, areas of competitive advantage that other brands did not occupy: hence 'refreshment' and the slogan 'Coke refreshes you best'. Refreshment, as a *rational* claim, out-positions all competitors. Over the years the refreshment platform has led to 'enjoyment', 'sociability', 'togetherness' and 'universality', the core of Coke's *emotional* appeal.

So it is with pharmaceutical brands: their positioning must perforce be based on effectiveness or they would not be viable. The promise, and delivery, of effectiveness engenders trust, perhaps the most powerful of all emotions. Beliefs about pharmaceutical brands and their effectiveness occupy a different corner of the brain than that of cola drinks. Relief from illness, pain or discomfort is a far higher needs state than the alleviation of thirst. Trust in pharmaceutical brands, therefore, is a more vital and hard-won commodity. But once gained it can be leveraged most successfully in the brand-building process.

Brand personality

Brand personality builds on the emotional appeal of brands and is the medium through which these, in advertising and through visual identity, are expressed. Therefore it is an important differentiating factor in positioning brands. Brands can be positioned as masculine or feminine, young or old, authoritative or light hearted, radical or conservative, according to how advertising and visual identity are used. Brands can reflect human personality traits and can align themselves closely with the aspirations of their target audience.

Advertising in medical magazines is replete with beaming geriatrics exemplifying the virtues of the latest treatment for incontinence, or amorous fifty-somethings whose marital bliss has been restored by Viagra. Such crass stereotyping may be effective in capturing – for the briefest moment – the attention of hard-pressed doctors, but the industry must appreciate that only a subtler touch is likely to succeed with modern consumers, sophisticated and sceptical as they are.

Brand values

These of course are the glue that binds the customer to the brand. They are referred to above. They *must* be linked to the brand's attributes – the reality of the offer – or they will have absolutely no credibility. Moments of truth are critical to the brand/customer relationship. (Some cynics, however, have commented that, in pharmaceuticals, *placebo* is often the most powerful brand.)

Mike Paling, in Chapter 7, reflects on how so much brand advertising – because it is aimed at GPs – focuses on product attributes, and how so little focuses on the patient's emotional needs. That this should be so is perfectly understandable, as it is a function of the supply chain of medicines. But what it highlights is that while the functional needs of doctors and their patients are very much the same, there is a whole layer of additional support – reassurance – that the patient needs. Information about, and access to, pharmaceutical products will soon be only a click away: this is when brands will really come into their own.

Unique attributes of the brand that support the values

What are the functional and emotional elements of the brand that can support the brand's core values? Where is the proof? With Rx products there should be abundant scientific evidence that the claims made for the product are true: this is mandatory. A number of official and quasi-official regulatory bodies exist in countries such as the UK to ensure that no bogus products slip through the net. With OTC products much the same applies; and as many OTC products have been on the market for decades, longevity – and the trust built up over the years – can also provide powerful emotional justification.

How the brand appears to its audience

This is the visual manifestation of the brand's role and purpose. It comprises brand name, packaging design and advertising. Not only should these reflect the brand's identity and positioning, they should help to express the brand's personality. The extent to which they can do this depends on whether the brand is available as Rx or OTC. Far fewer restrictions of course apply to the design and advertising of OTC brands; but the Rx sector, for the time being, remains tightly regulated.

Other chapters in this book discuss at length the art and science of brand naming and packaging design. It is significant, however, that the brand name is just about the only component of the branding mix through which the brand owner is permitted to convey brand positioning to *all* audiences. The choice of the brand name therefore is absolutely critical – particularly if the brand is earmarked for the OTC market.

Finally, a word or two should be said about internal commitment. Creating a culture where the importance of branding is understood is critical. No amount of careful market analysis, brand building and testing will succeed unless it is accepted implicitly within the organization that branding is of genuine commercial value and can help to optimize scientific success. Such a belief is spreading within the pharmaceutical industry, and a good example is that of Zantac. In his book *Brand Vision to Brand Evaluation*, Professor Leslie de Chernatony tells the story:

> When Glaxo had developed Zantac to compete against SmithKline Beecham's Tagamet, they anticipated a challenging battle, particularly because of Tagamet's dominant position in the anti-ulcer drug market. At the time of Zantac's launch, Tagamet commanded a 90% market share in the UK. Yet Glaxo's senior management had memories of not exploiting Ventolin when it was launched. A market research study recommended that Zantac should be launched at a price 10% below its rival. Recalling the higher price that Ventolin could have obtained, and forcing the organization to recognize the superiority of the brand, Sir Paul Girolami, Glaxo's CEO, ordered that Zantac should be launched at a premium over Tagamet. If the brand was to achieve its objective of becoming a brand leader, staff needed to be committed to delivering a quality offering at a quality price. Through a series of well-conceived strategies supported by a committed team, Zantac overtook Tagamet.

Timing

When should the strategy development process commence? For nascent prescription drugs, as soon as the new product's effectiveness has been proved, and its likely positioning therefore adumbrated. For prescription drugs, whose status is about to be changed to general sales list or whose formulation is to be adapted for the OTC market, as soon as such a change is contemplated. The virtual certainty is that, before too long, many pharmaceutical brands will appear on the Internet and in DTC advertising. In such circumstances it will be the duty of their owners to both maximize their commercial attractiveness and ensure that potential customers receive fair and honest information upon which to base their choice. The brand strategy development process – which will pinpoint positioning and communication imperatives – should therefore commence as soon as possible.

Patient power

The rationale for this book is that while the global pharmaceutical industry is undergoing fundamental change due to economic and demographic factors, the *rate* with which such change will occur will be driven by the Internet and DTC advertising.

The Internet has generated more wealth more rapidly than any other business trend. As a means for global communication it is unparalleled. Its omniscience has helped to create numerous virtual communities. These comprise patients with a common illness (for example AIDS and MS sufferers) who get together regularly online to discuss the latest developments in treatment and so on. (Recent research shows that more people now log on to search for healthcare information than for pornography.)

Under current regulations in the UK, DTC advertising exists for limited medicinal products, such as OTC cough medicines, analgesics and cold remedies. In other countries, notably the USA, direct access is far broader with television advertising increasingly being accepted as the norm. This might yet be a step too far for the UK, but indirect advertising via advocacy groups is allowable provided information is presented in a balanced way. Brand names should not be used, although there have been many exceptions to this. With the expansion of the Internet allowing free access to information, together with the European Parliament's Bill of Human Rights, this restriction must – and will – change. (Anne Devereux and Rob Benson discuss DTC advertising in much greater detail in Chapters 5 and 6.)

Between them, the Internet and DTC advertising will create among ordinary people far greater knowledge about drugs and healthcare. Consumers will be better informed than they have ever been, and armed with this knowledge will press for more widespread availability of pharmaceutical brands.

There is evidence that this is already happening. A study recently conducted in the USA by the Guideline Research Group revealed that more than 90% of US consumers are in favour of making more drugs available without a prescription (Table 1.2).

The research set out to discover whether there is widespread consumer support for the switch of a handful of prescription medicines, particularly those such as Pravachol from Bristol-Myers Squibb or AstraZeneca's Prilosec, currently under the US Food and Drug Administration's (FDA) microscope. In their September 2000 edition, *OTC Business News*, the leading healthcare publication, commented on the Guideline survey as follows:

> Just over three-quarters (76 per cent) supported AstraZeneca's switch application for its heartburn medication. A similar figure came out in support of granting OTC status to anti-allergy products, such as Clarityn (Schering-Plough) and Zyrtec (UCB Pharma), which have already been released for sale in other markets, notably Canada and the UK.

TABLE 1.2			
Receptivity to Rx to OTC switches			
	Good idea (%)	Bad idea (%)	Don't know (%)
Medication such as Prilosec to treat heartburn or acid indigestion	76	17	7
Allergy medications such as Clarityn, Allegra and Zyrtec	74	19	7
Oral contraceptives for adult women	63	25	12
Osteoporosis medications such as Fosamax	50	30	20
Medications to lower cholesterol, such as Pravachol and Mevacor	49	42	8
Medications to treat depression, such as Prozac or Zoloft	18	76	6
Source: Guideline Research Group			

There was equally strong support for relaxing the restrictions on oral contraceptives for adult women, with some 63 per cent of respondents – both men and women – declaring themselves in favour. Medications for osteoporosis, such as Fosamax (Merck) and medications that help to lower cholesterol, including Pravachol and Merck's Mevacor received slightly less backing, but with around half of all consumers questioned in support of their transfer to the non-prescription market, there is still a good case for their Rx-to-OTC switch.

By contrast, few consumers thought that it was a good idea to switch antidepressants such as Prozac from Eli Lilly or Zoloft (Pfizer). In fact, just 18 per cent voted in favour of OTC status for these drugs.

Encouragingly for the manufacturers of these prescription drugs, the support for their switch to OTC status is not simply notional. Indeed almost seven out of ten said that they would buy an over-the-counter version of Clarityn, Allegra or Zyrtec; 64 per cent revealed that they would be prepared to buy Prilosec. A little over two-fifths were prepared to buy non-prescription oral contraceptives or medicines to lower cholesterol.

The Guideline research revealed a broad consensus about the desirability of switching these medications to over-the-counter status across a broad band of income groups. Both men and women, more affluent (households with an income of over $75,000) and less affluent (under $20,000) households and consumers in each of the major regions of the US are equally likely to support switching these medications.

Significantly, consumers regardless of their declared level of household income said that they were prepared to pay considerably more than at present for the convenience of being able to obtain Clarityn without a prescription. Clarityn is available off prescription in Canada at a cost of $11 per pack (equivalent US price). In the US, patients currently pay a prescription co-payment in the region of $5. However, almost 60 per cent said they would be prepared to pay an extra $7 – a total of $12 – to be able to purchase Clarityn without the need for a doctor's prescription.

The main driving force behind the desire to see more OTC medications become available is high cost to the tax payer of prescription medications.

According to Robert Seidman, vice president of Pharmacy for the Blue Cross managed healthcare company in California, his organization covers over 800,000 prescriptions a year for low and non-sedating antihistamines. This results in a bill of over $84,000 for medications – and related consultations – that are, in fact, safer than the non-prescription antihistamines currently available.

Similarly a lack of prescription coverage by some insurance companies has a role to play. Nearly one in four adults (24 per cent) surveyed by the Guideline Research Group have no insurance cover. This translates to over 48 million US adults who are required to pay for prescription medication out of their own pockets. In fact, among households with an income of under $20,000, over four in ten (43 per cent) do not have prescription coverage. The lack of coverage is exacerbated by the relatively high co-payment that some consumers must foot for each prescription. The Guideline Research Group found that, on average, consumers with coverage pay over $10 for each prescription they fill.

The pressure to increase the pace of Rx-to-OTC switch activity is predicted to grow as a result of the Internet. According to Dr Whitcup of Guideline Research, younger consumers who have access to medical information over the Internet are especially interested in the switch of the products listed in the research. These consumers want to take an active role in their healthcare and have knowledge and desire to read about medications and treatments.

Conclusions

This has been a long chapter so we shall make the closing brief. We are nearing a junction in the history and affairs of the pharmaceutical industry. From one direction come the governments and health maintenance organizations, anxious to transfer as much of the growing cost of healthcare (of which the cost of drugs is a significant component) to private individuals. From another come the individuals themselves, informed by the Internet and DTC advertising, and anxious to influence the medication they are prescribed. From a third comes the pharmaceutical industry, forced into mergers to optimize R&D and sales effectiveness, and therefore profits, yet unaware seemingly of their own destiny. Does it lie in medicine or marketing? Instinctively they incline to the former. Yet the future is about both, and branding stands at the crossroads.

References and further reading

Blackett, T *Trademarks*. Macmillan – now Palgrave, 1998.
Blackett, T and Coke, C *Branding in the Pharmaceutical Industry*. FT Management Reports, 1998.
de Chernatony, L *Brand Vision to Brand Evaluation*.
Donovan, Dr A *DTC: What we do now. What should we do later?* Conference paper.

2 | The valuation of pharmaceutical brands

NICK LIDDELL Interbrand

Relevance of brand valuation to the pharmaceutical industry

The investment community's interest in the pharmaceutical industry has led to high stock market valuations for businesses that succeed in the sector. Such businesses have in the past amply repaid their investors, reflected in increased profits, dividends and share prices. The industry has relied for these profits on the ability of drug companies to pass on rising drug costs to the consumer in higher prices. This ability to charge high prices arises from the economic peculiarity of the industry.

The pharmaceutical industry is riddled with market imperfections, particularly agency imperfections, asymmetries of information and global sunk costs. These combine to create:

■ a reduced price sensitivity on the demand side
■ a degree of market power on the supply side
■ demand curves that do not reflect the social benefits.

Pharmaceutical demand is stronger and less price elastic than it might otherwise be since drug expenditures are often reimbursed by public or private insurers, encouraging overuse and higher prices. This problem is made more acute given the asymmetry of information between the prescribing doctor (the agent) and the insurer or health authority (the principal). Doctors can be expected to display a degree of risk-aversion, preferring the branded product in which they have gained experience during the period of patent protection; they may also lack incentives to alter their prescribing habits. Moreover, patients and doctors alike may have imperfect information as to whether lower priced generic products meet the quality of the branded drug.

These market imperfections have prevented governments and insurers from applying sufficient pressure on pharmaceutical companies to hold down price increases. Consequently, costs have soared; R&D investments have been doubling every five years since the 1970s. The industry currently invests approximately $13 billion on R&D, equivalent to 17% of total sales. Since one-third of the industry's 300 best-selling branded drugs, worth $37 billion in annual sales, will be vulnerable to competition from generic manufacturers when they go off patent over the next ten years, pharmaceutical companies are depending increasingly on R&D investments to yield new drug discoveries.

On the supply side, patents allow for substantial price discretion to firms who invest heavily in R&D to produce new drugs. This is not to say that pharmaceutical companies enjoy perfect monopoly of supply; firms compete via R&D to discover new products and subsequently compete with substitutable products via marketing and pricing strategies. It is evident that the focus here is on competition via R&D, rather than competition via marketing and pricing and that the reason for this emphasis lies in the belief that patents are by far the most important creators of profit. However, there are compelling reasons to believe that pharmaceutical companies are currently underestimating the potential value of branding.

The current emphasis on R&D in relation to the brand seems to neglect the fact that branded pharmaceuticals continue to command a price premium over generics following patent expiry. There is also evidence to believe that the loyalty enjoyed by branded drugs may even increase as generics enter the market. Branding is already recognized as a key element in sustaining competitive advantage for over-the-counter (OTC) medicines and as the market shifts in favour of OTC remedies, the importance of branding is likely to increase as time goes on. Moreover, concentration of R&D activity on a contracting number of areas for which there is not yet an effective cure will have the dual effect of reducing the marginal efficiency of R&D investment, while at the same time increasing the likelihood that alternative patented drugs will exist to address the same ailment.

Thus, branding is likely to become a source of competitive advantage which pharmaceutical companies ignore at their peril. The efficient allocation of pharmaceutical companies' resources between brand investment and investment in other factors such as R&D will become increasingly important to their success. Consequently, the success of pharmaceutical companies will hinge upon the ability to quantify the benefit accruing to companies resulting from brand ownership and investment.

The value of a brand

The value of a brand lies in its ability to generate and sustain demand for a company's products or services. Cursory examination of well-known global brands underlines their ability to secure repeat business, if properly handled, and often to permit the brand owner to charge premium prices. However, it is also evident that to create and maintain these global brands requires extensive investment. Consequently, the efficient allocation of pharmaceutical companies' resources between brand investment and investment in other factors such as R&D hinges upon the ability to quantify the benefit accruing to companies resulting from brand ownership and investment.

Interbrand's concept of brand value is based on the premise that brands generate and secure consumer demand. The financial value of brands is represented by the net present value of their expected future earnings, according to a discounted cash flow valuation technique. Cash flow-based techniques are currently the most common methods for valuing brands and are widely accepted internationally. The UK Accounting Standards Board (ASB) has brought out new accounting standards (FRS10 and FRS11) which permit the inclusion of acquired brands on the balance sheet. In determining the useful economic life of the brand, the ASB has endorsed the discounted cash flow method. Moreover, this economic use method of valuing brands reflects the real reason for owning and creating brands: generating and securing future demand and, as a consequence, future cash flows.

Interbrand's brand valuation methodology

In order to determine brand value it is necessary to:

■ assess the current earnings that can be attributed to the brand
■ forecast future earnings of the brand
■ identify an appropriate, brand-specific, discount rate.

To win the support of auditors, any brand valuation method must also do the following:

■ follow fundamental accounting principles
■ allow for revaluation on a regular basis
■ be equally suitable for home-grown and acquired brands.

Interbrand defines the value of a brand as encompassing the economic worth attributable to the trade mark, logo, packaging and get-up, as well as to the recipe, formulation or raw material mix and the reputation related to all these elements. In other words *brand value* embraces all the proprietary intellectual property rights encompassed by the brand. Thus, for the purposes of evaluation we consider a brand to be an 'active trade mark' – a trade mark actually used in relation to goods or services and which has, through use, acquired associations and value.

Interbrand has pioneered the development of brand valuation techniques. Over the last 13 years, Interbrand has completed over 2000 valuations of the world's leading brands, with an aggregate value in excess of $80 billion. When brand valuation first came to light, valuations tended to be based on historic brand profits. Now it is almost universally accepted that brand valuation should be based on the discounted value of future brand earnings and the following summary describes this current basis of brand valuation, based on a four-stage methodology:

- a segment analysis which groups the brand according to how it is manifested to the customer

- a financial analysis which identifies business earnings

- an analysis to determine what proportion of those business earnings are attributable to the brand

- a brand strength analysis, which assesses the security of the brand franchise both with respect to trade customers and end consumers. This security is expressed as a 'brand strength score' which provides a discount rate to apply to brand earnings.

Segment analysis

Brand value is created at the point of contact with the customer or the party that determines customer choice. As such, a customer may be either a trading organization, a private consumer, or an intermediary body. Interbrand's approach to conducting a brand valuation exercise is on the basis of separate product or service, geographical and customer segments. This is because the behavioural patterns of a customer's purchase decision are likely to vary depending on the product being bought, by whom the product is being bought and how the product being bought relates to the brand. In our experience, this front-end approach is the most effective way of valuing a brand, as it considers the difference between the component segments and provides the building blocks of brand value.

The pharmaceutical industry is not characterized by homogeneous products sold to a homogeneous set of customers. Clearly, the purchase decision will be affected both by the supply side of the market (for example the manufacturing capacity and distribution) and by the demand side (for example the purchaser's level of information about competing offers).

Consequently, the role played by the brand will vary in each case. For example, the brand is more relevant where a drug is off patent since it represents one of the few factors by which a product is differentiated from competitors' brands. Where a drug is on patent, the product can be seen to enjoy virtual monopoly rights to the market in question, depending on the degree of substitutability offered by competing remedies. In such a case, the role the brand plays may be limited to little more than expanding demand for a monopoly producer.

Also of relevance is the customer to whom the product is sold. There is a significant asymmetry of information involved in the consumption decision where a consumer is charged with the responsibility of selecting an OTC medicine and the selection process consequently places great emphasis on the brand. This is not to say that there is no role for the brand to play in determining selection by a prescribing doctor; in this case, the brand may play on the doctor's risk-aversity with respect to prescribing unfamiliar drugs or medicines from unfamiliar sources. However, the brand can be seen to play a lesser role in the second case.

The difficulty here lies not in the fact that pharmaceutical companies operate in a diversity of marketplaces but comes with the appreciation that, during its life cycle, the supply and demand conditions under which a particular drug is sold are almost certain to change. For example, any monopoly rights guaranteed by patents are certain to expire, given that patents have a finite lifetime. Consequently, the importance of branding for a particular drug is almost certain to change during its lifetime.

Financial analysis

Key financial data are used to fully identify cost-absorbed profit streams (by segment) for a business' branded operations: profit and loss accounts and often historical sales costs and earnings are used to project five-year brand revenues and profit flows. All brand valuations are carefully prepared to ensure that the earnings identified relate solely to the brands being evaluated. Thus any non-branded or other brand earnings and associated costs must be removed from the business earnings. To avoid overvaluation of the brand, it is necessary to make a fair charge against earnings for the value of the tangible assets employed in the business. These would include production facilities, R&D, investment and the distribution network.

Until a fair return has been made on the fixed assets and working capital tied up in the business, it cannot be said that the brand (or any other intangible) is adding value to the business. The charge made against earnings therefore eliminates the return on capital that would have been achieved on the production of unbranded goods. This leaves a residual return that reflects the return on intangible assets of the business (of which the brand is one).

This is represented by the cost of capital to the business that is applied to the operating profit after tax. Once corporation tax and a charge of the capital employed have been subtracted from the operating profit, we are left with the earnings that are attributable to intangible assets employed in the branded business. The next step is to establish what proportion of the total residual earnings are due to the brand rather than to other intangible assets.

Role of branding index

In some heavily branded industries, such as cosmetics or luxury goods, the residual earnings of that business are, in effect, the brand earnings since there are virtually no other intangible assets in the company. In a more technically complex industry, such as pharmaceuticals, the ability of the business to earn in excess of a base return on tangibles will depend partly on intangible assets other than the brand, including R&D expertise, patents, marketing and sales-force knowledge, and access to database information. Such intangibles will have an important effect on a business' earnings capacity. Consequently, Interbrand have developed an approach for assessing the extent to which the brand drives demand for a particular branded product.

This is achieved first by identifying key drivers of demand for the business. The degree to which the success of each driver is dependent on the brand is then ascertained through a weighting process that results in a single per cent figure. This is referred to as the 'Role of Branding Index' and reflects the overall dependence of the business on its brands and branded activities. Based on quantitative and qualitative analysis, this process provides a systematic way for approaching the issue of importance of the brand in relation to other intangible assets and produces reliable conclusions that can be tested. Once the Role of Branding Index is applied to residual earnings, it is possible to determine brand earnings.

In discussing branding in the pharmaceutical industry, a distinction must be drawn between the product brand and the corporate brand. It is common for pharmaceutical products to be identified and endorsed by a corporate branding structure. Having a corporate brand acts to reassure consumers and risk-averse doctors because purchase behaviour in the pharmaceutical industry, by the very nature of the products, is heavily dependent on reliability and reputation. Prescribing doctors inevitably develop an impression of particular pharmaceutical companies in their dealings with them. This is a function of their own experience with the company (for example in terms of the perceived effectiveness of previous drugs that the company has produced) and the reputation the company has earned through the experience of others (for example through adopting a predatory pricing policy). While tough restrictions currently exist in relation to the advertising of their products, pharmaceutical companies are at greater liberty to promote their corporate brands.

In the case of the pharmaceutical industry, the relative importance of key drivers of demand will vary according to the segmentation discussed above. The specific weighting and reliance on branding of each key driver is contingent upon the idiosyncrasies of the brand. The following drivers seem particularly relevant to demand for pharmaceutical products.

Awareness/familiarity

Given the lack of product knowledge on the patient's behalf and the plethora of alternatives available to prescribing doctors and chemists, a key element in the consumption decision rests in the ability of pharmaceutical companies to generate a degree of familiarity with their products in relation to competitors. In terms of the patient, this driver is likely to increase in importance over time as the continued growth of the Internet and abolition of restrictions on direct-to-consumer (DTC) marketing increase the scope for dialogue between pharmaceutical companies and the users of their products. For example, the easing of US regulations in 1997 opened the door to television advertisements of prescription drugs; now, drug companies spend in excess of $3 billion each year on consumer advertising campaigns. This driver is also likely to increase in importance with respect to doctors, as pharmaceutical companies back their brands with increasingly sophisticated marketing techniques. This is an inherently brand-related driver, as the brand is the medium through which awareness and familiarity are conveyed.

Availability/distribution

This driver is more relevant to OTC drugs sold to patients, given that this is a low-interest category and consumers are unlikely to search far and wide for their preferred brand of medicine. However, even in this segment it would seem that this driver plays a limited role. The existence of retail price maintenance (RPM is a vertical restriction that exists when suppliers require retailers to sell their products at, or above, a specified price) indicates that pharmaceutical companies are either prepared to sacrifice distribution for control over pricing, or they feel secure enough in their current distribution to make this driver of secondary importance. Given the high level of concentration in the industry, big players are unlikely to benefit from significant advantages in terms of distribution. Consequently, this driver is of minimal importance.

The role of the brand in this driver is high for products that are well known. This is due to consumer pull – it is expected that the drug would be on offer and people will ask chemists for the brand as a choice of preference.

Recommendation

Given the need for doctors to make decisions based on objective evidence of a drug's effectiveness, coupled with the low interest in this category on the part of consumers, this is likely only to be a minor driver. However, there is a belief that the role of recommendation could become more important with time as the growing proliferation of healthcare information on the Internet is likely to fuel growing public awareness of health issues. Recommendation is intrinsically a brand-related activity – without the brand there would be nothing to recommend.

Packaging

This is a minor driver for purchasers of OTC medicines who are likely to interpret package design as a signal of quality. As drugs are increasingly advertised to consumers, the importance of this driver will rise, as the packaging of medicines becomes a vital component of pharmaceutical companies' marketing strategies. Given that packaging signals the quality of the product it contains, this is an entirely brand-dependent driver.

Price

Given the current insensitivity of demand to pricing and the existence of RPM in the consumer market, this is a low driver. However, as medical bodies become accountable for the amount they spend on pharmaceutical products, the pressure to find lowest price alternatives will increase and the salience of this driver will consequently come to bear. The price of a product is a matter of fact and in most cases does not rely upon the brand for its interpretation.

Perceived quality

The *raison d'être* of a drug is to make people better (or at least to make people feel better). The perceived quality of a drug, in terms of its effectiveness, likely side effects, method of ingestion and dosage, is consequently of clear importance to doctors and patients alike. Quality perceptions are largely subjective assessments for patients; while they are capable of assessing whether or not a drug provides a therapeutic effect, often there is limited scope for comparison with competing drugs, particularly for ailments that do not recur or persist over time. The existence of placebos provides further evidence that the brand has an important role to play in this driver at the consumer level. However, since doctors benefit from a broader level of experience with respect to competing remedies, their assessment of the quality of a pharmaceutical product is more objective. Consequently the brand has a lesser role to play.

Sales quality

The success of marketing in the pharmaceutical industry rests not only in providing evidence of the quality of a drug, but also in providing such information in an easily digestible format. The importance of this driver to doctors is illustrated by Diovan, when falling revenue prompted the adoption of a new, simple, consistent marketing strategy, resulting in a 54% jump in sales. Doctors are afforded very little time to shortlist products for prescription; consumers have little medical knowledge and little interest in spending time researching drug effectiveness. Consequently, presenting evidence of the therapeutic effects of drugs in an accessible format is important for doctors and consumers alike. There is less scope for the brand to play a role in this driver. In the case of doctors, sales representatives of pharmaceutical companies are responsible for marketing drugs and a great deal hinges on the representatives' ability to provide clear and accurate information. There is a greater opportunity in the consumer arena to focus upon this driver as part of a strategy to market the product and as such, this is a more brand-related driver at the patient level.

Customer pull

Thomas Ebeling, head of pharmaceuticals at Novartis, claims that 66% of patients who ask the doctor for a particular product actually receive it. Although consumers are currently unlikely to have strong opinions regarding brand preference for pharmaceutical products, this is certain to increase as consumer interest in health issues grows over time. By definition, consumer pull relies entirely on the brand.

Product range

This is a more relevant driver in the OTC segment, where consumers have varying preferences, for example regarding how comfortable they feel taking potent drugs (leading to varying strengths of OTC branded drugs) or their

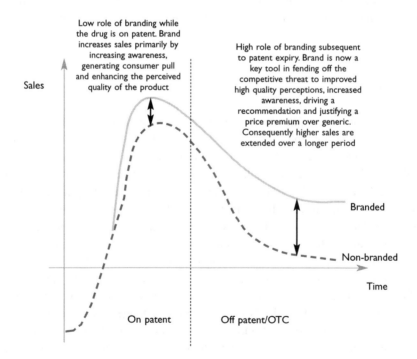

Figure 2.1 The role of branding in the pharmaceutical industry

preferred method of ingestion (for example patch, gum or inhalator for Nicorette). Given that the brand is the common element which ties a range of products together, the role played by the brand is high for this driver.

Assessing brand strength

Two brands that offer the same future earnings profile may have completely different values. If one is a powerful, well-established market leader and the other is a highly fashionable brand launched only last year, yet both have the same financial forecasts, it is the well-established market leader that would have the greater value. This is because the risk profile of the new brand is much greater than that of the more established, proven market leader. The value of a brand reflects not only the level of earnings it is capable of generating in the future but also the likelihood of those earnings actually being realized.

The brand's strength is the primary determinant of its risk profile as a marketing asset. The stronger the brand, the less the risk that its future cash flows will not be realized. The weaker the brand, the less secure the future cash flows. Consequently, an analysis of the strength of the brand is required to determine its risk profile. The analysis should include a comparison of the brand to its competitors as well as to a notional ideal, risk-free brand. Inter-brand's approach to this task is to assess a brand's strength against seven key attributes as follows.

Market

Brands in markets such as food, drinks and publishing are prima facie stronger than brands in, for example, high-tech or clothing areas, as these markets are more vulnerable to technological or fashion changes. A brand in a stable but growing market with strong barriers to entry will thus score particularly highly.

Stability

Long-established brands that command consumer loyalty and have become part of the fabric of their markets are particularly valuable and are normally afforded high scores. In the pharmaceutical industry, brands in the OTC market with a long heritage should score highly. This is a criterion which is particularly difficult for pharmaceuticals; there is often considerable optimism over new developments but this does not necessarily ensure success. For example, the introduction of Tacrin for Alzheimer's disease caused great excitement, but its early potential was not realized.

Leadership

A brand which leads its market or market sector is generally a more stable and valuable property than a brand which is lower down the order. To score highly in the area of leadership a brand must be a dominant force in its sector with a strong market share. It must therefore be able strongly to influence its market, set price points, command distribution and resist competitive invasions. This would best have applied to Tagamet in the late 1970s and early 1980s, followed closely by Zantac and more recently by Losec. The pharmaceutical industry is one of the few sectors that has reliable global audit data on competitive products. The same level of information detail is lacking in the hospital sector, but data can be estimated.

Trend

The overall long-term trend of the brand is an important measure of its ability to remain contemporary and relevant to consumers, and hence is an important measure of its value. In pharmaceuticals, scoring highly for trend is increasingly difficult where the approaching expiry of patent coverage in major markets starts to erode future branded product development. The potential to extend the brand into the OTC market is important as a basis for a strong trend. This was achieved by Zovirax, Canesten and Tagamet and the strength of the manufacturer's name is also important in facilitating this move.

Support

Those brands that have received consistent investment and focused support usually have a much stronger franchise than those that have not. While the amount spent on supporting a brand is important, the quality of this support is equally significant.

Geography

Brands which have proven international acceptance and appeal are inherently stronger than national or regional brands. Significant investment will have been incurred in the geographical development of such brands and they are less susceptible to competitive attack. They are, therefore, more robust and stable assets. Moreover, by no means all brands are capable of crossing cultural and national barriers so those that are must be considered as particularly valuable assets. The pharmaceutical industry has an inherent strength in that all its products have the ability to transcend international borders, as health is a global issue. For pharmaceuticals, significant investment is needed for geographical development of brands; this is especially true with regard to obtaining approval for marketing in major markets.

Protection

A registered trade mark is a statutory monopoly in a name, a device or in a combination of these two. Other protection may exist in common law, at least in certain countries. The strength and breadth of the brand's protection is critical in assessing its strength. Indeed, if the legal basis of the brand is suspect, it may not be possible to apply a value to the brand at all for balance sheet purposes.

A global brand such as Zocor or Losec presents the analyst with additional variables that should be taken into account. No matter how well established the brand may be in multiple markets around the world, its brand strength will vary from country to country.

Factors influencing the inter-country variation in brand strength will include differences in:

- the nature and dynamics of each market
- the longevity of the brand in each country
- the competitive environment
- market share and brand trajectory.

The risk profile for each market is assessed and these are applied to the brand earnings stream in each market. By combining the net present value of brand earnings for each market, a brand value can be determined.

Calculating brand value

The relationship between brand strength and brand value is not linear. A new brand, no matter how much support is put behind it, is highly vulnerable and any forecast cash flows must be viewed with considerable care. A very high discount rate would be applied to such future cash flows. Frankly, this position does not change very much as the brand goes through the early part of its development. The brand is still inherently risky. It is only once the brand has begun to establish itself in the market that the security of its future cash flows looks more assured.

As the brand increases its marketing strength and becomes a market leader, its risk profile improves yet further. But once the brand is a dominant player in the market, it becomes irrelevant how much more support is put behind it; its risk profile does not change very much. A brand such as Coca-Cola is already very strong and the discount rate one would apply to that brand's cash flows is not going to change significantly, regardless of how much more market share it is able to gain.

The relationship between brand strength and brand value therefore follows a normal distribution and can be represented graphically in an S-curve. Having determined the shape of the S-curve, the next task is to determine appropriate discount rates. The bottom point on the curve is simple to determine – since one can have no confidence that a weak brand will be able to realize any of the future revenues it has been forecast to generate, we would apply an infinite discount rate. At the other end of the scale we have the

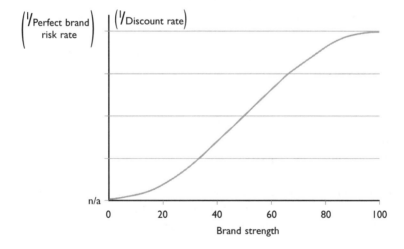

Figure 2.2 The Interbrand S-curve

notionally ideal brand. The notional ideal brand is, in its risk profile, close to the risk-free rate represented by the return on government bonds. It carries a small premium over the risk-free rate as it is not a traded security. The risk assessment for each brand is based on the brand strength score; the higher the score, the lower the risk premium and thus the discount rate. The calculation of brand value is effected by applying the discount rate identified during the brand analysis to the future brand cash flows identified during the financial and market analysis.

Conclusion

It cannot be denied that patents allow for substantial scope for firms who invest heavily in R&D to set high prices for new drugs. Clear evidence of this is found in the ability of pharmaceutical companies to generate substantial profits despite spiralling R&D costs. However, in the context of an industry coming under increasing pressure to reduce price (and therefore cost) inflation, the importance of the patent relative to the brand seems to have been somewhat overstated.

Patents have fixed, short lives which are further abbreviated by the time lag between patent registration and the introduction of the drug into the market. The point can be made that the effective life of the patent will expand in the future as leaps in IT have the scope to cut this time to market. However, this scope is restricted by the need for regulation of new drugs that are released into the marketplace; it costs an average of £350 million and 10–12 years to bring a drug through the regulatory procedure. Thus, the role played by the patent is limited by its fixed lifetime and by the length of time taken by the regulatory process.

Brands, on the other hand, do not suffer from such constraints. Given an appropriate level of support, a brand is capable of generating and securing profit far beyond patent expiry. The current smash and grab approach adopted by pharmaceutical companies implicitly assumes that pharmaceutical brands are incapable of surviving competition from generic entrants following patent expiry. However, there is strong evidence to believe that a more long-term, brand-sensitive approach may prove more profitable, given both current and expected market conditions.

Following patent expiry, one would expect an increase in price competition and lower prices for branded drugs resulting from the entry of generic drugs. In the long run, it seems reasonable to assume that prices will be forced down towards the marginal costs of drug production. In practice, however, Scherer's 'generic paradox' seems to hold true. Evidence points to a high degree of brand loyalty for pioneering brands, with the result that brand names are able to successfully defend high market shares, despite prices which continue to rise above inflation. A number of authors have noted that 'several firms' products had prices more than 50% greater than the minimum and still had a significant share of the generic market'. In their article, 'Generic Entry and the Pricing of Pharmaceuticals', Frank and Salkever observed that 'increased competition from generics was not accompanied by lower prices of brand-name drugs; on the contrary, evidence suggests small price rises tied to expanded competition.'

According to the Schmalensee model of first-mover pricing advantages,

> the image advantage that comes from consumer recognition as the first mover in some product category may permit its possessor to hold prices above costs for significant periods of time while retaining a large share of the relevant market.

Evidence of the scope for branding also lies in the apparent ability of the first generic entrant to retain a substantial market share with a higher price than later generic entrants.

A further insight into the scope for branding comes with the observation that doctors, patients and pharmaceutical companies all recognize that there are costly consequences of assuming every patient is the same. The heterogeneity of patients in terms of drug effectiveness, preferred method of application and possible side effects affords pharmaceutical companies a multitude of opportunities for product differentiation. There is an appreciation that it is uncommon in most cases to be able to identify a best cure for any single ailment, regardless of patients' idiosyncrasies. Indeed, if this were a common phenomenon, then we would no longer require the expertise offered by a doctor in order to prescribe a cure.

Patients also differ in their attitudes towards the pricing of pharmaceutical products. In their article, 'Pricing, Patent Loss and the Market for Pharmaceuticals', Frank and Salkever suggest that entry of generics leads price-sensitive buyers to shift to generics, leaving only price-insensitive buyers to purchase brand name products. Thus, the demand for branded products following entry by generic actually leads to *less* price sensitivity of demand for their products, allowing them to raise their prices further without a substantial contraction of demand or loss of market share.

It should also be noted that generic entry is not the sole competitive threat to producers of branded pharmaceutical products. While a patent confers upon its owner exclusive access to a valuable piece of intellectual property, this does not necessarily translate into a monopoly position within the market. Patent rights do not preclude the existence of branded remedies that employ entirely different formulas to address the same ailment. For instance, Prozac competes with other patented drugs, including amphetamines, methylphenidate (Ritalin), and pemoline (Cylert) for the treatment of depression. Moreover, the degree of this overlap can be considerable; pharmaceutical companies tend to concentrate their R&D activities in similar areas and fierce competition arises from the race to bring the next blockbuster drug to market. Concentration of activity on areas where demand for pharmaceuticals is particularly strong thus leads to an oligopolistic climate in which companies will increasingly rely on branding to gain competitive advantage.

It is important, however, not to undermine the role that the patent plays in building a successful brand. Up to this point, discussion has revolved around the role played by the patent *as opposed* to the role played by the brand. However, the patent can be interpreted as an intrinsic element of the brand and the period of patent protection can be seen as vital to its success. While there are many factors involved in building a strong brand, a critical consideration in the pharmaceutical industry is timing. As illustrated by Schmalensee, the success of a pharmaceutical brand lies in obtaining first-mover advantage. In the credit market, Visa first claimed a convenience positioning based on broad merchant acceptance. Prospective cardholders flocked to the brand, spurring a demand-led increase in the number of merchants joining the network, creating a self-perpetuating source of competitive advantage. In the same way, a period of patent protection can be seen as more important in terms of brand building through the establishment of relationships with doctors, patients and intermediary bodies, rather than in terms of affording pharmaceutical companies the opportunity to derive short-term gains from monopolistic pricing strategies.

It is important to note that shifting the focus of attention more in favour of branding is not to argue for reduced spending on R&D. The economics of the industry are changing and so must the economics of the companies which form the industry. The reliance that the pharmaceutical industry has historically placed on the patent as a sole means of securing income cannot continue indefinitely, as advances in IT reduce information imperfections and consolidation of purchasers into large private organizations increases price sensitivity of demand.

Thus, there are strong theoretical and empirical reasons to believe that the potential value of pharmaceutical branding is currently underestimated. Brands represent an important signalling mechanism in an industry characterized by asymmetry of information and risk-aversity. Moreover, the pressure to market drugs will increase as will the pressure to drive down costs and prices. Branded prescription drugs will be marketed directly to the consumer via television advertisements, Internet marketing and telemarketing. Pressure to hold down price rises will force pharmaceutical companies to allow their return on equity to fall and deter them from engaging in predatory behaviour with respect to pricing and investment in R&D. The increasing costs associated with bringing new drugs to market will force pharmaceutical companies to take a more long-term interest through building strong brands which guarantee profits far past patent expiry.

The evidence presented in this chapter also provides strong reasons to believe that the short-term focus on the patent has produced sub-optimal profits within the pharmaceutical industry. Consequently a shift towards a long-term, branded approach could release latent profit through increased demand over a longer period, even in the context of lower prices, which would in turn provide additional funding for R&D. Pharmaceutical companies will thus be forced to focus attention on the value of their brands in order to withstand the gale of competitive destruction currently sweeping through the industry. A key to survival will lie in determining the future contribution of brand value to business value through the use of brand valuation techniques.

References

Frank and Salkever 'Generic Entry and the Pricing of Pharmaceuticals', *Journal of Economics and Management Strategy*, **6**(1): 75–90.

Frank and Salkever 'Pricing, Patent Loss and the Market for Pharmaceuticals', *Southern Economic Journal*, **59**(2):165–79.

PART II

Rx to OTC Switching

3 | The Rx to OTC switch – creating the climate for change

GARY LYON Evidence Based Marketing

10 years ago...

WordPerfect was the world's favourite word processing program.

There were 160,000 Internet hosts (the total at the beginning of the year 2000 was 72,000,000).

New Coke was launched.

■ In 1990, we were at the beginning of the Rx to OTC 'switch revolution': the deregulation of previously prescription-only (Rx) medicines to over-the-counter (OTC) status

■ Nurofen (ibuprofen) had just switched in the UK and Boots was committed to creating a pan-European OTC brand

■ Advil/Nuprin had already switched in America, along with 0.5% hydro-cortisone (Cortaid) and several cold remedies

■ The outlook for switches and the OTC market generally was bullish – even rapturous. Most experts predicted that the OTC market would explode, led by switches and the coming harmonization of European Union (EU) regulatory mechanisms in Europe, beginning in 1992.

If you had to pick a sport that would be symbolic of the growth curves most OTC people had in mind, you might choose hockey. Now, as a Canadian, I prefer the variation played on ice but even if you prefer the field version, the shape of the stick is roughly the same and this is how most sales projections looked. So what happened? Perhaps the moral is, be careful what you wish for. The healthcare industry overall has clearly grown but in ways that were probably unthinkable ten years ago. Other authors in this book have helped us understand trends such as the consumerization of the prescription market via direct-to-consumer (DTC) promotion and the Internet. There has also been an enormous increase in consumer interest in alternative, prevention-oriented self-treatment. If we had all done our Michael Porter 'competitive forces' analysis ten years ago, perhaps this impact would have been better understood. So where do we go from here?

This chapter will explore:

■ Current business trends in the global market for OTC brands

■ A comparison of Rx to OTC brand switches in the USA versus the rest of the world

■ The key success factors for switches

■ The emerging OTC business strategies of the major sector players

■ The outlook for OTC brand growth and Rx to OTC switches over the next five to ten years and

■ A summary of the implications from a branding perspective.

First, let us recap some of the important, current business trends.

Market overview

The global OTC market is growing at about 4% a year, according to industry researchers Nicholas Hall and Co. (1999). While such growth would perhaps be acceptable to most FMCG (fast-moving consumer goods) players, the challenge for the OTC industry is that most OTC business groups share accommodation with large pharmaceutical players. The Rx market grew +8% in 1999 and the published results of companies with both Rx and OTC divisions suggests that the pharma side is growing up to three times faster than their OTC/consumer divisions. Most of the Rx growth is attributed to the red-hot US market that has been on a ten-year winning streak.

On a brand basis, unlike many FMCG categories, there are still relatively few power brands in the OTC sector, particularly outside the USA:

■ The top ten brands in Western Europe only accounted for 10% of the total OTC market in 1999, according to Nicholas Hall, and 8/10 of all brands were over ten years old.

■ The largest European brand (Aspirin) had sales of under $210 million across Europe and features an active ingredient that has already celebrated its centenary.

■ Another global OTC brand, Vicks, is found in 85 countries, according to its manufacturer, Procter & Gamble, but the most common form (chest rub) is found in only 41 and the same formula is present in only 29 countries.

■ By contrast, the top 10 brands in the US accounted for 22% of the total OTC market in 1999.

The top 20 brands in Western Europe and the USA by dollar sales that have been growing in excess of underlying CPI inflation during the period 1997–99 are shown in Table 3.1.

TABLE 3.1
Top 20 Western European and US OTC growth brands

Western European power brands

■ Aspirin (Bayer)	■ Vicks (P&G)	■ Nicorette (Pharmacia)*
■ Halls (Pfizer)	■ Nurofen (Boots)*	■ Rennie (Roche)
■ Supradyn (Roche)	■ Anacin (AHP)	■ Panadol (SB)
■ Ricola (Ricola)	■ Clearasil (P&G)	■ Strepsils (Boots)
■ Centrum (AHP)	■ Gaviscon (various)	■ Efferalgan (BMS)
■ Fisherman's Friend (L'house)	■ Benylin (Pfizer)	■ Imodium (J&J)*
■ Otrivin (Novartis)*	■ Nicotinell (Novartis)*	

US power brands

■ Tylenol (J&J)	■ Advil (AHP)*	■ Centrum (AHP)
■ Nicorette (SB)*	■ Robitussin (AHP)	■ Tums (SB)
■ Excedrin (BMS)	■ Alka-Seltzer (Bayer)	■ Benadryl (Pfizer)*
■ Motrin (J&J)*	■ NicoDermSQ (SB)*	■ Sudafed (Pfizer)*
■ Halls (Pfizer)	■ Aspirin (Bayer)	■ Nature Made (Otsuka)
■ Monistat (J&J)*	■ Sundown (R Numico)	■ Imodium (J&J)*
■ Osteo-Bi-Flex (R Numico)	■ One-a-Day (Bayer)	

*Rx to OTC switch brand/ingredient   *Source:* Nicholas Hall & Co. DB6

While eight of the US top 20 growth brands contain switched ingredients, only five of the European brands contain ingredients that were formerly (and recently) prescription only. Switches have clearly been the engine for the higher US growth rate. Only four trade marks (Aspirin, Halls, Imodium and Nicorette) appear in both lists. Even within the European arena, there are few pan-European brands. It is clear that the penetration of European switch brands has lagged behind the US in most product categories. Some might argue *vive la différence*, but for marketers attempting to create multi-country brands, the differences are important to understand.

Key European versus US market differences

■ *The limited ability of consumers to self-select* – Unlike the USA where OTCs are sold broadly, virtually every other major market restricts access (by regulation) to pharmacies only and often behind the counter out of consumers' reach and vision. The impact on sales can be dramatic as shown by the mid-1990s switch of H_2 antagonists (Zantac 75, Pepcid AC and Tagamet 100) that saw the highest market share gains in countries with the most open access (USA, Sweden and Canada) and weaker sales in more restrictive markets (UK, Australia and France).

■ *Availability of reimbursed (prescribed) alternatives* – As long as reimbursed options exist for treating mild to moderate conditions, the OTC market in Europe will continue to be underdeveloped. This is discussed in more detail later in the section 'Outlook for OTC brands'.

■ *Weak business case for switch investment* – The persistent underdevelopment described above impairs the business case for promotional investment since many costs such as advertising are essentially fixed. Since most OTC marketers are ultimately competing with their prescription colleagues for seed money, many potential OTC brands in Europe go unswitched or are weakly (and unsuccessfully) promoted.

Successful Rx to OTC switch strategies

While Europe may be lagging behind the USA in terms of switch penetration, clearly there have been several successful Rx to OTC switches on both sides of the pond. According to OTC strategist James Dudley, the specific factors that underpin most successful switches, defined as achieving at least 50% of the market share of the incumbent, leading brand are:

■ Creating and delivering a breakthrough consumer benefit

■ Transferring the prescription heritage to the OTC brand

■ Being first to switch in a particular therapeutic class

■ Having sufficient promotional weight with targeted consumers – a minimum 25% share-of-voice of category advertising spending.

Branding obviously plays a key role in transferring the prescription heritage. If the Rx brand name cannot be used with the OTC switch (as is still the case in several European markets), this transfer is made all the more difficult. Moreover, Rx trade marks have been traditionally assigned with little consideration for their ultimate application to an advertised OTC brand. While this will always be an area of intense debate and ultimately driven by practical considerations such as registerability and language issues, we might at least agree that some prescription trade marks are more suggestive of end benefits than others. Such trade marks provide an opportunity to generate brand name awareness and core benefit awareness *simultaneously*. Clarityn (Schering-Plough) and Singulair (Merck) are two such examples in the respiratory products area that come to mind.

The end result of this generally low growth OTC environment and the clear success factors for Rx to OTC switches can be seen in the emerging business strategies of key sector players.

Key players' strategies

Some of the main strategies that have been pursued by key sector players are summarized in Table 3.2 and can be described as follows:

■ *Focusing on core brands and markets* – For the most part, this means prioritizing on switch and number one or two brands in growth categories in multiple/core markets while divesting marginal/national brands. The emerging maxim might be described (somewhat harshly) as 'The UK is worth 20 Austrias'. New business structures are emerging that attempt to manage OTC brands as global assets.

■ *Attempting to build critical mass in the key US market* – Acquisitions and joint ventures have been the usual means.

■ *Pushing for improved business efficiencies* – Three routes have been followed:

TABLE 3.2	
Examples of key players' strategies	
Strategy	*Examples*
Focus on core brands and markets	SKB, P&G (divestitures, global category teams)
Build critical mass in USA	Pfizer (acquisition); Bayer, Roche (joint-venture)
Improve business efficiency	Hoechst, Rhône-Poulenc (merger); Glaxo Wellcome, SKB (shared infrastructure with Rx business units)
Target VMS and functional foods	Warner-Lambert (Quanterra branded VMS), Novartis (Aviva functional foods and Altus joint-venture with Quaker)

- Mergers and acquisitions
- Consolidating infrastructure with the core Rx business
- Outsourcing specialized support functions (for example retail coverage of smaller pharmacies).

■ *Targeting vitamin and mineral supplements (VMS) brands and nutritionals* – Some players are attempting to use existing brand platforms or partnering with food companies to gain distribution leverage. In Europe, the appeal of pursuing functional foods/VMS launches can also be seen at least in part as an attempt to circumvent the restrictive pharmacy-dominated, highly regulated OTC market. The weak response (thus far) to Novartis' Aviva launch suggests that functional foods are as challenging as any product launch and that all elements of the marketing mix (including price) have to be right.

Outlook for OTC brands

So what *is* the outlook for OTC brands and particularly Rx to OTC switches over the next five to ten years? It would be foolish to suggest that sales will grow at an accelerating rate so that we end up with our hockey stick sales forecast again. The one exception is likely to be brands in the VMS category, which we will come back to later. My crystal ball is very cloudy looking ahead ten years, so let me be mostly wrong rather than totally wrong and focus on the next five years and the main drivers of Rx to OTC switch growth.

Driver 1: Reducing/eliminating Rx reimbursement of same ingredient

This is a huge limiting factor in Europe as previously highlighted where continued reimbursement by state-funded schemes of the Rx ingredient in the same or higher doses has led to consumers effectively boycotting the OTC variant.

Outlook:

■ This continues to be a political minefield so the best we can hope for is modest improvement, that is, higher patient co-pays. However, the potential exists for setbacks as well as gains (for example Germany, where the co-pay actually *decreased* in 1999). Consumers will generally continue to resist paying for their OTC drugs when reimbursed, prescribed options exist.

Driver 2: Accelerating breakthrough ingredient deschedulings for self-treatment

Outlook:

■ Look to the Rx market to define the biggest new targets (for example asthma, cholesterol reduction, high blood pressure management). The entrenched physician/pharmacy lobby exerts significant, negative influence to move outside the traditional OTC mindset of mild to moderate disease conditions. For example, there has been only modest descheduling momentum in some major markets (0.25% hydrocortisone in Germany and 0.5% hydrocortisone in France were approved in 1996, ten years *after* approval in the UK and Italy). While the OTC switch advisory committee in the USA has turned down cholesterol reducers once already for descheduling, breakthroughs are still more likely to take place there and in the UK for the foreseeable future.

Driver 3: Harmonizing a binding descheduling process

Outlook:

■ National regulatory agencies in the EU continue to exercise their prerogative despite the acceptance of the principles of mutual recognition, particularly on the Rx side. The EU Pharmaceutical Directive is up for review again in 2001. The potential exists for true harmonization with OTCs but the practice is highly politicized with especially active physician/pharmacist lobbies in France, Germany and Spain.

Driver 4: Using the Rx trade mark for the switch brand and expanding the use of umbrella branding

Outlook:

■ There is little likelihood of change on the Rx trade mark issue in the short term in hold-out European markets (France, Spain, Italy and Portugal). Restrictions on the use of umbrella OTC trade marks are similarly entrenched. It could be possible as part of a more comprehensive industry/government pact that delivers some guarantees of overall healthcare cost containment. The key question is whether the Rx-dominated pharma companies would make such a deal to benefit their smaller OTC divisions. A more likely goal would be to pursue legalizing DTC promotion, as described more fully below.

Driver 5: Loosening restrictions on advertising and promotion

Outlook:

■ Some further progress is likely on speed of review although most regulatory agencies have not adopted rigorous performance standards. Further industry participation and self-regulation is likely in Italy and possibly Spain. The EU Pharmaceutical Advertising Directive is up for review in 2001 but the OTC industry is still divided within its own house as to whether restrictions should be maintained or relaxed, displaying the multinational versus local company fracture which still exists in many national markets.

Driver 6: Increasing distribution and loosening pricing restrictions

Outlook:

■ Clearly, retail price maintenance (RPM) will disappear in the UK during the next five years. However, expanded distribution into non-pharmacy outlets of licensed medicines will occur probably only in markets where it is already permitted (such as the USA, Australia, New Zealand, Canada, the UK and the Netherlands) due to pharmacy lobbies. Surprisingly, perhaps, there continues to be little underlying call by organized consumer groups to increase access. Any breakthrough in Europe in this area will probably be retailer led, for example Wal-Mart and Carrefours/Promèdes, and build upon prior expansion of VMS and functional food offerings. Finally, Internet impact (for example drugstore.com) as a sales channel will probably be limited in the short term (apart from VMS brands) by the relatively low cost/infrequent purchase cycle of most OTCs and the patchwork of legislation on the practice outside the USA. Nonetheless, there is huge interest and long-term potential. For example, American consumers can already achieve savings of $30 (30%) per prescription on chronic care drugs such as Lipitor. Inevitably, the Internet will accelerate the culling of marginal pharmacies that do not provide sufficient value-added service to consumers.

Other factors (the wild cards)

In addition to the six factors just described, three additional leading indicators of change in the consumer healthcare arena need to be watched: the expansion of DTC promotion for Rx products, the growth of home-based healthcare and continued industry consolidation.

Direct-to-consumer (DTC) promotion

DTC advertising of prescription brands in the USA and New Zealand, which has been a major sales influence since 1998, is already having a significant effect on OTC brands globally. The *promotion sans frontière* nature of the Internet has made a farce of regulators' attempts to limit its impact to Americans. The scale of this activity is staggering. The leading global allergy remedy, Schering-Plough's Clarityn had US sales of $2.3 *billion* in 1999 and was supported by over $200 million in promotion, consumer advertising taking the lion's share – an amount equal to the sales of the company's *entire* OTC portfolio. What makes this surprising to most Europeans is that Clarityn is a prescription brand in the USA and an OTC brand virtually everywhere else. In fact, three of the top ten DTC spenders were allergy brands. While part of the DTC debate has been focused on the advisability of promoting so-called lifestyle drugs which provide quality of life benefits, it is interesting to note that only Merck's Propecia for male pattern hair loss (the number two advertised brand) could be considered to have no medical benefits among the top ten DTC brands in 1998.

From a business perspective, it is clear that DTC promotion of Rx brands could be viewed as both a threat and opportunity for OTC business organizations. The threat is that DTC effectively delays the need to switch (for example Clarityn in the USA) and creates a ready-made, consumer-based franchise that requires only modest adjustments when it eventually goes OTC. The bigger threat is that DTC activity soaks up scarce promotional resources that otherwise could go into existing and future OTC businesses. For example, Schering-Plough's own OTC medicines business has stagnated in recent years, assisted, in part, by the cannibalization of Schering's own OTC allergy brand, Chlor-Trimeton. Another example is that the direct consequence of a successful Relenza/Tamiflu DTC launch for the prevention and treatment of flu will be a direct hit on the OTC analgesic/cough and cold markets. The fact that this has been largely described so far as a zero sum game scenario betrays much of the history of how OTC brands have been traditionally managed as stand-alone silos distinct from their Rx counterparts. This traditional thinking is clearly out of step in a world where the skills set for successfully branding Rx products via DTC campaigns is now essentially the same as branding OTC products.

Outlook:

▪ In my view, there is a better than 50% probability that DTC promotion will be permitted by 2004 in major markets in Europe plus Canada and Australia, but it could be category specific (for example cholesterol-lowering drugs). This outcome will be tied to a continuing US success (that is, low body count) and Rx cost (reimbursement) containment strategies in Europe. A similar fracture line exists within the Rx sector between (mostly international) firms that are in favour of DTC versus (local) firms that are opposed. In the meantime, there will be a proliferation of disease management or patient awareness efforts in all markets which will attempt to brand as many elements of Rx promotion campaigns as possible without mentioning brand names and overt product benefits. Look for OTC-like packaging, key messages and user database acquisition efforts as manufacturers enjoy another Canadian pastime: skating as close to the edge without falling through the ice!

Home-based healthcare

Acceleration of PC/web-based health monitoring and management systems in a home care setting is almost certainly likely, as funding-constrained payers move patients from hospitals to outpatient settings wherever possible. This will have a positive influence on OTCs, given the persistent undertreatment of many conditions and their adjunctive role in easing pain and other symptoms. Early leaders in this emerging market include America's Health Hero Network with its 'Health Buddy' system of plug and play health monitoring devices. Payers such as government health plans and private insurers as well as the pharmaceutical industry are eager to tap into the data provided by such systems in order to develop more cost-effective treatment protocols and provide real time clinical surveillance data. These applications are building on the more established role of the Internet as a source of healthcare information.

Outlook:

■ Internet access is expanding rapidly but the quality of currently available healthcare information is highly variable and it is mostly a one-way (data in) transaction. Consumer studies indicate that many consumers are still reluctant to place personal health information in a shared environment, and confidence in the security of the Internet – already shaky – could be eroded further by breaches, should they occur. This will improve with the development of credible, branded healthcare portals such as Healtheon/WebMD but setbacks are likely. The technology exists now to greatly expand the range and usefulness of in-home health monitoring. OTC businesses have the opportunity to partner with software and point of care players to promote the adjunctive use of OTCs. OTC organizations are also well placed to provide the necessary marketing skills for gaining insights into consumer needs to accelerate the acceptance of these new technologies.

Continued industry consolidation

Corporate amalgamations completed or announced since 1995 have involved companies representing almost 50% of the OTC industry. Several of these pairings now find well-established OTC players in bed with consumer neophytes: SmithKline Beecham with Glaxo Wellcome and Warner-Lambert with Pfizer come to mind. In both cases, the stronger consumer partner has the weaker equity position in the merged entity. There will be considerable pressure to divest non-core assets in addition to duplicate products in order to satisfy competition watchdogs. These restructurings provide a unique (and time-limited) opportunity to rethink organizational, drug development and pre-marketing strategies, including branding considerations for their enlarged portfolios.

Outlook:

■ Continued consolidation within the pharma sector will create a steady stream of brand divestments, which has kept acquisitive players such as Seton-Scholl (now SSL) growing at a brisk pace. Whether the consumer units of the merged companies can retain their OTC talent pool and impact upstream drug development efforts to build in self-medication considerations at an early stage remains to be seen. In almost any scenario, these mergers will create considerable internal disruptions that competitors will be able to exploit.

Conclusions

I offer the following, main conclusions along with the implications for branding consumer healthcare products.

- First, it is difficult to see OTC sector growth matching Rx growth over the next five years. This will create some discomfort for OTC managers who share resources and executive support with their faster growing Rx business colleagues. Mergers and acquisitions, new product development and general brand-building investments such as advertising are likely to be scrutinized more carefully as long as the US prescription market remains the most attractive return on investment prospect. Business development and licensing routes are the only real means to outperforming anaemic category growth levels. My advice: put away your hockey stick and brush up on your Monopoly skills!

- Pan-European brands will continue to be relatively few and medium sized. The European switch environment will improve only slowly. Global branding which is being redefined by major FMCG companies will be less of a consideration in the OTC sector with the key exception of switches. Global *category* strategies aimed at developing R&D and claims platforms with national/regional branding variants appear to be more viable.

- DTC promotion of Rx brands will inevitably leak out of the USA and will eventually (if reluctantly) be formalized by other regulatory authorities. Rx trade mark selection, proposition development and other branding initiatives such as packaging must therefore be subjected to the same disciplines employed by consumer marketers.

- VMS and functional food entries will be another source of pan-European brands but the more successful ones will build off existing brand platforms such as Centrum or come from outside the pharma sector entirely, for example Weight Watchers.

- Large pharma players will focus on achieving greater efficiency gains and attempt to harness Rx/OTC synergies. This comes down to recognizing that brand-building skills have become a core competency requirement for the *entire* business. The key opportunity therefore is to leverage consumer-based, business-building capabilities from the OTC side, achieve supplier/skill efficiencies, extract and apply as much learning as possible from big-budget DTC campaigns and effectively achieve a seamless strategic and operational architecture. What is needed most is a common *language* that the two business groups plus senior management can use to engage in these discussions. An evidence-based approach anchored by superior insights into consumer needs must be the hallmarks of clinical development, NPD and marketing planning that is accepted across the entire organization.

In summary

The OTC business units of the major pharma companies possess the old (but tried and true) skills of brand-oriented, consumer marketing. In the new world of consumer-directed healthcare, the Rx divisions of these same companies need these skills. It does not mean that the OTC players have all the answers but why not learn from the successes as well as the failures? As comedian Sam Levenson once said, 'You must learn from the mistakes of others. You couldn't possibly live long enough [*or afford*] to make them all yourself!'

Acknowledgements

The author recognizes and appreciates the assistance of Dr Jerome Reinstein (WSMI), Nicholas Hall, James Dudley and Godfrey Axten in the preparation of this chapter.

4 | Successful switch strategies

HUGH FERRIER Sudler & Hennessey

Brands are returning to their roots

As we have turned the corner into the new millennium, we have found famous brands returning to their product roots – a timely reminder that a successful brand was, and is, simply a very relevant product idea, well executed.

We find Coca-Cola not just driving sales with its original flavour, but reminding us of its historical roots, with a logo incorporating the famous Coke bottle, itself a great example of functional packaging design. This bottle, made with thick, curved glass, had been created to withstand the impact of being dropped from refrigerated vending machines. In the middle of the 20th century, not everyone had refrigerators, so the Coke delivery system was an integral part of the brand's core promise of 'pick-you-up' refreshment. Coca-Cola is still successfully nurturing this brand icon.

Medicines, too, are about function and good design. If we could fast rewind to a country doctor in Smithfield, North Carolina, after the American Civil War, we might find a certain Dr Joshua Vick using his camphor, menthol, and eucalyptus oil preparation in his practice – and his enterprising brother-in-law Smith Richardson, a pharmacist, putting that preparation into its distinctive blue jar and selling it as Dr Vick's pneumonia cure. Nowadays, the celebrated Vicks VapoRub (Figure 4.1), with its promise of natural, soothing vapours, is such a relevant and powerful brand icon that its current advertising recaps with a visual device, the magic vapours in action, even when it is for a newer Vicks line, such as a nasal spray.

The challenge for marketers nowadays is to introduce new products, relevant to today's needs, which will become the new brands of tomorrow. This often boils down to introducing new lines under an existing brand name. The commercial reality faced in particular by large, global corporations, with

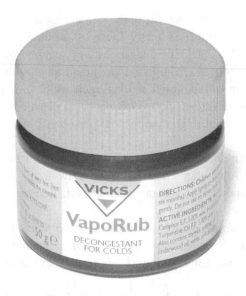

Figure 4.1 Vicks, today

constant pressure on bottom-line performance as well as sales expansion, is that it is less risky to make the necessary advertising investment for an existing brand name than for a new name.

If we accept that most new product briefs in consumer companies, such as those mentioned above, actually specify the use of an existing brand name, can we persuade the pharmaceutical industry – which famously has adhered to the principle that each new ingredient/generic compound should mean a new brand name – to take a more evolutionary approach to brand building, in order to maximize the return on its existing brand assets, developed over a longer period of time?

The role of product in the brand mix

In consumer marketing, there is the oft-quoted axiom that 'People buy brands, not products'. This, of course, is true. And it is just as true in over-the-counter (OTC) medicines, where in well-studied OTC sectors it has frequently been demonstrated that consumer brand-buying repertoires exhibit higher than average levels of brand loyalty, compared to other fast-moving consumer goods (FMCG) markets.

But we should not forget the role of the product itself in the brand mix. We know that a brand comprises many facets – product, packaging, price, communication, and a bundle of imagery values acquired over time – all of which work as a whole to create its unique brand identity. Nonetheless, it is self-evident that, in a functional market such as medicines, the product remains the dominant part of the overall package. (This contrasts with other markets, for example fine fragrances, where personality and image drives the brand business.)

But does the importance of the product itself make it easier or harder to brand medicines? And what lessons can we draw from observing existing OTC medicine brands in the self-medication market on how to innovate and enhance brand value?

This chapter attempts to show not only the importance of building brands in the self-medication market, but also of paying attention to the product itself, and using product innovation as the turnkey to expanded brand sales and profitability.

We shall look first at particular issues, arising from being a licensed medicine, that affect OTC brand planning, and then look at a particular Rx to OTC switch in 1999 which exemplifies some of the factors that need to be addressed in order to achieve success. In this example – from the analgesics market – not only was the use of an existing Rx brand name the foundation for future success in the OTC market, but, crucially, product differences in terms of superior features were the key to successful brand differentiation. This differentiation was carried through from product performance, through packaging, into advertising communication, and is the foundation for the brand owner in extending the brand's user base and future profitability.

The problem of sameness of indications for OTC brand positioning

A significant challenge for the OTC marketer, compared to his FMCG counterpart, is to understand how to work within regulatory constraints while still setting out to achieve a distinctive positioning for his brand. A major element of any consumer brand's positioning relates to its communicated usage and not just its typified user. Because a licensed medicine can be sold for use only for those indications that appear on the product licence, it follows that there is often little room for manoeuvre on usage positioning at a strategic level. This constrains differentiation versus competition, which is likely to have gone for the maximum list of (similar) allowable indications for the product segment.

Interpretation of advertising communication claims – when measured by regulatory authorities – can be subjective, depending on the market.

For example, from 1997 to 1999, the Novartis nasal decongestant brand Otrivine attempted a more emotional selling platform across all its European markets, focusing on the product's sensory properties at clearing the user's head of feelings of stuffiness. They used the copyline 'Sets your senses free'. In at least one Nordic market, however, a very strict interpretation of the product delivery – that Otrivine was licensed as a *nasal* decongestant – was used to refute the copyline on the grounds that it was claiming activity on all the senses; hence, they refused to admit the legitimate secondary effects that could be experienced, from using the product.

This requirement to position one's brand against only its licensed indications underscores the importance of careful product planning. If one active ingredient is able to gain an extra indication versus another ingredient in the same product class, then an advantage can open up. We will pick up this theme later on.

The problem of parity of product performance for OTC brand differentiation

In parallel with this constraint, health departments, looking at OTC dossiers, tend to regulate towards parity of product strength per established OTC indication, and this further hampers the marketer's attempts to differentiate.

Taking the example of OTC analgesics – the oldest established self-medication sector – we find that the products' active ingredients have been adjusted at OTC dosage level to the strengths that are equal, literally equivalent, to each other. An active ingredient, even if more potent, has only been allowed at a lower amount per dose.

This paradox – that OTC products directed at the consumer can find it harder than their Rx cousins to build in product superiority – can be illustrated by looking at OTC dose levels of analgesic tablets. The standard dose of paracetamol (acetaminophen) is 1000mg, usually delivered as 2×500mg tablets per dose. Because the newer substance ibuprofen (switched from Rx in its inventor's market, the UK, in 1983) is gram for gram more potent than paracetamol, the dose deemed sufficiently potent for the OTC indications allowed is 400mg, usually presented as 2×200mg. Another non-steroidal anti-inflammatory, ketoprofen, obtained US switch approval for most of the usual OTC indications in 1995. Its equivalent dose to ibuprofen 400mg, was proposed as 50mg. The more potent the pill, the smaller it becomes in size.

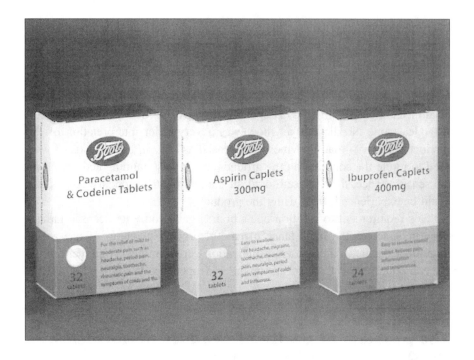

Figure 4.2 A range of dose levels for OTC analgesic products

The result of this adjustment to standardization of strength in OTCs has an immediate consequence for the marketer. His ability to make true superior strength claims is usually removed entirely, since his more potent ingredient has been effectively reduced in size, thereby neutralizing his competitive strength argument. One consequence of these analgesic trends has been, in Anglo-Saxon markets, to concentrate strong product developments on combination ingredient products in order to allow double action claims. Such a direction has bucked the trend in continental European markets, where medical opinion and consumer safety concerns favour a single ingredient product approach in self-medicated pain relief.

Clearly, if no other means of competitive differentiation is available, the emphasis on differentiation via brand message will become all the more critical. However, because the nature of competitive marketing requires us to find a competitive edge, the thorough preplanning of an OTC dossier in order to find a unique indication becomes a route worth pursuing, wherever possible. What do we mean by this?

Finding new product indications to gain a competitive edge

To return to our earlier example of analgesics: the substance of choice for consumers for most everyday pain relief indications, as supported by most Western medical opinion, has been paracetamol. Provided this ingredient is used correctly, well within its safety window, it is a highly effective, well-tolerated pain killer and antipyretic. Its use has largely supplanted that of aspirin, previously the ingredient of choice in self-medicated pain relief. But, unlike aspirin and ibuprofen which are NSAIDs (non-steroidal anti-inflammatory drugs), paracetamol has no anti-inflammatory properties. Could the relevant brand owner have exploited this difference between ibuprofen and paracetamol?

The daily (24-hour) OTC dose of ibuprofen is set by most brands, in most countries, at 1200mg – three doses of 400mg. At this dosage level, the OTC dossier does not normally support any anti-inflammatory claims, although pain relief claims for indications such as backache are accepted. The point is – could the marketer of an ibuprofen-based brand push more aggressively for a daily maximum dose of 1600mg, thereby adding (competitive) anti-inflammatory claims to the brand versus a paracetamol-based brand? This is the kind of competitive edging through product analysis that OTC marketers need to adopt more frequently.

A good example of competitive outflanking, is made by the Reckitt & Colman OTC brand Gaviscon in the OTC gastrointestinal market. At first sight, its different product type (sodium alginate, a rafting agent) and mode of action (which prevents acid reflux in the oesophagus, rather than neutralizing acid lower down in the stomach) appear to offer little difference, in terms of practical end result, for the consumer with indigestion – if the brand's indications would be identically phrased to those of single or double antacid ingredient indigestion remedy brands, such as Rennies or Maalox.

However, by developing communication around a unique problem, such as heartburn (essentially a layman's description of higher up stomach pain), Gaviscon was able to position itself as a remedy quite distinct from antacids. Normally, a head-to-head fight against a brand as strongly defended as Rennies (an effective product, reasonably priced, heavily advertised and with satisfied users), would have been fruitless for a newer entrant such as Gaviscon. But by choosing to fight on different territory to the antacids, by inventing a new problem and offering a new solution, Gaviscon built a new OTC franchise. The key to success was its maximization of product difference, linked to differentiation at key indication level, and exploiting this through consistent communication to pharmacists and consumers.

Such is the kind of planning challenge facing the OTC marketer, who must not only understand consumers' language for relevant insights, but also ruthlessly interrogate his ingredient and its clinical efficacy data, so as to find an indication-based competitive advantage, however hard this may be, in the OTC regulatory climate.

If this thesis holds true, it follows that the key to competitive success in OTC marketing will be highly product based. So, Rx to OTC ingredient switching (for it is the generic that is switched, not the brand) with the securing of the relevant, competitive indications can become the product innovation driving force that can build for a new brand franchise OTC.

Product innovation and brand building through Rx to OTC switching

Unlike many other industries, the consumer market for medicines has a useful parent market from which newer product ingredients can be drawn, in the right circumstances – the Rx medicines market. Just as R&D-based innovation has to be the driving force in Rx medicines, so there is a need, too, for new, competitive substances to provide brand differentiation in the self-medication market. This can provide a useful pipeline of revenue for the pharmaceutical company, since investment focus on new Rx medicines results in loss of interest in marketing those products which have moved to off-patent/generic status while Rx. Clearly, if they can be seen as brands, not just products, then they can be seen to have an extended life after patent expiry (Figure 4.3).

But what should the OTC innovator look for from an Rx product and will a product superiority in the Rx sector translate into certain success when it appears OTC? Experience suggests that the mere existence of an ingredient not yet used OTC and whose useful Rx life has ended, does not, per se, offer a reason to switch that substance. It is more important to ask if there is a real opportunity to build a new brand, versus the existing brands in the segment. At this point, we should remind ourselves that we need to ensure that there is a relevant self-medication indication, as well as a product to go with that indication. To quote the old marketing adage, 'There may be a gap in the market, but is there a market in the gap?' We have already referred to the success of Gaviscon at entering the gastrointestinal self-medication market hitherto dominated by tablet and liquid antacids. However, a later competitive launch into the same market, by no fewer than three competing new brands, has been less successful. It is worth considering why, thus far at least, this new segment has been less successful for the pharmaceutical companies concerned than they would have liked.

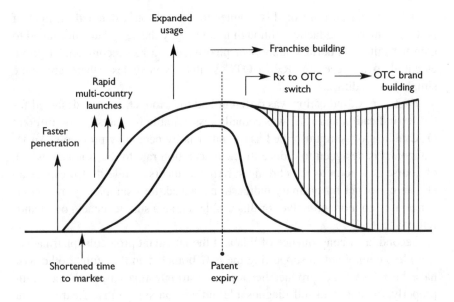

Figure 4.3 The life cycle of a brand
(Sudler & Hennessey, by permission)

The importance of having a real consumer benefit

This was the OTC launch in Europe – initially in the UK market – of the H_2 antagonists, which arrived from a successful Rx market, where the products had been prescribed for chronic sufferers of ulcers. First came Johnson & Johnson's Pepcid AC (famotidine) and SmithKline Beecham's Tagamet 100 (cimetidine), followed by Glaxo's Zantac 75 (ranitidine). The latter was more successful, partly as a result of tactical learnings from the first two.

After heavy spending launches in the mid-1990s – including TV advertising as well as the gamut of print and in-pharmacy promotion – this new subsegment still had not achieved even a 10% share of the total OTC indigestion remedy market by the end of 1999. Usually, the advent of three new brands of a new type of product will, with the combined effect of increased marketing effort, have driven up consumer penetration and hence the total market size. Certainly the H_2 brand launches had a positive effect on total market size, as did the activity undertaken by the existing gastrointestinal brands, which had launched their own added value line extensions to defend their positions. But why, given the contrasting success of Gaviscon, have the H_2 brands not made a greater impact?

It is not the purpose of this chapter to embark on a detailed critique of particular marketing tactics, although undoubtedly the early launches failed to gain the initial, important support of pharmacists, a key recommender group essential to a successful Rx to OTC switch. Nonetheless, there are some simple key findings.

First, the Rx indication was different and the product, so well designed for the Rx indication and role, was actually less suitable for the slightly different OTC indication, circumscribed as the latter is by necessary protocols. An H_2 antagonist is designed to reduce the acid secretion rate to the stomach, which of course is a boon to the chronic sufferer of ulcers. While it also can be an effective product for ordinary indigestion, caused, for example, by overindulgence, it is no more effective for this problem than a simple antacid or an antireflux agent.

Second, as a consequence of this and the attendant protocols, pharmacists were less committed to supporting the new brands than they might otherwise have been. An OTC product licence in gastrointestinals is restricted, quite properly, to acute and self-diagnosable indigestion symptoms. Clearly, if one has a recurring stomach pain, a visit to the doctor is sensible, as it may be an undiagnosed ulcer. Worse still, there is a small, albeit remote, chance of an underlying carcinogenic condition – and the prolonged use of any type of acid controller might mask such a problem. This distinction between an indication and product for chronic use, as compared to an indication and suitable product for self-medication, was a tension that was not totally resolved at the time of the H_2 brands' OTC launches.

Third, in gastrointestinal, just as in any other market, a high tech product per se (such as our example of an H_2 antagonist) does not automatically confer brand superiority over a low tech product (such as an antacid, the basic chemical nature of which is very simple). Success depends on the accurate identification of a consumer need and how well the brand meets that need in terms of product, pack, price, availability and communication.

The pre-existence of performance Rx ingredients, therefore, offers an interesting potential armament for the OTC marketer's brand-building ambitions – but only if the product's features and advantages offer the consumer a real, tangible benefit.

The value of a well-known name

However, the central questions for the OTC brand marketer relate to brand values. What proposition and what name will build a successful brand franchise? What is his commercial remit? Is it to build on a brand owner's existing consumer brand franchise? Is it to transfer the brand values of an Rx brand, or to create from scratch a completely new brand? Is there a reimbursement issue that affects whether the Rx name can be used in practice?

If there is an existing consumer brand franchise, and a switched ingredient is being used to relaunch that consumer brand, or produce a new top of the range variant with improved efficacy, this is often the happiest scenario. The existing consumer brand is, in effect, relaunched by dint of the innovation. This enhances the brand value from the point of view of the business. The consumer, being attached to the original brand is usually delighted that his or her brand has done something new and better, since this confirms his or her judgement about the brand and the emotional bond is strengthened.

For a consumer company in self-medication which has no Rx pipeline, the opportunity is always to go shopping for an Rx ingredient, usually at a pharmaceutical company that has little or no interest in entering an OTC market itself.

But this chapter is concerned to focus principally on the potential for a pharmaceutical company to improve its branded assets by extending an (Rx) brand franchise with an introduction of a brand version for the OTC arena.

So what particular problems and opportunities exist to exploit the consumer awareness of an existing Rx brand for the OTC market?

The low salience of Rx brand names outside North America

In the USA, the permitted use of branded direct-to-consumer (DTC) advertising to promote Rx brands has dramatically changed the landscape of brands, in terms of their levels of consumer awareness and the claimed level of prescriptions that have been made out by doctors as a result of branded consumer requests. In the USA, Rx brands are able to achieve levels of spontaneous awareness – a measure of the salience of a brand – closer to those enjoyed by OTC brands.

Outside the USA, the picture is different. It is true that, owing to general media interest in certain therapies, there has been an unusual degree of awareness created for (Rx) brands such as Prozac or Viagra. Even so, such public relations and general publicity has boosted largely aided awareness. Spontaneous awareness, driven by factors such as mass availability and mass advertising, remains low. The existence of unbranded DTC advertising in Europe and elsewhere does not help to raise awareness and salience of Rx brand names.

Extensive consumer research has revealed this passive nature of Rx brands. Because a doctor has in effect chosen your Rx treatment for you – it was not selected by you by name, in the pharmacy (as you only needed to hand over a prescription to the pharmacist) and it was dispensed, very often, in a generic-type package, with little or no colour graphics – you as a consumer have been deprived of all the usual tactile and visual cues you would normally get when selecting, buying and using a brand.

It is this active engagement by the consumer, in personally choosing a brand on the grounds of its product appeal, packaging, price, and so on, which is absent from the Rx brand usage process.

A good example of this normal absence of Rx brand salience can be found with the old Ciba brand, Fenistil (dimetindene maleate), which has a large sales base in many European markets, for example Switzerland, Germany, Portugal and Spain. The Rx version – a systemic – is indicated for the usual allergy problems you would expect for an antihistamine, but is particularly prescribed for skin allergy problems, due to the unsuitability of its ingredient (which can cause sedation) for potential daytime use in allergic rhinitis.

By contrast, the Fenistil OTC variant is a topical gel treatment. It is a sector leader and has reasonable levels of spontaneous and prompted aware-ness. It is positioned for insect bites, with secondary usage for nettle rash or sunburn allergy. The brand colours of orange or red are similar for the Rx and OTC products. Consumer research in its largest market of Germany revealed virtually no awareness among the larger (OTC) consumer franchise of the existence of the Rx version at all. In consumers' minds, there was no connec-tion. The supposed brand connection was based entirely on the ingredient from the laboratory, since in other respects – distribution channel, advertising, usage positioning – there was little to connect the two. Fenistil is not an unusual case. There could be countless examples of the virtual invisibility of Rx brands in consumer perception.

Nonetheless, within a particular therapy area, there may be some residual awareness of the Rx brand name among a core target group of chronic sufferers – the ulcer sufferer has heard of Zantac or Losec, the allergy sufferer has heard of Clarityn and so on.

Some factors in brand name choice

In addition to the issue of brand awareness, what about brand imagery values? What aspects of the Rx brand's reputation can be exploited to the benefit of a future OTC brand? Here, the name really should have an important role.

The future endorsement value of using an Rx brand name is obvious. The name carries with it connotations of being approved by doctors, efficacy, being the real thing, and when the OTC sales intermediary, the pharmacist, is added to the equation, it is clear that there is a huge advantage if the Rx brand name can be used, or a recognizable adaptation of it (perhaps to define to the professional that it is a lower OTC dose version, or to circumvent any reimbursement issues, if reimbursement is still in place for the Rx version).

So, when should the same name be used and when not? Not a bad starting point is the rule that if the indication is identical, use the same name, but if it is different, proceed with caution.

In the case of Nurofen (ibuprofen), it had been decided not to use the name which the brand owner, Boots, used for its Rx brand – Brufen – which, prior to the genericization of ibuprofen, had been very much a leading antirheumatic in many markets. Although it had been an expensive exercise to create a new brand – Nurofen – from scratch, the different array of OTC indications, from headache through neuralgia to period pain, doubtless justified the decision as correct, especially as Brufen's core indications and usage in osteoarthritis and rheumatoid arthritis were not available as OTC indications (Plate 4.1).

Provided, however, that a launch case can utilize a proven Rx ingredient, for more or less the same indication as the Rx brand and use the same brand name (or very similar), one has the opportunity to truly maximize the best asset of all – the reputation of the Rx brand.

How can the OTC marketer best exploit this reputation? Certainly, we are now in the field where brand marketing comes most to life – that of communications. But before we consider the role of advertising in creating brand personality, we must keep our feet on the ground. As we observed earlier on, medicines are function-driven products. Bluntly, they are bought and used because they work, and they are rejected very quickly, if they do not work. What mechanisms or channels are available through which brand credibility and reputation can be built?

The pivotal role of the pharmacist

The irony of medicine marketing is that the best quality brand endorsement one could hope for – the endorsement of a doctor or medical specialist – is not available. Regulations worldwide protect the objectivity of the system, for the greater good of patients and consumers, by prohibiting doctors from publicly backing one medicine brand over another. The same applies to dentists and other medical specialists.

Nonetheless, although brand advertising and promotion may not use professional endorsement, the verbal endorsement, in the counter selling of one's Rx to OTC switched brand, by the retail professional the pharmacist, a trained expert in pharmaceutical products, is not just desirable but essential. Even if consumer advertising or word-of-mouth suggestion is the original reason why a consumer seeks out the newly switched OTC brand to try it, he or she will invariably seek the reassurance of the pharmacist as to its efficacy.

Hence, any Rx to OTC switch launch will extensively detail the pharmacist on the brand launch, the product ingredient and OTC indication, highlighting the product's benefits and setting out a recommended protocol for the pharmacist to follow. It is probable that a training package for the pharmacy assistants will be included. Last, but not least, the brand's launch programme will ensure that the trade profit margin will be suitably generous to compensate the pharmacist's business for his or her valued endorsement of the brand.

The FMCG marketer, unfamiliar with medicines, might question why such resources should be put behind the trade, essentially, a push marketing element of the mix. Conventional marketing wisdom directs the marketer to put the majority of a brand's promotional effort above the line, seeing this revenue allocation as an investment in the future reputation of the brand. But the pharmacist wears two hats – he or she is not just a commercial trader but also a valued professional adviser. It has been famously remarked, in the context of the increasing down-regulation of drugs' status and the emphasis on self-care and self-medication, that if pharmacists and pharmacies did not exist, it would be necessary to invent them.

The role of the pharmacist in a successful Rx to OTC switch is pivotal. If a brand's early reputation as an endorsed (the implication is 'preferred') professional brand can be established in the OTC market, then future brand imagery on efficacy and reliability is already underway. Moreover, a new OTC market entrant needs, if faced with an OTC sector that is already heavily advertised and in which existing brands are bought with some degree of loyalty, a fresh weapon with which to break into the existing consumer purchasing repertoire. The pharmacist should be cherished, because his or her active role in being able to endorse a new brand, in effect switch a consumer from his or her existing behaviour pattern, should not be underestimated.

Perhaps the most dramatic example of this pharmacy power has been the UK experience of Nurofen in the OTC analgesics market. OTC analgesics has become the largest, yet in many ways remains, the most conservative, of OTC consumer markets. After all, as consumers we may be prepared to experiment with a new packet of sauce mix or a new brand of ice cream, but when we suffer an unpleasant problem such as a tension headache, why would we want to alter our choice of analgesic brand, if it works!

Boots' Nurofen, at launch, and in subsequent years, was heavily advertised. But the brand achieved a very high level of active pharmacist endorsement, both from pharmacists at Boots (the multiple high-street chemist), and at independent chemists. This was driven partly by the need for the brand to communicate to pharmacists that ibuprofen was not only a product for muscle and joint pain, due to its history, as they knew, but also was very effective for headache, dental pain and other everyday pains. However, the brand's main purpose in employing a pharmacist recommender programme was to gain trial from users of other OTC analgesics. Now, over 15 years later, the brand is close to being the UK brand leader, leaving aside generic products. The role of the pharmacist in helping to cement the reputation of this brand has been inestimable.

Advertising: a vital tool in building an OTC brand

Finally, but by no means least, the tools of advertising and public relations exist to enable the OTC brand marketer to build not just short-term sales, via awareness and first-time trial, but also to reinforce, year in, year out, existing users' feelings of satisfaction with the performance of their brand.

Indeed, much advertising research over the years, across a wide variety of markets, has demonstrated that advertising is at its most effective when delivering brand messages to brand users that reinforce their existing behaviour. In this way, advertising can slow down the frequency with which these users try alternative brands. It is this consistency with which brand leaders are able to attract a greater share of any particular consumer's personal spending, which is translated into a leading sales position.

It is true that short-term promotional pricing used to drive short-term sales, is not permitted with medicines (following the general principle that consumers should not be encouraged to consume more medicines than they need): but there is plenty of evidence from the more mature OTC sectors that consistent advertising spend, behind a proven advertising property, can and does translate into brand preference, even when there is little or no product difference compared to rival brands. In this respect, the addition of emotional values through building advertising personality does have a role to play in medicine advertising, just as in other FMCG sectors.

Although we have acknowledged that medicines are a function-driven category, bought to address a problem, it is equally true that health is an emotive and personal subject. Countless qualitative research groups or interviews, on the subject of particular sectors and brands in self-medication, have recorded consumers saying that such and such a brand is 'right for me'. This notion has the consumer explicitly admitting that he or she feels his/her choice is right, not because there is objective third party proof that their brand is better, but because they feel it works for them and they feel comfortable using it. Such declarations of trust place OTC advertising in the heartland of other advertised consumer markets, where the advertising message as a whole is an emotional as much as a rational sell.

The second part of this chapter will now look at a particular Rx to OTC switch example, which goes to illustrate some of the points made above.

We now move to a case study of a brand called Voltaren (diclofenac), launched as a full OTC by Novartis Consumer Health. The ingredient and the brand were previously the property of Novartis Pharmaceuticals. The topical brand variant Voltaren Emulgel was approved for internal transfer to the Consumer Health division in December 1998, and the brand was launched OTC in Germany in mid-1999, with advertising support in September 1999. The brand support was rolled out in Belgium (where as a semi-ethical, it was already on sale without prescription), Poland, Hungary, the Czech Republic, Italy, Switzerland and Israel, before the end of that year.

Key factors in the switch of Voltaren Emulgel/Schmerzgel

Voltaren (diclofenac) had become, by the early 1990s, the world's leading prescription NSAID, operating in the Rx anti-rheumatic market. In 1994 it was the only analgesic in the world's top ten selling drugs, by dollar value. Its success was founded on the ingredient diclofenac, an NSAID that outper-formed the previous leading NSAID, ibuprofen, in terms of potency and hence efficacy, while not unduly impairing tolerability for the patient (its record on gastrointestinal tolerability placed it no worse than middling, in terms of gastrointestinal tract irritation, when compared to several other strong NSAIDs which had a harsher profile in this respect) prior to the more recent advent of COX-2 (cyclo oxygenase) inhibitors. Thus, Voltaren had built up impressive credentials in the treatment of osteoarthritis and rheumatoid arthritis in its prescription market.

Some key questions became pertinent. Could the same substance repeat this success in the highly competitive OTC analgesics market? More impor-tant, could the same, successful *brand* be used to make an attractive proposi-tion in the consumer analgesics market? And if so, should its proposition be aimed broadly (in line with conventional thinking on OTC analgesics) at all pain relief indications, including the high frequency of usage indication, headache? Or should the brand be more specifically targeted at its heartland indications that relate to musculoskeletal pain – in consumer language, muscle, joint and back pain?

Regulatory preplanning work in several markets had revealed that there would not be universal or immediate approval for a lower dose OTC tablet. But there was an immediate opportunity for Voltaren Emulgel, a unique and trade marked gel/cream formulation, also mainly still Rx, for topical application. This variant would have a further advantage, from the point of view of the marketplace, that a loss of reimbursement would not be an issue in most countries, although it was decided for the German launch market, where ethical sales of the Emulgel were still very substantial, to name the brand Voltaren Schmerzgel (pain gel being a category recognized labelling). Elsewhere, it would be sold OTC as Voltaren Emulgel (Plate 4.2).

Although there were concerns of some 'cannibalization' of Rx sales, the prescribing trend favoured a switch as soon as possible. Other Rx to OTC switch cases of dominant sector leaders leading such down-regulation trends– notably Glaxo Wellcome's Zovirax (aciclovir) – had shown that switching tended to produce greater (Rx plus OTC) aggregate sales, and often showed uplifts in the Rx brand sales, after the OTC brand had been advertised.

Planning the core components for a successful brand: principal research stages

Preliminary analysis of the main topical analgesic markets in Europe showed grounds for optimism. First, the topical analgesics segment (pain relief gels and creams) was buoyant, due to the arrival of topical NSAIDs, which were offering something different from the older pain relief rubefacient products (heat rubs, creams and ointments) and the slightly more recent freeze sprays.

Second, and more important, Voltaren Emulgel appeared to have some relevant product benefits: its active ingredient, diclofenac, was second to none in efficacy, and the brand was widely respected by doctors and pharmacists alike; and it had a unique and trade marked gel/cream formulation, which had a scientific story about its efficacy as a delivery system for the active ingredient. Originally, Novartis' scientists had evolved and patented the Emulgel, which combined hydrophilic (water attractant) and lipophilic (fat attractant) properties. The benefit of this formulation was to facilitate deeper and more rapid penetration of the product, through the epidermis, to the site of the pain and inflammation. In this way, it could offer a real, competitive point of difference versus existing gels (which tend to be sticky and stay on the skin surface) and versus creams (which can be greasy, and less pleasant in use).

Thus, although originally designed for the Rx market, the fact was that Voltaren Emulgel had been designed thoughtfully around real consumer benefits.

But what essential strategic disciplines were required, to test whether the theory could be translated into a successful OTC launch? The pre-launch communication planning comprised four important stages, all designed to plan in distinct branded imagery, from the outset.

First, there was a search for relevant and motivating consumer insights. A major consumer study into pain was commissioned, conducted in three of the larger European markets, Germany, Italy and the UK. It would utilize some fresh research tools, which are discussed further below.

The second element was an audit of the main competitors' communications, in the shape of a communications landscaping study. This would be used to ensure that the communications territory occupied by Voltaren Emulgel would not only deliver the relevant product message, but would use a distinctive tonality via its creative approach. It was imperative to follow an axiom of consumer advertising – 'it's not just what you say, it's how you say it'. The aim was to find a distinctive executional idea or device to ensure that, in communications mapping, the new brand would occupy the right territory and sit distinctively from its competitors.

The third preplanning research stage entailed concept evaluation. Written concepts utilizing a strong consumer insight, brand promise and reason to believe (drawn from the supportable scientific data from the Rx brand) were developed and tested in two phases – a qualitative phase to iron out communication issues and refine the statements, and a quantitative phase to measure which concept was not only preferred, but would best drive purchase intention when turned into communication.

The technique that was used is one that is designed to optimize message before the niceties of creative execution are added. If the bare concept looks successful, then accurate execution should only increase the effectiveness of the advertising. Previous knowledge and goodwill towards a brand name is thereby excluded, in case it leads consumers to flatter, unwittingly, a product idea which otherwise they would judge poor.

Fourth, advertising pretesting was built in. Once advertising executions had been developed, these too would be taken to consumers to assess their takeup.

Gaining consumer insights

The consumer insight work sought to circumvent some of the overrational effects now being experienced in qualitative focus groups. It employed techniques that allowed a truer, more instinctive picture to emerge. It interviewed friends and family groupings, together and as individuals, and used affinity groups, whose lead members had recruited their own friends and colleagues.

Projective techniques – such as cartoon drawing and children's paintings – were used to unlock deep-rooted concerns and attitudes. The study, replicated in three markets, identified some key triggers that would be important for the Voltaren team to address with their topical analgesic communication.

Topicals were seen as generally less effective than tablets – consumer language provided seminal clues. Tablets were called painkillers, whereas topicals provided pain relief. Because all topicals were seen as safe, any new entrant would need to establish efficacy credentials. Crucially, it became clear that topicals were still – despite the advent of other NSAID formulations – being judged by the standards of traditional rubs (rubefacients), in terms of delivering a strong, warming sensation at skin surface level. They provided temporary relief. This explained why consumers still did not especially believe that a topical was truly a painkiller. It also became evident that, in the absence of sensory clues, such as a hot or cold sensation on the skin, efficacy demonstration, in some form, would be a vital component of communication, so as to build brand belief. Furthermore, it became clear that, because the first generation products worked at surface level, it might be necessary to actually demonstrate the deep penetration of the new topical NSAID in the advertising.

Although there were cultural differences between the three markets – with the notably green German consumer preferring topicals in principle as being closer to natural or home remedies – the similarities between countries were far greater. This lent confidence that a common executional approach should be possible.

In parallel, the Voltaren team commissioned their agency to audit communications in the sector. A landscaping approach was used, which effectively would allow the viewer to stand back and see the big picture, in terms of what kind of messages and tonal approach was being adopted by the key players in the market.

Understanding the competitive communications context

First, conventional media spend auditing was undertaken of the main brands in the sector which were media spenders in the key markets in Europe. This shortened the category list, so that only the important, media-driven brands in the sector were ultimately included in the mapping exercise. Analysis was done of the product main promise and supporting message – a reason given to believe (if available) – and brands were first mapped on a vertical axis. Those presenting themselves as strong/powerful acting, or an innovation/breakthrough, were placed towards the top: those presenting themselves as effective, but via a gentle/caring action, or with natural remedy action, towards the bottom (Figure 4.4).

But the single, vertical axis 'powerful action' versus 'gentle action' only helped to differentiate the competitors' communications, on *product* grounds. Brands, by contrast, have a richer texture, as a result of *how* they communicate. By analysing the overall creative approach the planner was able to discern what basic communication territory the competitive advertisers were seeking to occupy with their brands.

A distinction was made, therefore, once all the advertisements had been viewed, to distinguish brands which were tonally presented as 'new'/'breakthrough'/'aggressive'/'product-feature oriented'. These were designated 'high tech'. By contrast, brands' communications that were 'trust-based'/'human-centred'/'sympathetic'/'consumer-benefit oriented' were designated 'high touch'. By replotting the horizontal aspect of these same brands along this horizontal axis, a more interesting landscape appeared, which provided this greater tonal contrast between the brands (Figure 4.5).

In short, it would be as important, once concept evaluation had been completed, to determine whether Voltaren Emulgel should launch with a

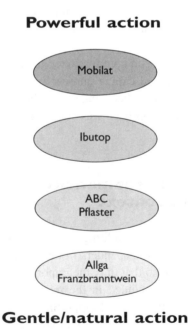

Figure 4.4 Brand mapping – 'strength of action' dimension

communications style that would position it as a 'high tech' brand, or a 'high touch' brand. Even at an early stage, consumers make instinctive as well as rational reactions to new brand propositions.

The technique offered the Voltaren marketer another tool, that of helping to ensure that his own brand's communication would position his brand in the part of the market he wanted, and that this would be clear, relative to the competition. In the instance of the German launch market, such differentiation was vital. A quick tally of products on the market – from herbals through to licensed medicines – for relieving muscular aches and pains unearthed over 50 brands.

In a general sense, there is no right or wrong brand personality. But careful planning can weigh up the pros and cons of a particular brand adopting a certain style, early on. Just as a person will decide whether a sharp Italian city suit or a conservative British country style is right for him, so does a brand adopt the clothes most suited to differentiate its personality.

The research thus far confirmed the way forward for Voltaren Emulgel. The product's proven active and unique cream/gel delivery system, argued for it to be positioned at the high end of performance in the OTC market. To sell it as gentler/more natural would not have been credible: to mirror the

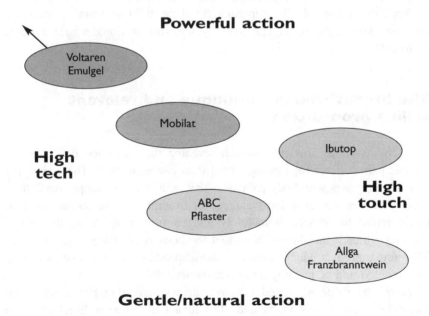

Figure 4.5 Brand mapping – the 'human' dimension

'family'/'end benefit' stance of an existing and successful OTC competitor Ibutop, would have been indistinct, and would have undersold the brand's Rx performance heritage and to position it purely against the end benefit of joint mobility would have too closely copied the rival Mobilat proposition.

Crucially, there was sufficient residual awareness of the Voltaren name from the ethical market, where it successfully stood for power and efficacy. And the brand's Rx usage in arthritis pain and back pain sat easily with the planned OTC indications of muscle, joint and back pain. While the pack colours of the Rx Geigy pack needed to be more consumer friendly, there needed to be a colour code link for the brand, hence the orange colour provided continuity.

Based on the earlier research into insights, and the clinical and Rx marketing experience, the product story was potentially established: the fast and deep penetration could be turned into a consumer story.

At the third stage, of written concepts, when the final proposition would be finely honed and tested, the manufacturers of Voltaren knew they had a strong insight built around the desire for muscle, joint and back pain sufferers to have a more effective topical remedy without the need for pills. They also knew they had a strongly differentiated and competitive product message, which could be supported by a demonstration of the penetrative power of the product to work where it was needed, beneath the skin's surface.

Yet although tonally the approach could be different from competitors' communications, the message, essentially, was similar. Could a unique aspect be found?

The breakthrough – a unique and relevant selling proposition

A rescrutiny of the Insight research revealed the continued desire of the chronic pain sufferer for healing, rather than just pain relief. The underlying fear of consumers with body pains was that pain relievers simply mask their pain. This was seen as a disadvantage, for example, for the sportsman, who might return to activity prematurely and so further aggravate the injury. Another research insight had been that the body needs time to repair itself. Therefore a product which could promise a speedier recovery time as well as pain relief would be meeting a hitherto unmet need.

Here, the value of mixed R&D/regulatory/marketing personnel brain-storming sessions was vindicated. The idea that Voltaren Emulgel could promise quicker healing emerged. Logically, a product which reduced the inflammation surrounding muscle and joint tissue would enable the body's natural healing process to get started sooner than otherwise would have occurred. A more aggressive concept was created, alongside those which merely promised deeper product penetration. The proposition was that Voltaren Emulgel not only stops the pain, but also speeds up the healing process. In both qualitative, then quantitative, research, this unique proposition proved a winner. Thus, it confirmed the value of a depth study into consumers' real needs, which the product's inherent design was able to meet.

Finally, creative work – both in TV and print media – was developed. While several approaches looked promising, one special technique which used a thermographic camera stood out. Its vivid and dramatic graphics not only delivered the demonstration message of the product, but, as important, created a high tech imagery which fitted exactly the desired position for the brand in the communications landscape map. Consumer pretesting of a very highly finished storyboard had confirmed this.

In the marketplace, the communications preplanning was quickly vindicated by the early in-market results. In Germany, the brand moved quickly to a leadership position, following two waves of advertising. In Belgium, where the brand had languished in fourth position as a semi-ethical, it quickly doubled its share and moved to brand leader. Similar results of dramatic market penetration and significant brand share movements were recorded wherever the brand and its TV advertising was taken.

The classic ingredients for OTC success, to which we alluded earlier in the chapter, had been blended and cooked together. A good product ingredient and delivery system had been carried across from the Rx market. Virtually the same indications – in consumer terms – had been retained. As many as possible of the transferable brand values of power and efficacy had been retained in the OTC launch. The communications approach had messaged a unique double promise of pain relief and healing, while using the latest executional techniques, to create a truly distinctive/modern/state-of-the-technical-art look and feel to the consumer brand, so that it would position itself clear of the existing, overcrowded market.

III

The Rise of
Patient Power

5 | Direct-to-consumer branding – the US perspective

ANNE DEVEREUX Merkley Newman Harty Healthworks

In the early 1990s, direct-to-consumer (DTC) advertising in the USA was the luxury of the rich – the big brands that had the funding and the volume of patients or prospects to justify mass consumer spending over and above professional promotion. Those mass brands, in broad-reaching chronic care categories such as allergy, cardiology and metabolics as well as quality of life categories such as hair loss, developed an expertise in reaching and motivating their best prospects to request and even demand their drug.

Entering the new millennium, DTC advertising has ballooned throughout the industry. It is one of the mandatory strategic considerations for a successful launch or product branding effort for almost all pharmaceutical brands – large and small.

■ DTC promotional spending by pharmaceutical companies in the USA has grown 400%, from $266 million in 1994 to $1.3 billion in 1998, and is projected to exceed $7 billion by the year 2005 (MPA, 1999).

■ In 1998, six of the top ten US pharmaceutical companies invested more than half their total promotional budgets to reach consumers – and spent 44% more in advertising to consumers than in promoting their brands to physicians (MPA, 1999).

■ Advertising expenditures by the biggest brands exceed those of the world's most aggressive packaged-goods marketers. Clarityn, for example, is estimated to have spent more than Coke – and did so with spending bursts during peak allergy season, thereby dominating the airwaves.

■ DTC advertising in the USA replaced the advice of a friend or relative as the primary source of information a consumer uses before requesting a specific brand from a physician (MPA, 1999).

What fuelled this marketing revolution?

Many authorities attribute the growth of DTC advertising to the key market factors shown in Figure 5.1.

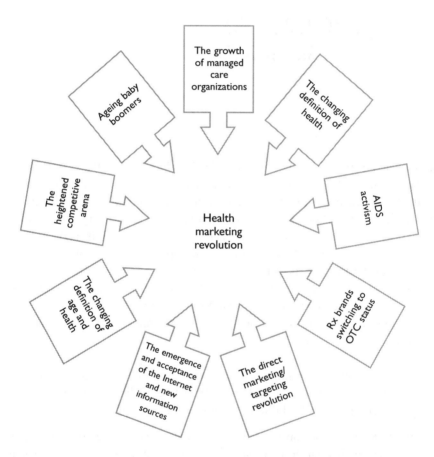

Figure 5.1 Key market factors attributed to the growth of DTC advertising

The growth of managed care

Most Americans grew up with a medical system where private doctors treated patients, who were then reimbursed by their insurance carriers for the care they received. With the emergence of managed care over the past ten years, the role of the doctor as the authority has been somewhat undermined by the requirements of the managed care organizations with which they are aligned. These institutions determine treatment algorithms, prioritize (and sometimes limit) specific drug use and have altered the way in which physicians are compensated. While quality care is still valued, physicians within the managed care arena must also manage (and maximize) patient volume and the use of over-the-counter (OTC) options as part of the treatment process.

The result of this treatment evolution is that many patients and their loved ones are becoming educated about treatment options. Now they can ask for the medicines and care that they were once denied as part of the system. They can also seek answers and information from alternative sources because their physicians no longer have the time to answer their questions.

The changing definition of health

If you had asked a middle-aged American in 1975 what it meant to be healthy, they would likely answer 'my arthritis isn't bothering me anymore' or 'my sore throat has gone away.' Health was defined as the lack of symptoms.

Roll the calendar forward 25 years, and that same middle-aged American would define health as holistic, as mental *and* physical. A few forward-thinkers might even suggest that, 'without healthy relationships and a healthy environment, I'm not totally healthy'.

Physicians are held to these standards. Despite decreased available time and an increased number of treatment options, physicians are expected (as a standard of care) to understand how a given illness relates to the patient's total life, and to make suggestions for modification/improvement of that lifestyle beyond writing a prescription or applying a cast.

DTC advertising, especially in the form of in-office promotion or patient education, often helps to fill the gap between patient expectations/patient definition of health and the role physicians can possibly play given the constraints on their time.

An increasingly holistic view of health and the emergence of herbal remedies

When physicians and educational resources within the practice do not meet patients' needs, they often turn elsewhere for treatment or relief. Results from a survey conducted by *Men's Health* magazine in 1999 showed that 40% of US adults are now more likely to treat themselves before consulting a physician than they were 12 months earlier. Many of those adults turn to herbal remedies as their first-line therapy. This trend is a result of the growing respect earned by a few of the country's leading homeopathists and herbal experts such as Dr Andrew Weil, and the growing acceptance of the medical community (including both doctors and pharmacists) in herbal remedies as valid treatment options.

The availability of OTCs

The patent expiration of leading Rx medicines has also put increased power in the hands of patients. Drugs such as Zantac, which once held the position of the world's largest brand (as measured in sales), opted to launch OTC versions of their brand in order to extend use and protect market share.

As a result, patients gained access to new classes of medicines never before available to them, and approached these offerings with enthusiasm and caution. Armed with warnings from their healthcare providers that misuse of these medicines could mask more serious problems or cause serious side effects, consumers sought education and information for themselves, becoming a more educated, curious and demanding audience.

The growth of direct marketing and targeted marketing

In all business categories (including healthcare), direct marketing experts have perfected and evolved their ability to identify, reach and convert consumers based on their interests, behaviours and purchase patterns. Database companies such as Carol Wright have accumulated behavioural information on millions of US households, including disease incidence and medical treatment. Retail marketing giants such as Catalina can make offers at the point of purchase, based on consumers' previous purchase decisions. As a result, pharmaceutical marketers can purchase names and efficiently reach target populations with their specific drug information and offers.

The ability to target has become so refined that not only do healthcare marketers target based on disease state, but they target based on key psychographics, ethnic skews, OTC behaviours and even by store purchases in real time.

The emergence of the Internet

The Internet provides instant access to health information never before available to the average consumer and allows for the customization of material to meet specific needs.

Once diagnosed with an illness, patients and their loved ones use the Internet to search for answers, opinions, alternate treatment options and even clinical data that allow them to personally evaluate options and bring questions to their physicians. The Internet is now used *most often* for gathering health-related information. As a result, DTC marketers now view the Internet as an ideal venue for reaching the highly involved patient or caregiver at the time of peak interest, using their site and links to related sites as an inexpensive and effective mechanism for brand building, patient acquisition, enrolment in loyalty programmes and referral to related physicians and pharmacies.

The heightened competitive arena

Over the past ten years, marketing pharmaceutical products has become increasingly competitive. The availability of parity drugs or products has motivated marketers to use new techniques in order to create allegiances and establish differentiated positions. One of these techniques has been to reach consumers and motivate them using less traditional means (other than clinical benefits such as safety and efficacy) in order to create demand, preference and product differentiation.

For consumers whose drugs are not fully reimbursed by their insurance company (or for those who have no insurance), manufacturers' offers, including coupons, rebates and free trials, often mean the difference between parity drugs or provide a reason to continue therapy during tough financial times.

The AIDS epidemic

The AIDS epidemic is another factor undeniably associated with the birth of patient activism and DTC (or in this case, direct-to-patient) advertising. Leaders in the AIDS movement helped to demonstrate the power of patients by motivating changes in healthcare, accelerating funding of research and drug approvals and raising issues related to quality of life, which are often pushed aside in the world of science and research. As a result, drug companies responded with ads targeting their active audience and a dialogue began.

The coming of age of the baby boomer generation

The huge generation of baby boomers are now coming of age and healthcare is becoming a top priority for them. Born between 1946 and 1964, this generation is currently searching to optimize healthcare for themselves and their families. In a recent survey on generation marketing, Yankelovich notes that boomers are constantly challenging the system, doing things differently and seeking customized attention. They are looking for 'the perfect thing for them' and, in the case of healthcare, DTC marketing allows them access to more information so they can make decisions that are right for them. *Time* magazine (June 12, 2000) reports on a Del Webb survey of boomer attitudes, noting that boomers feel

> their greatest contribution in retirement will include demanding funding for medical research. The red ribbon for AIDS and the pink ribbon for breast cancer will be replaced by gray ribbons of gerontology.

Entering the new millennium, the evolution continues

DTC has become a required tactical consideration for most brands in the USA. Yet the definition of DTC and how it can be implemented is evolving daily. To the layperson, the first definition of DTC is mass advertising via print (as was the case in the mid-to-late-1990s, when print was the dominant form of advertising) and TV (where the bulk of US advertising dollars are spent today). The reality, however, is that many brands cannot afford (and are not best served by) these media, which cast a wide net in order to reach the desired patient populations. Or, if they are well served by mass advertising, it cannot work effectively without being supplemented by more targeted mechanisms for ongoing communication.

Mass advertising

Decisions as to whether to take a mass advertising approach are often made based on an assessment of key variables:

■ the size of the target patient population
■ the chronicity of the disease state
■ the relevance of that disease state to its sufferers
■ the average value of a patient taking medication.

For example, disease states with large patient populations such as cardiovascular disease or diabetes make national advertising efforts logical because it is relatively easy to reach the patients in question. Patients with chronic diseases, where the problem is a constant reminder to the patient that their disease (such as arthritis) is not well controlled, also make DTC information welcome. Life-threatening disease states such as cancer or Alzheimer's are so alarming that many people are often on the lookout for information that could help their friends or loved ones. In categories where the cost of therapy or patient value is high, DTC spending often pays off despite having a relatively small target population.

The role of direct marketing

There are many brands that fit none of the above criteria but have used targeted DTC to drive their businesses. Marketers of HIV drugs have been able to control costs because AIDS populations are relatively easy to reach – both geographically and through existing AIDS organizations. With disease states such as multiple sclerosis, where the patient population is small yet actively involved in treating their disease, marketers have succeeded by creating proprietary communications venues (the Internet, newsletters and MS associations) where new patient acquisition as well as compliance/persistence messages can be sent.

Non-traditional patient communication

For pharmaceutical marketers outside the USA, branded mass consumer advertising may never be permissible due to government restrictions. For that reason, it is important to look at the other forms of consumer communication that inevitably accompany (and often substitute for) mass advertising efforts, including:

- patient education
- caregiver communications
- loyalty marketing (retention, persistence, compliance, protection)
- public relations
- celebrity testimonials.

These less traditional approaches help marketers to reach consumers while keeping within regulatory guidelines.

Patient education, in the form of in-office brochures, posters and interactive games, can serve to educate patients and drive them to ask questions of their doctors that might otherwise have gone unasked. For example, millions of patients are taking medication to control their diabetes, but the reality is that with monotherapy, many of them are not reaching government-recommended levels for control. Yet these patients have no idea what that level should be, and the physicians are not specifically discussing those levels with their patients. By instigating a discussion between doctor and patient, a new therapy is often added, benefiting the company manufacturing that add-on drug and benefiting the patient by putting him in better control.

In many disease states, the patient is not the primary person taking responsibility for controlling their disease. That role often falls to their caregiver – a spouse, child or friend who helps to manage the health of that sick person. In chronic disease states such as hypercholesterolaemia, good dietary control is an important aspect of care. Appealing to the caregivers by giving them tips on healthful cooking, as well as an overview of possible treatment options, will not only help to initiate discussions about therapy, it may well increase patient compliance and persistence as well. With scary diseases such as cancer, many family members often launch searches for information about drugs that might help their loved one.

Compliance and persistence with therapy are essential for patients' successful treatment, yet for most patients, whether on a short-term antibiotic or on lifetime therapy for a chronic disease, medicines are not taken properly. Loyalty programmes set up to communicate with patients throughout the course of their treatment can offer huge benefits to both patients and pharmaceutical marketers. Loyalty programmes allow for the exchange of information, voicing of concerns and migration to new and improved therapies. They can be value-added services that help a physician to differentiate one drug from another or help to keep patients taking their medicine past traditional drop-off points. In the USA, most marketers using traditional mass media approaches to DTC supplement their efforts with loyalty marketing. As they say, it is a lot cheaper to keep an existing patient than to find a new one!

Occasionally, marketers need to be more subtle with their promotion. Many have chosen less direct routes, such as public relations or the use of celebrity testimonials, to supplement – or substitute for – traditional communications. Those venues, while harder to control and measure, can allow less regulated discussion of brands and their benefits than can happen within the highly regulated bounds of DTC.

Another more subtle approach to patient communications is disease-state or unbranded advertising. Probably the most common (and the only legal form) of DTC advertising in Europe, disease-state advertising is used by marketers to provide the public with information on a disease (not a drug). In the USA, when a consumer calls a free phone number to inquire about an unbranded ad they saw on TV or in print, they can be offered branded materials about treatment options via the mail. Disease-state advertising is most commonly used by market leaders for whom the risk of the patient going directly to their doctor without waiting for the branded materials is low.

Top-line evaluation: will DTC work for your brand?

In the USA, brands determining whether they might pursue a DTC strategy evaluate numerous variables before proceeding. A few key questions are:

- *Opportunity:* What is the size of the market and current level of patient satisfaction? (A crowded, satisfied market makes DTC expensive.)

- *Doctor acceptance:* Do physicians have enough confidence (or see minimal enough risk) to provide patients with the requested drug?

- *Competitive set:* Is our product unique enough to be differentiated? Can our benefits be made meaningful to patients? How much will we need to spend to achieve a loud enough voice?

- *Value:* How much is a patient on therapy worth? (And how much can we spend to find, convert and maintain them?)

- *Targetability:* How easy is it to find and reach our audience? What existing media venues exist?

- *Involvement:* How involved in their disease are patients and their loved ones? (Apathy also makes DTC a challenge.)

- *Compliance:* Is there a substantial problem with patients dropping out of therapy or inadequately taking their prescriptions? (If so, DTC can often help.)

Possible applications to Europe/global

While current restrictions make branded DTC impossible, progress has already been made in bridging the communications gap between manufacturers and patients. Disease-state advertising has been effectively implemented in Europe, herbal products are becoming more mainstream and in-office patient education is effectively serving to stimulate conversation in-office.

But it is unlikely to stop there. Most of the factors that have helped DTC to succeed in the USA – the availability of OTCs, the emergence of technologies such as the Internet and direct marketing resources, the heightened competitive arena and the coming of age of the baby boomer generation – exist globally as well.

References

MPA (Magazine Publishers of America), Summer 1999.
Time magazine, 2000.

6 Direct-to-consumer branding – Europe and Asia

ROB BENSON Bates Health World

The extension of direct-to-consumer (DTC) advertising of prescription drugs beyond the US marketplace to other commercially attractive world markets such as Japan and Europe is an intensifying battleground for change. Advocate and reactionary interest groups continue to line up either side of the debate, which is complicated by the political and health professional conservatism that surrounds the business and economic arguments. Pressure is building within the fast-growing pharmaceutical industry now valued at $350 billion worldwide. At its simplest, it is a contest between free-market thinking and the various complexities of socialized welfare philosophy and health precedents that have been structurally unchallenged for the past 50 years. With so much at stake, it is perhaps inevitable that, outside the USA, the DTC advertising debate has been highlighted by more polarized opinion than consensus argument, and the volume and tone of the debate more emotionally charged than rationally centred.

DTC opponents point to the hard-sell directness and implied manipulation they perceive in the nearly $2 billion now being spent per year on US advertisements for prescription drugs that treat heart disease, cancer and other life-threatening conditions. They criticize even more intensely the advertisements for life-enhancing pharmaceuticals for hair loss, obesity and other so-called new 'lifestyle' conditions, where advancing science can now offer consumers new choices.

Countering this, consumer advocates make the point that:

> Medical drugs are amongst the most important commodities we have – our very lives often depend on them. Yet we have less control over whether we get them, less say in which ones we are allowed, and less knowledge about them than about almost anything else we consume. (Carter, 2000)

While the DTC debate can wrap itself around lofty themes such as personal freedom and social equality, in order to understand its origins as well as its emergent and future direction – involving a whole range of consumer communications of which advertising is only a part – the central forces of change within the inter-relationship between globalization and consumerization need to be recognized as providing the template for growth for the world's leading pharmaceutical companies.

The globalizing world of pharmaceuticals

Compared with the car industry, airlines, computer manufacturers and other businesses, pharmaceutical companies are late starters in facing the challenges and opportunities presented by the wider world market. With illness, disease and the desire for good health indiscriminate and homogenized aspects of life, the historical fragmentation of healthcare provision is a reminder of its time-deep and local roots. Regardless of this, the pharmaceutical industry is now actively addressing the global issue in terms of both supply and demand.

On the supply side, the economic reality of delivering double-digit growth in a business where a major new drug costs, on average, $600 million and 10–12 years to get to market has focused industry attention on new strategies. Such supply-side change has been built on speed-to-market efficiencies and a tighter therapy focus designed to concentrate R&D effort and lead to enhanced return on investment (ROI) post-launch.

Equally, the prospect of genomic-based innovation continues to spur supply-side restructuring, none more so than industry consolidation from acquisitions and mergers, all designed to boost the critical mass now considered necessary to compete with advantage at a global level where the top 20 companies now command nearly 70% market share (Figure 6.1). However, no amount of channel restructuring on its own can deliver the growth expectations now in place for both the pharmaceutical industry and its leading companies as set by the world's financial markets. This is where the spotlight falls on the desire to accelerate the expansion of DTC to the world market for drugs.

Influencing the demand side against the background of such non-geographical fundamentals as ageing populations and the ever-rising thresholds of consumer expectation is a powerful catalyst that is transcending the nationally rooted world patchwork of healthcare provision. Such demographic and attitudinal demand-side change is well documented, as is the maverick influence of the Internet, the global health information explosion and the rise of patient power. This places the world's leading pharmaceutical companies at a crossroads, with the DTC debate centre stage.

Size and scale create the choice to compete, achieving success still remains the challenge

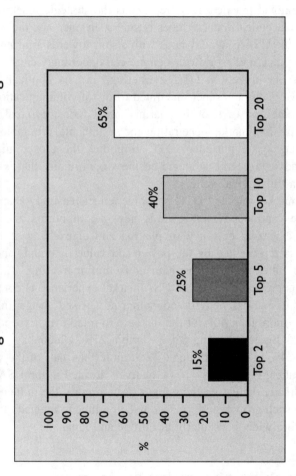

Figure 6.1 Leading pharma companies' share of world market (2000)

Source: Med Ad News, 1999

With mergers and acquisitions, a new corporate mandate and now portfolio management efficiencies leading to a tighter brand focus, most leading manufacturers now urgently need to bring changes in supply and demand together to leverage the growth they desire and need to be seen to deliver. In short, they need to change the rules of drug marketing on a worldwide basis to accommodate the patient as both end-user and consumer in parallel to all their other promotional communication activities. Far from being a marketing addition to current promotional practice, DTC represents the strategic redefinition of the way the pharmaceutical industry does business. In this way, the extension of DTC beyond the USA is synonymous with a shift towards a far more market-oriented future that links worldwide commercial opportunity creation, development and its maximization. DTC marketing, and its application through consumer advertising and other integrated forms of communication, helps to create significant new ways for the pharmaceutical industry to realize its goals of rapid new product market penetration and sustainable, profitable growth. In essence, in corporate parlance, DTC embodies the closer alignment of competitive advantage with strategic business opportunity that is at its most desirable on a truly global scale.

With the market-oriented DTC phenomenon increasingly shaping awareness, attitudes and behaviour towards new health norms and healthcare choices, the emerging currency of pharmaceutical exchanges, actions and involvement is represented by the power and value of brands and branding best practice inherent in mainstream consumer marketing. The evidence propelling this process beyond the USA market experience is compelling. In 1999, 25 of the most heavily consumer-advertised drugs in the USA accounted for more than 40% of the increase in retail drug expenditure, with brands such as Lipitor growing 56%, Clarityn 21%, Glucophage nearly 50% and Prilosec 24% in that year alone. With more than half of the world's top 20 pharmaceutical companies' HQs effectively located in the USA, and such companies already delivering the highest growth rates, the influence of DTC marketing on such growth performance will continue to intensify the pressure for change worldwide, particularly in Europe and Japan.

DTC – reaching the wider horizon

The pharmaceutical industry's harnessing to date of the global business potential offered by DTC marketing outside the USA needs to be considered at various levels, characterized by various inherited factors from the pharmaceutical industry of the distant and recent past.

Shaping this are three dominant parameters, all of which are themselves in the flux of change with an eye to the future:

1. First, the overall sub-optimal level of shared understanding of DTC, such that confident best practice and consistency of approach have yet to be fully defined for broadscale company action to take place, even where corporate and top-level management support for DTC exists in principle.

2. Second, the compounding effect of widespread decentralized company and key organizational structures that fragment common effort along budget control and profit responsibility lines, often anchoring DTC initiatives at local, regional or country levels.

3. Third, the inherent conservatism of an industry still heavily dependent worldwide on government health expenditure for reimbursement-sourced revenue and product licence approvals, all controlled by powerful regulatory forces resistant to anything that they perceive might upset the public balance sheet.

These three interconnected factors compound a shared overall industry caution, but not inertia, towards DTC, as an emerging breed of leading pharmaceutical manufacturers is now beginning to demonstrate. As a result, DTC activity to date outside the US market is moving forward but at different speeds and, as yet, with no common initiation focus but several. These collectively indicate an accelerating industry appetite for change that favours genuine DTC adoption as both desirable and inevitable. This transitional process is also being promoted and fuelled by the continuingly growing influence of the Internet and its rising challenge to the legal pharmaceutical status quo on a worldwide basis, especially in developed markets such as Japan and Europe.

In parallel with this, however, three discernable levels of DTC engagement can be identified to date as increasingly the active norms outside the USA. These are not mutually exclusive, as they can involve the same pharmaceutical companies and brands, indicating perhaps a faster exchange of DTC practice within the most DTC active companies.

DTC and strategic planning

With Europe and Japan representing well over half of the world's pharmaceutical market, it is inevitable that, beyond the USA, these regional markets should represent the next primary DTC targets for an industry committed to growth and increasingly accepting of change. This appears especially true of the world's top 20 drug companies who now control approaching 70% of the world market. This interest is fuelled by a new determination to exploit more aggressively the commercial potential of efforts being made to create increasingly innovative new product pipelines, even if fed from non- or part-owned biotech alliances.

Such a business perspective is beginning to introduce DTC marketing considerations significantly earlier in the brand development process, certainly pre-launch and increasingly as early as Phases II and III, a trend that will grow as earlier consumer involvement is further legitimized as part of best R&D practice, econometric modelling and outcome benchmarking.

The role of DTC in such contexts is directed at market conditioning and can be engaged outside the USA within the current regulatory frameworks at the level of non-product specific disease and symptom awareness activity, often backed by third party and patient group support. The commercial objectives in such circumstances include raising awareness to expand or modify treatment expectations within targeted markets into which new products are later introduced. This approach is intensifying as the leading pharmaceutical companies clarify their areas of therapy interest, core competence and R&D priorities for the future.

Thus, DTC marketing outside the USA is increasingly being adopted corporately at the senior level of strategic planning, particularly in the arena of new product development and market introduction. This is being further encouraged as, even for non-US companies, the US market, as the world's largest, is increasingly the market of choice for the launch of new products destined to become the global brands of tomorrow and where DTC marketing is an inherent and major campaign component. Behind such actions lies a quietly growing confidence and belief in the inevitability of regulatory change in both Europe and Japan. Evidence supporting such growing belief continues to emerge from various sources whether it is the UK's Association of the British Pharmaceutical Industry (ABPI) Informed Patient Initiative directed at legislative change at EU and national level and its increasing influence within the wider European market, or the British Medical Association's (BMA) policy shift on DTC to: 'want to shape what happens rather than just oppose it [DTC]'.

This represents a growing realism outside the USA towards the strength of the DTC argument even if it remains disliked in principle:

> We [the BMA] believe that what is happening in the US now could be happening in Europe within the next 5 to 10 years. (BMA, July, 2000)

Add to this the now famous *Lancet* editorial and the DTC in Europe debate shifts from 'no never' to 'when and how':

> It is time to take a mature view about marketing ethical pharmaceuticals direct to the public.
>
> Physicians should be strong enough to cope with more informed patients and the patient needs to realise that with empowerment comes the opportunity to take a truly informed part in the prescribing process.
>
> The time is right for an extension of direct-to-public advertising for prescription-only medicines from the USA to other countries, at least on a trial basis. (*Lancet*, 28 March, 1998)

To this point, the ABPI Informed Patient Initiative develops a rational call for change in Europe:

> The current restrictions at EU level should be reviewed in the light of technological advances and increasing demand from patients for information to assist with their understanding of medicines ... responsible and fact-based communication should be provided directly to the patient. (APBI, 2000)

Local market DTC adoption

While the DTC situation in Europe and Japan continues, DTC marketing has already been adopted outside the USA, most notably in New Zealand. With over two years' experience, the New Zealand opportunity has been enthusiastically taken up by the pharmaceutical companies active there, proving a relatively low-cost and valuable test-bed for DTC campaign experimentation outside the USA. From a worldwide perspective, the New Zealand case illustrates in practice how difficult it is for regulatory authorities to reverse the growth of DTC when the genie is well and truly out of the bottle. As a result, amid criticism of executional interpretation of the rules, the New Zealand DTC debate is now focused on refinement and more consistent and robust industry self-regulation in its implementation. It is about the shape of adoption and not strategic or conceptual reasoning and justification of its very existence.

Far from being a distant, local DTC sideshow, the New Zealand experience is particularly significant in the symbolic sense, as it helps to dilute the emotionally charged US stigma of free-market profiteering often quoted by the most extreme opponents to DTC. Indicative of this is the very recent change in Australia where a recommended legislative review is now proposed which, if accepted, would permit a limited relaxation of the advertising rules within that market currently restricting DTC adoption. On closer analysis, this move illustrates again the global macro-effect of the Internet, the health information explosion and the increasing desire of people to become more actively involved in their own health and healthcare. In such circumstances, DTC advertising and its other expressions are but the voice to the words.

Innovative DTC initiators

While the debate for legislative change supportive of DTC marketing continues outside the USA, several leading pharmaceutical companies have undertaken important and innovative DTC initiatives that have legally operated within the current law. This is especially the case in Europe, and in particular the UK, where common cultural and language links with the USA, plus a relatively open approach to self-medication and the use of mainstream consumer media to promote OTC brands have created a climate favourable to DTC initiatives.

Such initiatives operate on the unbranded disease and symptom awareness DTC model. This recognizes the potent role of health information as a catalyst for both consumer empowerment and relationship-building dialogue between the company (or corporate brand) as product brand owner and the consumer as end-user or carer.

It is important to recognize such an approach as:

■ A communication process, not an event

■ Involving information as opposed to promotion

■ Built around the disease or medical condition, not a particular treatment or named product brand.

As a result, the European Directive 92/28 is not breached or compromised in its definition of what is not promotion: 'Statements relating to human health, not products.'

Case example – Novartis

Novartis recognized that people suffering from fungal nail infections often did not recognize the symptoms of their condition, resulting in significant underdiagnosis and therefore undertreatment, especially early treatment intervention with the appropriate prescription medication.

With Lamisil, a highly effective as well as innovative brand within its prescription portfolio, the company adopted a DTC disease-awareness approach that utilized consumer press, TV, direct mail and telephone helpline support to alert consumers to the condition and its symptoms. This use of consumer communication stimulated awareness and self-reference in the wider population as well as providing sufficient information and education to encourage sufferers to see their doctor. At no time was the brand Lamisil mentioned, but its strong market positioning created a powerful link whereby the brand would, by association, become a beneficiary of any subsequent increase in prescriptions for the condition.

To engage consumers as potential and actual sufferers, the DTC programme centred on the 'Stepwise' consumer support theme. This enabled the route to diagnosis and treatment to have a personality and image that effectively filled the product brand space, enabling the programme to carry important information to the target market. This simple and highly effective DTC approach, based on disease and symptom awareness, has reportedly generated over 250,000 consumer responses and continues to run in the UK. It has also proved illustrative of the current status of DTC in Europe:

■ First, it underpins the strategic role and scope of DTC within current EU law to add incremental growth to a brand via market expansion. It can also powerfully prepare the ground for an eventual Rx to OTC switch.

■ Second, it validates the desire of consumers to be proactive and take greater responsibility for their health, an awareness, attitudinal and behavioural shift best managed as a process with the use of a range of integrated communications rather than a simple advertised event.

■ Third, it illustrates the potency of simple and clear health information and its significant scope to enhance both the quality of the patient–doctor dialogue and encourage better compliance post-prescription – two common, well-documented and costly weaknesses in the health systems of most major world markets.

It should be noted that this Novartis DTC programme was challenged legally by a small group of doctors who complained that Lamisil enjoyed monopolistic advantage as one of only two oral treatments available and that it put pressure on doctors to prescribe. The legal outcome validated the company's action, stating there was no breach of the legal code. The legal verdict also acknowledged that:

Novartis [in their submission] had gone to some length to explore the issues surrounding the code ... and recognised that there was a fine line distinction between education and promotion ... but Stepwise was not encouraging patients to ask for a specific medicine.

Case example – Pharmacia & Upjohn

Pharmacia & Upjohn adopted a similar DTC approach in Europe targeting incontinence sufferers but with a bolder campaign style synonymous with a market leader stance and a mission to legitimize and develop the incontinence category within which their Detrusitol brand competed.

The consumer media mix utilized in the UK included TV, national press, a telephone helpline and direct mail fulfilment with further information packs (Figure 6.2). Of additional interest were the following:

■ The involvement and campaign pre-vetting with health professionals such that problematic issues could be fine-tuned in advance and doctor and nurse audiences prepared ahead of the consumer advertising and its impact.

■ The inclusion of additional consumer respondent data components, as part of the fulfilment pack sent back to consumers who contacted the helpline, provided the company with valuable information in order to track campaign performance and commence customer segmentation analysis for future marketing.

■ The inclusion of the Pharmacia & Upjohn corporate brand as a sponsorship tag in the communication.

■ The copy references to treatment choices and specific symptom references to help to shape the profile and mind-set of consumers encouraged to see their doctor and the doctor–patient dialogue at consultation (that is, language that opens the way to condition differentiation without mentioning the product by its brand name).

All the above DTC elements can be found in the early disease-awareness advertising that took place in the USA in the 1980s and 90s, illustrating a new level of convergence and shared learning between Europe and the US market.

This Public Health Education Campaign aims to help people who suffer from bladder problems. If you are a sufferer, it would help us to reach other sufferers by answering the following questions.

1. Did you learn about the freephone number from

   a) A poster or notice on a wall   YES / NO

        Where was the poster / notice?   Shopping Centre
                                                     Bus Station
                                                     Motorway Service Area
                                                     Doctors Surgery
                                                     Other

   b) An announcement in a newspaper / magazine? YES / NO

   Which newspaper/magazine was it   ....(Please write in the title)

   c) Television announcement   YES / NO

2. Before seeing the current campaign, did you ever discuss your bladder problem with any of the following? (Please tick more than one box if needed.)
                                                     GP   ☐
                                                     Nurse   ☐
                                                     Continence Advisor   ☐

3. Have you received any of the following for your bladder problems in the past? (Please tick more than one box if needed.)
                                          Pads / pants   ☐
                                          Surgical operation   ☐
                                          Device inserted in the bladder   ☐
                                          Advice on special exercises   ☐
                                          Advice on special diets   ☐
                                          Tablets/pills which were prescribed   ☐
                                          Tablets/pills bought from a chemist   ☐
                                          (without a prescription)

5. Are you   Male   ☐
                                          Female   ☐

6. Which of the following best describes your age?
                                          Under 30   ☐
                                          30 – 44   ☐
                                          45 – 54   ☐
                                          55 – 64   ☐
                                          65+   ☐

Thank you for taking the time to answer these questions. If you would like to receive further educational items on this subject in future, please fill in your name and address below. This information will be treated in the strictest confidence – your details will not be passed on.

    NAME   _____
    ADDRESS   _____
               _____
    POSTCODE   _____

Once you have completed this questionnaire please return it via FREEPOST in the envelope provided. Thank you for your help.

Health Education Sponsored by Pharmacia & Upjohn   P4592B/6.99

Figure 6.2 Pharmacia & Upjohn DTC campaign
(mail pack respondent questionnaire)

DTC – US/European convergence

There is significant evidence of a growing strategic DTC convergence between the USA and Europe when market-leading brands with innovative benefits, especially those owned by the top ten pharmaceutical companies, are considered, from Viagra to Detrusitol, Lamisil to Xenical, Zyban to Relenza. In the USA, the top ten brands account for 41% of all DTC expenditure, while the top ten drug companies account for nearly 80% of total DTC market spend. In non-US markets, where non-product branded DTC campaigns are introduced, this picture is likely to be replicated while current legislation remains unchanged.

Outside the USA, therefore, DTC investment in the short term is likely to advantage such major players in commercial situations where the following criteria and conditions apply as a whole or in part:

- Undertreated markets
- Chronic condition with no cure
- New, more effective therapy/good safety profile
- Patients and carers are information hungry
- Scope for leadership brand position
- Quality of life issues are important
- A public health benefit is recognized.

This recognizes a strategic and symbiotic relationship between the scope of DTC marketing and enhanced health outcomes for patients (see Table 6.1).

Beyond such strategic considerations, executional DTC campaign style, tone and content are likely to remain very different between the USA and other world markets, even after regulatory liberalization. That said, there

TABLE 6.1	
DTC marketing – patient and brand owner benefits	
Patient benefits	*Brand owner benefits*
■ Earlier diagnosis	■ Market growth/legitimacy
■ Quicker treatment intervention	■ Faster penetration
■ Most appropriate treatment option	■ Strong market share
■ Enhanced compliance and persistence	■ Brand loyalty
■ Improved outcomes	■ Corporate and brand reputation enhancement

remains a strategic continuum that already links the US DTC environment to the rest of the world, when the full spectrum of DTC communication is aligned from the most generic non-branded stage to the full-blown branded DTC scenario as exists in the USA (Figure 6.3). On this basis, the degree of DTC ascendency of the European marketplace legally positions it at 'corporately supported disease treatment awareness' (Level 5).

However, as witnessed by DTC initiatives such as those undertaken by Pharmacia and Novartis, wide scope within the current European regulations already exists, especially if third party or patient group support is elicited and underpinned by public relations programmes working in harmony with paid-for advertising and direct marketing (Figure 6.4).

This can be enhanced further by linking off-line communications with new online media opportunities, which are evolving speedily to create the new reality of online, one to one, relationship-based patient communities built on partnership and permission marketing. Such developments will in time have sufficient critical mass to make them corporate assets that can assist in both brand marketing and even clinical research programmes, creating a new strategic cyclicity to pharmaceutical marketing built on DTC communications and the involvement of the consumer (Figure 6.5).

Following the 80/20 Pareto principle, such refinements are equally attractive as they create new scope for brand owners to target and capture the most

DTC Communication Platforms

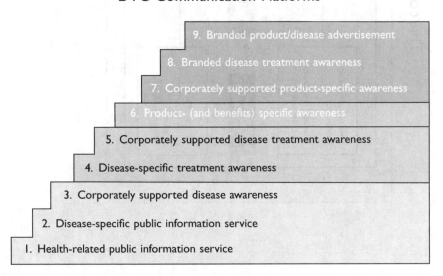

9. Branded product/disease advertisement

8. Branded disease treatment awareness

7. Corporately supported product-specific awareness

6. Product- (and benefits) specific awareness

5. Corporately supported disease treatment awareness

4. Disease-specific treatment awareness

3. Corporately supported disease awareness

2. Disease-specific public information service

1. Health-related public information service

Figure 6.3 The way forward

The communication matrix

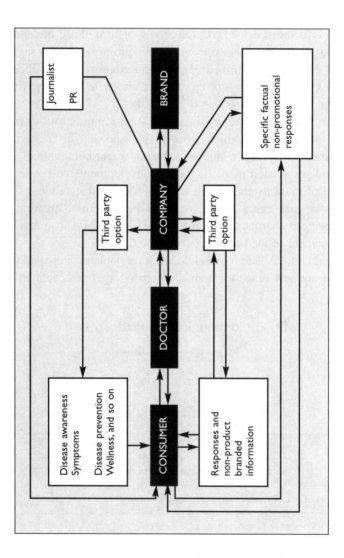

Figure 6.4 The European DTC model

Online patient communities are a growing reality

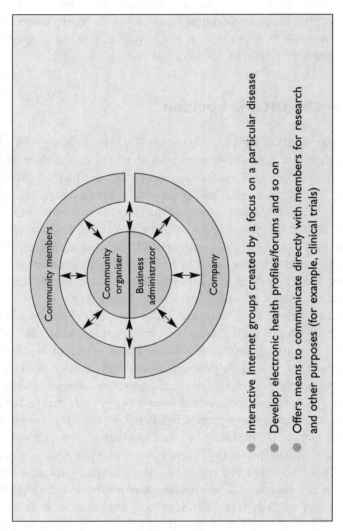

- Interactive Internet groups created by a focus on a particular disease
- Develop electronic health profiles/forums and so on
- Offers means to communicate directly with members for research and other purposes (for example, clinical trials)

Figure 6.5 New online DTC

profitable consumer segments of any market – the 20% of customers that represent 80% of profits. This is of particular relevance to the future advance of DTC as ROI on new DTC expenditure is now a critical upfront campaign planning issue.

Even without European legislative change, the stand-back evidence suggests that DTC is proving to be an effective prime mover that is in many ways reshaping the pharmaceutical business and marketing model, aligning it ever closer to the best practice approaches developed and adopted by mainstream consumer marketers the world over.

DTC – the future horizon

With Japan an anticipated front leader for DTC legal change after Australia, legal change in Europe is expected realistically in two to three years' time. Regardless of this, DTC scenario planning is now part of virtually every marketer's remit, not least because it can influence every pharmaceutical market. DTC, and its adoption beyond the USA to other major world markets, is a key part of the globalization of pharmaceuticals. It sits well within the new business model that links smarter R&D innovations to the full potential offered by worldwide demand. It is the key communication driver converting an industry with products to one endowed with power brands that can shape and dominate the markets they compete in (Figure 6.6).

The link between the role and influence of DTC communications to create such brands with market power recognizes that only with deep consumer insight and involvement can the business goal of lifetime customer value generated from high penetration and high loyalty be aimed at and secured within the business. Moreover, as industries mature in terms of globalization (and pharmaceuticals still have a way to go) change intensifies at all levels. The key emerging challenge is not whether DTC is going to be a part of a company's business, or even whether it is right for a particular company, it is fast becoming 'How is your company going to cope with DTC?' This recognizes that regardless of the market, powerful competitors with powerful brands will be applying a new consumer marketing philosophy as part of their total enhanced business mission from now on. In summary, it is a question of growth and survival as to how quickly and smartly pharmaceutical brand owners adapt to the growing and irreversible global reality of DTC.

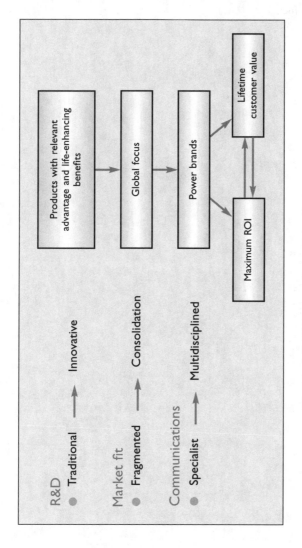

Figure 6.6 The emerging new businesses

References

BMA, July 2000.

Carter, R, 2000.

Lancet, 28 March 1998.

7 | The role of advertising in branding pharmaceuticals

MICHAEL PALING Paling Walters Targis

Introduction

We live in a world where the branding of fast-moving consumer goods (FMCG) surrounds us almost wherever we are, most notably through the medium of advertising. In sharp contrast to this, the world of prescription pharmaceuticals is, in the main, just starting to embrace this phenomenon. Despite this, the debate as to whether the pharmaceutical industry can really succeed in creating brands out of its products through advertising, or whether it even needs to, has gone on for many years. The issue appears to revolve around what we mean by *branding through advertising*.

In the consumer goods market, it surely means making a connection with the audience through communication of the brand's values. The key to making that connection is through having a *real insight* into the audience and by tying in the brand's values to the customer's values.

Next time you pick up a medical magazine, look at the advertisements and judge for yourself if we are doing this effectively. That does not necessarily mean that all advertising in consumer markets is doing this either, or even setting out to do this. Let us not forget that advertisements can also set out to sell straight off the page. But if we want to develop a long-term branding approach to advertising a pharmaceutical product, we must establish a connection with our audience.

In pharmaceutical marketing, it is sometimes said that there are unique market forces and circumstances that may lead to the conclusion that expending lots of time and money on developing long-term branding for prescription drugs is a waste of time. I would not agree with that sentiment for one minute. Good, and more importantly, *relevant* branding of any product is worthwhile because it helps us to add value to drugs in intensely crowded markets. Indeed, the role of branding is certainly to increase differentiation and in that sense, simplify the decision-making process for customers.

But you could be excused for thinking that the industry is not interested in trying to brand its products. Just observe some of the feature listing/ever-changing communication strategy/value omitting approaches to brands that are so readily visible in advertising communications to doctors and other healthcare professionals around the world.

In this chapter I will concentrate on looking at this subject through above-the-line advertising, which should surely represent the purest exposition of the brand proposition. Each advertisement should set out to deliver the brand and its values in a nutshell, and in doing so put the brand into the reader's mind. After all, that is the place where brands exist.

The pharmaceutical marketing environment

So, what are the circumstances that can be said to make the pharmaceutical market a unique marketing environment? Let us start by looking at the sort of businesses that produce the products in question.

The large global pharmaceutical companies are vast and powerful busi-nesses. They are full of immense business talent and some of the greatest scien-tific brains. This industry's lifeblood is discovering new medicines for today's, and tomorrow's, illnesses. It is also clear that in this industry, the stakes and risks are high. It is a highly competitive business – and never more so than now. Currently, it is estimated that it costs between US\$ 200–300 million in R&D to bring a new drug successfully to market. The vast majority of potential new products will die along the way and never recoup any of their investment.

We are also seeing a consolidation of these already vast global businesses, which control the supply of medicines via healthcare professionals to the man in the street. These Rx medicines are the key to the industry's success, with the vast majority of all sales of medicines globally coming from this market sector – the balance being drugs which can be purchased without a doctor's prescription. What is more, the growth, in terms of volume and cash, is also coming from the prescription sector, right now.

The mega mergers, Glaxo Wellcome with SmithKline Beecham, and Pfizer with Warner-Lambert, result in companies with annual sales of around \$22 billion and \$25 billion respectively. However, these new companies still only have less than 8% each of the total global medicine market. The global share of the largest pharmaceutical companies is thus much smaller than their coun-terparts in many other business categories, such as computers or automobiles. This relatively old, but changing, industry seems only now to be entering a time of maturity and consolidation. Size and financial muscle are the order of the day.

One would normally expect that such a competitive environment would throw up many new products, all battling to gain supremacy for the company marketing them, and this is so, as each new and established class of drugs quickly attracts more and more competitors. But, for such a competitive marketplace, the desire to create strong brands is relatively weak. In consumer markets, the more competitive it gets, the more important is the need for strong branding and hence strong brand-led advertising to defend market share. But as stated above, this is often deemed to be less important in pharmaceutical markets. There may be a number of reasons for this view:

- There are pressures on doctors, in most countries, to prescribe by the generic name, rather than by the brand name, because of price. Can you imagine being in a supermarket and someone tapping you on the shoulder when you pick up a can of Heinz baked beans and saying you must buy the own label can as it is half the price? In a supermarket this function is performed by the juxtaposition of the own-label product and branded product, not by the government or by a managed care organization.

- There is also the concept that drug selection by a doctor is seen as a totally *rational evidence-based* choice. This would negate the values brought to the fore by a brand. After all, the doctor is a trained scientist, so what use would he have for branding? Having said that, this is no different to the average consumer buying any brand. Do we not all think our brand decisions are based on logic and intelligence?

- A situation also exists where the end-user is not the prescriber/one who chooses the medication (although the person who chooses is becoming more difficult to define in some markets). It is unlikely that the prescriber will try the product on him or herself, and so usually relies on feedback from the patient or from the observation of results.

- The various regulatory controls that exist can be seen as creating barriers which stop the creative branding process. Prescription drugs have a short patent life before generic substitutes are allowed on the market and in some countries there is no patent protection at all. This leads to a quick sell being more important than long-term brand building through advertising and so on.

- The fact that the quick sale is so important means that the pharmaceutical industry is sales – rather then marketing – driven. Classically, 50 to 70% plus of a company's promotional budget will be spent on the salesforce and this is universally seen as the business' most effective promotional tool. In a market the size of the USA, salesforces are numbered in *thous-ands* of medical representatives. The number of salesmen visiting primary care doctors can be so great in some countries that each representative may only have 50 or so customers to call on. There may also be situations where three or four representatives will be selling the same product to an individual doctor. *But the representative is never going to be the best vehicle to communicate the brand.*

Therefore, the window of opportunity for a new product is narrow in phar-maceuticals, because intense competition in each medical category works to bar entry and prices can fall when products lose patent protection. This wipes vast sums off the sales line and intensifies the need for a quick sell.

While a move to over-the-counter (OTC) status is sometimes seen as a way of extending the life of a product, in reality, few will get this opportunity to move to a position where a doctor's intervention is not required. This is usually because of safety and regulatory reasons. Those that do make a switch are not guaranteed the sales of the previous prescription brand. Witness the H_2 anti-ulcer drugs Zantac and Tagamet. When they switched to OTC for heart-burn, from prescription-only, UK sales came nowhere near expectations for either brand.

The picture is not always so negative, of course. Some brands are highly suited to a switch, for example Bayer's Canesten (clotrimazole) and Diflucan (fluconazole), for the treatment of vaginal fungal infections (an easily self-diagnosed condition, easily self-treatable, limited in duration and so on). In the case of Canesten in the UK it also had the benefit of dominating the prescrip-tion sector in terms of market share. Zovirax (aciclovir), for use in cold sores, would be another good example of a product suitable for switching. But, OTC brands have to shoulder the burden of greatly increased advertising and promo-tional budgets, as the target audiences grow in size from relatively few doctors to many more consumers. Consumers read and view media that are more expen-sive for an advertiser than the traditional medical trade press.

Is there a role for brand advertising in prescription pharmaceuticals?

Before continuing with this train of thought, let us confirm what we under-stand by brands and branding. A brand is composed of:

■ *The name:* This is often very important in this area, as markets are so crowded and *differentiation* is vital.

■ *The packaging: (usually* of limited importance in prescription medicines).

■ *The product itself and its features:* In other words, the hard facts (even these are complex in pharmaceuticals where there are so many details and so much conflicting reality from one product to another, in terms of clinical support and so on).

■ The experience of the product (or the observed experience in this marketplace) and the ensuing word-of-mouth communication.

■ *The advertising and promotion* that is put together to *portray* the brand and to bring its *values* to life. This is the part of the mix that can most readily connect with the audience's feeling and desires.

If branding is the process whereby these brand values are conveyed to the target audience, advertising is the most important vehicle for carrying the brand message to the consumer – or purchaser – and implanting the brand's values in his or her mind. Hence, advertising has a key role in the branding process. So, a brand is the complex synthesis of all the parts listed above, be they tangible or intangible, rational or emotional. Advertising, within the mix, is able to work more effectively in terms of communicating the intangible and emotional than say, the company representative.

For the brand to work, the final result must be appropriate for the audience and differentiated from the competition. This is by no means an easy task. A brand is not only created through marketing and advertising, it also has to be cherished and nurtured along the way, as it goes through life. Hence, a brand can be thought as existing in the mind of a customer, whereas the product could be thought of as 'existing on a laboratory bench or leaving via the factory gate', to quote Stephen King.

So much for the theory. But returning to the intensely sales-driven pharmaceutical marketing environment outlined above, if this, in broadest terms, really is the environment in which pharmaceutical marketers and their advertising and communications advisers find themselves, we have to ask the following:

■ Is there *really* a place for branding in such a sales-driven marketplace?

■ Can we avoid, through branding, medicines becoming just commodities?

■ Can we build brands on a less factual basis, that ties into psychological needs, as we see in consumer markets? (Do doctors really need to know *everything* before they prescribe a brand? And even if they do, does that negate the need for branding, because it assumes factual knowledge is the *only* driver?)

■ Can we really create *value* for a brand and establish branding as more than merely the creation of visual *identity* (logo, colour and so on)?

■ Is it possible to create that critical relationship between a brand and the customer, that is the basis of true branding, in the pharmaceutical market environment?

My categorical response to all these questions would be 'yes'.

In some respects, the value of branding in pharmaceuticals is becoming more accepted and the evidence for this can be seen in some contemporary advertising. However, as stated above, little advertising encountered in the medical (rather than consumer) press would bear witness to this: we still rarely struggle to create brands out of products.

Perhaps none of this is really surprising, when one considers some of the drivers in the marketplace, in particular the largely recognized fact that the two most important goals in marketing prescription medicines are *speed to market* and *speed of adoption*, in order to optimize the ROI that is so vital to fund research. In pharmaceuticals it is rare for a brand to be successful unless it becomes so *quickly*: few brands have a second bite of the cherry. Without a doubt, the pharmaceutical industry is achieving these two goals more efficiently than in the past. Lead times for major new drugs are being shortened and newer drugs often take off at a much faster rate than did their blockbuster predecessors.

Of course, advertising has a most important role to play in terms of speed of adoption, as rapid and widespread awareness is vital in leading to high levels of trial. Advertising always delivers the best means of frequent contact with doctors and healthcare professionals in the early stages of a brand's life. This is always an issue with even the most zealous salesforce.

But the bigger, and more contentious, question is, what else can advertising per se achieve for the brand and for the brand's longer term future? Back to the 'Is branding necessary or possible?' question.

Perception is reality

In the world of consumer advertising, most would agree with the observations of Trout and Ries, gurus of brand positioning, when they said:

> There is no objective reality. There are no facts. There are no best products.
>
> All that exists in the world of marketing are perceptions in the minds of our customers.
>
> The perception is reality.

Perhaps, in pharmaceuticals there is too great an emphasis placed on having the *best* product. Was Zofran a better molecule, in the treatment of nausea and vomiting, than second-to-market $5HT_3$ anti-emetic Kytril? Scientifically the answer is probably 'No, absolutely not'. But, in the UK, at least, Kytril sales have only ever been a fraction of those of Zofran. Perhaps it was because Kytril took a product focus based on greater potency, while Zofran captured a value position in the hearts and minds of doctors, based on a brand stance. Who knows? It did help, of course, that Zofran was first to market. But it defended its sales remarkably well against such a strong competitor, and against later, and much cheaper, entrants. We will look at this brand again later.

So, do the observations of Trout and Ries hold firm in pharmaceuticals? Even in a market where facts, training and experience are important in determining choice, subjectivity still has a role to play in the prescribing process. However, brand advertising still needs to convey a fair amount of product information, as well as making a value connection with the reader.

But there remain many factors which constrain the prescriber's freedom to choose and prescribe a medicine. As we have said before, these are most often based on cost arguments, with pressure coming from governments and managed care organizations, depending on the country's health system. Doctors throughout the world are beginning to see attempts to curb their individual freedom of choice of a patient's medication.

But clearly – and in conclusion – while advertising is just one part of the complicated marketing and branding mix, it can, and must, have a role to play in building a brand's unique position rather than just stimulating awareness. It must represent the *best* opportunity for encapsulating the brand's proposition and shaping the development of its personality over time.

After all, your doctor is the same person who decides on your medication and then decides on which car, washing powder or beer to buy. Does your doctor ask to see all the evidence on each product in the local supermarket? Does your doctor read all the literature? Or is their brand choice more intuitive, based on how the brand is perceived – most importantly, how it has been perceived through the advertising?

Can a medical representative create a brand?

Most FMCG brands build their position within a market over a period of time, utilizing a long-term advertising strategy, combined with point-of-sale display, pack design and so on. It is largely a controlled and non-personal form of communication. The brand is largely built up in the consumer's mind without a series of dialogues taking place, and without direct contact with a salesperson.

But in the promotion of pharmaceuticals the key player is the salesperson. A salesperson's role is to get that sale. He or she wants quick results and is less interested in building a brand over a long period of time. So the representative wants to be armed with the facts, the details of the argument, the convincing story – and that is what they have in their hands when they enter the doctor's office or clinic.

Then the next salesperson goes in with another carefully honed set of facts, selling argument and convincing story, albeit often very similar to the last competitive sales pitch. Where are the values coming from in this process? How much of the success of the sale is down to the brand and how much of it is down to the salesperson? Which is the more important to preserve, the salesperson or the brand itself? What happens with all the doctors who never see salespeople? What would happen if governments decided that doctors should no longer see salespeople? That may seem too bleak a picture, but some companies are already working on the basis that, in the UK, over 30% of GP *practices* will not see a representative by the year 2003. In the USA, while the number of pharmaceutical sales representatives has almost doubled between 1993 and 1999, the number of sales calls was pretty much flat, at least between 1993 and 1997, when they went from 38 million to 42 million. Further USA data tells us that nearly half of all calls get no further than the receptionist's window.

But, how much easier would the selling process be if above-the-line advertising, with its more frequent contact and a single-minded message, had already set up the brand's values and point of view? Even in the pharmaceutical marketplace, selling and brand building can work hand in hand, with the same ultimate goal – sales.

One thing is certain – the true emotional *values* of a pharmaceutical brand are rarely communicated through below-the-line literature or by the salesperson. *The greatest challenge will be how to take the brand values desired and created through below-the-line advertising.* Sales training, motivation and company culture will have a vital role to play here in trying to create a salesforce which is the living persona of the brand. When this is achieved the potency of the whole campaign will be greatly enhanced.

Much of the best advertising to healthcare professionals does set out to create a brand and to build a defendable position in the customer's mind – just as in the world of advertising to consumers. But the majority of advertising to healthcare professionals tends largely to deliver the same facts and product features which might appear in the sales aid or brochure. Some ads even look like a sales brochure in a medical magazine. This can be especially true in the USA, where multiple page advertisements have been commonplace in the past. Eighteen pages of detailed information is the longest one I can recall.

When we look at an advertisement for a car, we don't expect to see reams of minutely detailed information about each moving part. We are given the whole, the big offer which the advertiser hopes will interest us (assuming we are in the target market, of course). The offer will relate more to our needs, desires, aspirations, dreams and so on, than to the minutiae of the brand's features. We want the 'Ultimate Driving Machine', in BMW terms, not 26.2 miles to the gallon in carefully controlled on-the-road tests. (Although, when we have bought our overpriced BMW, we might use the petrol consumption facts to reinforce our choice.)

Case example – Zofran

Figure 7.1 shows the launch advertisement for Glaxo Wellcome's brand, Zofran (ondansetron), which ran in the UK. It is for the treatment of nausea and vomiting as a result of chemotherapy or radiotherapy treatment for cancer.

Zofran is a fine product, but it wanted to be a fine brand as well. It was not going to do this by just listing its features and facts. More importantly, Zofran looked at what the audience *felt* and related to this. This was the basis of its strategy which drove the advertising and, more importantly, the brand. In a therapy area where patients are very ill and frequently will die, and where treatment is often very unpleasant because of side effects, it is the latter that often becomes the key focus in the patient's mind – and thus in the doctor's or carer/nurse's mind, as well. Patients openly say that 'the vomiting is far worse than the pain or the fear of death'.

Not surprisingly, there is a lot of guilt associated with administering treatments for cancer, because many of these drugs are so unclean and create such awful side effects. The Zofran brand was born out of this understanding, rather than out of a 97% efficacy claim. It allowed the brand to connect with the target audience far more deeply and in a more meaningful way than a mere feature ever could. The next product in the market, Kytril, had some advantages over Zofran, but it took a classic *product stance* and sold via the feature of potency to deliver effectiveness. (Also a risky stance when the next product could be *more* potent, of course.) Kytril was also cheaper than Zofran. But Zofran said 'I understand your problems, your worries, your dilemma. I will be your partner in solving these.' This empathy with patients' psychological distress led to understanding and trust. Zofran built a position that could be defended over time, because it related to the customer's true needs and concerns.

Figure 7.1 Zofran launch ad

This was borne out by some very probing qualitative market research, which clearly indicated just how far Zofran had gone in forming a relationship with the user. All the values of the brand advertising were readily played back and defended by users. In the UK, Zofran still dominates the $5HT_3$ antiemetic sector.

The value of advertising research in understanding and creating brands

The most important role market research can play in the branding process is as a planning tool, in terms of gaining vital insights to aid the development of the brand platform. To quote Bill Bernbach, the founder of Doyle Dane Bernbach:

> At the very heart of an effective creative philosophy is the belief that nothing is so powerful as an insight into human nature, what compulsions drive a man, what instincts dominate his action.

Similarly, while I am not against researching advertising concepts, it is also important that advertising research moves away from just finding out how effectively detailed messages are being conveyed through the brand and moves more towards researching what values are being conveyed and what values need to be conveyed. It is also paramount to get beyond the behavioural barriers that a doctor, or other healthcare professional, typically puts up in discussion groups. Doctors often conceal their true feelings in a cloak of professionalism: why should we accept this from doctors when we would not accept that from any other another group of consumers? Surely it cannot be argued that they are only acting as an intermediary and therefore always behave logically? Nor can it be argued that their attitudes are purely the result of their scientific training.

It is interesting to note that the Zofran advertising concept above was not tested prior to the campaign running. It was, however, extensively tested when the campaign was in place and then tested against the *values* the advertising was trying to convey, in order to check if the brand was also capable of living up to the communication objectives.

The real value of research must surely be more in the planning phase, when we need to know how target doctors and other healthcare professionals view patients, and their role and responsibilities towards these patients and the category of treatment. This information will be by far and away the most help in developing the branding – providing it is able to get below the surface, as in the case of Zofran.

With Zofran, extensive background attitudinal research was done to aid understanding, prior to any advertising concepts being developed. This included a series of one-on-one interviews and focus groups in hospital oncology departments and hospices, with patients, carers, doctors and family members. A wealth of *real* understanding was gained and the key motivators and drivers in this treatment area emerged, factors which would determine how the brand would talk to the audience and what would be the basis of the brand proposition.

This process helps to decide on the direction the brand should take and thus focuses the communication strategy. Any subsequent advertising research should then be testing against the brand's agreed value set and not *just* against the communication of a string of specific messages, such as fast, effective and so on. After all, it is relatively simple to communicate a tangible point, such as 'fast', off the page. Put it in the headline and in research the doctor will feed back 'the product acts fast'.

Case example – Zestril and Carace

Tom Blackett referred to these two brands in Chapter 1. This is the advertising story.

The launch advertising for the same molecule, with two different brand names, is similar to the birth of non-identical twins. Let us look at the UK advertising approaches for two parallel products, both were for lisinopril for hypertension. I believe that only one really strived to take a branding approach to its advertising.

One was launched by Merck Sharp & Dohme under the brand name Carace (with recognition in the name of the product being an ACE inhibitor) and the other was launched by Stuart Pharmaceuticals (now AstraZeneca). Stuart's lisinopril was launched with the brand name Zestril – the first plank of its branding and a name that already encapsulated a value which suggested a positive outcome for patients. The 'Zest' element of the name positively exuded good health and normality.

Manufacturers in this category (ACE inhibitors) had already spent a lot of time and money through a number of product launches trying to emphasize the fact that the ACE inhibitors were clean and hence did not affect adversely patients' quality of life as much as other anti-hypertensive therapies. But no one product had really captured this offer successfully and built a brand out of it.

Then along came Zestril with advertising that did not try to be the sales aid and did not list details, facts and figures. It created an overall brand identity and very strong values.

Sales at launch for the two brands, Zestril and Carace, told an interesting story. Zestril outsold its counterpart by four to one in the launch phase and maintained that dominance over many years. I would strongly contest that a great part of Zestril's success was because it became a brand. It created a highly positive value beyond the *explicit* and well into the *implicit*.

From Atlanta to Zurich, from Adelaide to Zagreb – a different approach?

We are often being reminded that consumer attitudes are converging around the world. Hence, the similarity in approach seen by, say, Coke or McDonald's from one country to another. It is often said that an important characteristic of most major FMCG brands is that they are international in scope. This is manifested in consistency in brand name, brand packaging design, brand colours and logo, and in brand values and brand attitude (advertising). You *recognize* the brand through its identity, but you *understand the values* through its advertising.

There are many FMCG brands that follow this approach worldwide and are able to do so because of the convergence of consumer needs, tastes, expectations and aspirations.

That is not to say that the advertising should be exactly the same creative execution in 80 countries. But if you put together all the worldwide advertising for brands such as Marlboro cigarettes, Coke, Absolut Vodka and many hundreds more, the commonalities in style, tone, values and brand essence would sing out.

How is this reflected by prescription pharmaceuticals? Surely, if the target group is the physician, are they not already a fairly homogeneous group? They are similar in being well educated, in the top income quartile, middle class, and largely well respected. They are also mobile and travel the world, some to work in other countries. At a senior specialist level, particularly, they are functioning more as a global group, through international meetings and learned journals and so on. There is also the impact of the Internet, which is a global medium which will become considerably more important over time. With some notable exceptions the treatment of ill health is fairly consistent around the world too.

The way any company's advertising and other branding elements (such as name, logo and livery) look around the world is largely a function of the way its central management approaches the global market. Some are centralized in structure, some decentralized, in terms of branding controls. In general, there seem to be fewer central controls within global pharmaceutical companies than there are in most other global businesses, when it comes to controlling the brand strategy or brand identity.

But Coke fiercely controls its brand identity and advertising around the globe. Can you imagine the Coke logo being, say, green in some countries? Or that Coke's values, as communicated through advertising, would differ from place to place?

Viagra, the world's best-known drug

Viagra is probably the world's most famous pharmaceutical brand – along with Prozac. Even before Viagra was launched the non-medical media were talking of nothing else – or so it seemed. Every radio and TV channel was full of it, every newspaper had it on the front page, every comedian had a joke about it, and the Internet screamed it. It was global news.

So what of its advertising as an expression of its global branding? Pfizer follows these principles:

- The name is the same everywhere in the world.

- The brand colour is usually blue (the tablet colour throughout the world for those who are not regular users) – but the brand colour/logo is sometimes white, sometimes grey and even red in Australia.

- There is some consistency in the logos, but in a couple of countries it is unique and very different, for example Australia.

- The advertising executions around the world (see Plate 7.1) are fairly distinctive, but share the common strategic approach to branding that Viagra is all about *preserving stable relationships between men and women*, rather than being about the flippancy of sex. (Even here the award-winning German execution may stand out.)

It appears that each country has given the brand a value through its advertising, rather than making it merely feature led. Furthermore, this has been done against a background of a prurient media pulling Viagra in a different direction.

So not all elements are the same from country to country. If one puts all the ads side by side, from all over the world, Viagra would not necessarily appear to be the same brand. But the bottom line is, has this adversely effected sales on a worldwide basis? Does it matter that a doctor in Perth, Australia sees a different ad to the doctor in Perth, Scotland?

Does Viagra end up being the same product, but not the same brand around the world, thanks to its advertising? If not, is this merely a function of its inconsistent visual identity rather than the values portrayed? It would seem that while we live in a world where vast global brands exist in consumer markets, a global approach to branding is much rarer in pharmaceuticals – at least at the moment.

Some brands <u>are</u> going global

While it is impossible to say how much benefit it will have on bottom-line sales, some pharmaceutical brands are attempting to adopt a global stance to branding, especially through their visual identity. This is expected to increase. There should at least be some cost savings by taking such a centralized approach. This will usually manifest itself in a common visual identity and could well entail a totally prescriptive set of promotional materials, including the press advertising campaign.

Ideally, for this approach to have maximum effect, it should be accompanied by a branding manual. The latter would set out to explain the rationale behind the brand's stance and convey and explain what drives its branding. Everyone in the company who is involved with the brand, anywhere in the world, will therefore understand the branding approach being taken.

An example of a centrally controlled approach to the brand, and a common creative expression around the world, is seen in a number of Merck Sharp & Dohme brands. Maxalt, for migraine treatment, is one example.

Plate 7.2 and Figure 7.2 show two of the many different treatments of Maxalt in advertising. But the key launch communication is the same and all feature a distinctive visual style (there were tight controls on the use of this). A global brand stance is being taken around the world, albeit one which is driven by identity and commonality rather than by a strong approach to branding through the creation of distinctive values for the brand. It is still relying on a feature-driven message (fast, effective, convenient), rather than a brand message based on values.

This is in sharp contrast to many global consumer companies such as Coke, McDonald's and many others. Their branding comes from a very different place, and is based on the brand's relationship with its consumer. These brands are driven by values and not just by identity and have followed the sequence of:

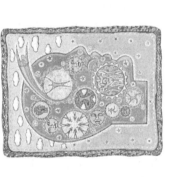

Figure 7.2 US Maxalt launch ad

- *brand strategy:* where are we going to take the brand?
- *brand essence:* what is our offer?
- *brand identity:* how do we visualize this?
- *brand advertising:* how do we communicate it?

So often in pharmaceutical marketing the identity – and even the communications – is set in stone long before the strategy and brand essence have been defined.

Conclusion

Advertising should generally be regarded as the key medium for transferring brand values to the customer. Branding can only work if it is at the heart of the advertising communication. While the pharmaceutical industry has been slow to realize, or perhaps more importantly, value this, there are signs that this is beginning to change. After all, a major pharmaceutical brand will have a promotional spend in the order of $600–700 million in its lifetime and a fair chunk of this will be spent above the line.

We have been both poor at branding and poor at branding in a global sense. Eventually, all pharmaceutical brands will need to behave like the most successful consumer brands and that may mean taking a global approach to branding, through advertising and brand identity.

Continuity in brand advertising should also become more important. This will only become reality if there is continuity in the strategy and the branding approach taken. This should be based on a consistent rather than changing strategy, wherever possible – but this does not mean that exactly the same advertising should run forever, or everywhere in the world.

These factors will have a major impact on how advertising is perceived and produced, and on how it works to create pharmaceutical brands.

Reference

Trout and Ries *Positioning: The Battle for Your Mind*, 1981.

8 Public relations and its role in pharmaceutical brand building

DAVID CATLETT Ketchum

In the information age, the power of public relations as a pharmaceutical marketing tool is being appreciated as never before. If you ask different people, you will probably get different answers as to why this is the case: its credibility; its flexibility; its efficiency in using the mass media and the Internet; its utility as both a pre-launch and post-launch marketing tool in a regulated environment; its ability to cut through the clutter to reach and influence diverse populations, including increasingly important consumer audiences; its capacity to leverage the multiplicity of communications outlets that have proliferated in recent years. Any or all of these answers would be appropriate. Public relations has blossomed as a marketing discipline in recent years to gain strong acceptance as a brand-building device.

This chapter will explore the value of public relations, its use in pharmaceutical marketing, as well as trends and opportunities. Because public relations continues, in many respects, to be a misunderstood discipline – even to those who are close to it – we will start with the basics and work our way into the pharmaceutical arena. We will cover the following subjects:

- *What is* public relations – really?
- Public relations as brand builder
- Public relations in a regulatory environment
- The cascading effect of key influencers
- Public relations as a DTC tool
- The question of celebrity spokespersons
- History and future.

What is public relations – really?

So just *what is* public relations? Although the understanding of public relations has increased in recent years, many marketers still have a fuzzy perception of what public relations can do, because they are usually much more familiar with – and better grounded in – other aspects of the marketing mix such as advertising and sales promotion. Public relations also suffers from something of a self-inflicted wound in that its name is rather nebulous and it covers a broad and ill-defined spectrum of disciplines, including, but not limited to, media relations, corporate communications, marketing communications, community relations, third party advocacy work, issues management and crisis communications. Thomas Harris, a leading public relations expert and author of *The Marketer's Guide to Public Relations*, describes the problem:

> The definition of public relations has been so elusive that in 1975 the Foundation for Public Relations Research (now the Public Relations Institute) enlisted 65 public relations leaders to sift through 472 different definitions and write one of their own.

The definition created by the Foundation is as follows:

> Public relations is a distinctive management function which helps establish and maintain mutual lines of communication, understanding, acceptance and cooperation between an organization and its publics; involves the management of problems or issues; helps management keep informed on and responsive to public opinion; defines and emphasizes the responsibility of management to serve the public interest; helps management keep abreast of and effectively utilize change, serving as an early warning system to help anticipate trends; and uses research and sound and ethical communications techniques as its principal tools. (Harris)

The clumsiness of this description recalls the proverbial horse created by a committee. It also does not acknowledge public relations as a strategic marketing tool. Thomas Harris offers a more focused definition of public relations in a marketing context:

> Marketing public relations is the process of planning, executing and evaluating programs that encourage purchase and consumer satisfaction through credible communication of information and impressions that identify companies and their products with the needs, wants, concerns and interests of consumers.

This definition is more in line with our interests, but it is self-limiting in terms of target audience. A more simple definition – and one of the oldest – is given by the father of modern public relations, Edward L. Bernays, the author of such classics as *The Crystalizing of Public Opinion* (1923) and *The Engineering of Consent* (1955). The title of his latter book sums it up: *Public relations is the engineering of consent*. This definition connotes the use of persuasion and education to gain acceptance and/or change behaviour. It applies to any target audience: consumers, physicians, allied health professionals, legislators, regulators, payers, industry analysts, investors and others.

The many tools and conduits used in public relations – ranging from a simple press release to electronic media kit; from the use of company spokespersons to outside opinion leaders and advocacy groups; from public forums to satellite press events and interactive web casts – may change, but they still involve a basic philosophy of informing, educating and influencing.

Many people confuse advertising with public relations, although the differences are quite simple. Advertising involves the purchase of space or time in a particular medium, with the benefit that the advertiser has complete control of the message, its reach and frequency. Public relations reaches its target audiences not through paid space, but through a variety of communications methods typically involving interaction with the news media or other third parties as a conduit. Public relations uses the credibility of its messages, images and spokespersons to educate and persuade its audiences. As gatekeepers, the news media function as both an audience and a conduit for public relations. Therein lies much of the art in public relations – a well-crafted publicity effort can result in great media coverage or visibility, whereas a poorly crafted effort can result in no visibility or worse, a negative reaction. The lack of control with public relations is often more than made up for by the highly credible impact of the finished product, if it is intelligently planned and successfully executed.

Public relations as brand builder

The power of public relations often goes unnoticed because it does not call attention to itself in the same way as advertising and other marketing disciplines. But that is precisely why it can be so effective, and it has earned a following among some prominent converts.

One of the most vocal is advertising authority Al Ries, co-author of such groundbreaking books as *Positioning: The Battle for Your Mind* (1981) and *Marketing Warfare* (1986). In 1998, Ries and his fellow author had an awakening about public relations as a brand-building tool, and articulated their point of view in *The 22 Immutable Laws of Branding*. They said:

> Today brands are built with publicity and maintained with advertising. (Ries, A. and Ries, L., 1988)

Ries and Ries explain that the third party credibility of public relations, through the use of opinion-leaders, advocacy groups and the news media, had become instrumental in creating brands, and that the reach and frequency of advertising was better suited to reinforcing brand awareness:

> What others say about your brand is so much more powerful than what you can say about it yourself. That's why publicity in general is more powerful than advertising. And why over the past two decades, public relations has eclipsed advertising as the most powerful force in branding.

Ries and Ries are not alone in thinking about the power of public relations as a branding tool. In *The Marketer's Guide to Public Relations*, Philip Kotler, Professor of Marketing at Northwestern University's Kellogg School of Management and author of the best-selling textbook *Marketing Management*, voices a similar opinion. He is quoted as saying:

> Marketing practitioners are very likely to increase their appreciation of PR's potential contributions to marketing the product because they are facing a real decline in the productivity of their other promotional tools.
>
> Marketing public relations in the future can only go one way: up. (Harris, op. cit.)

With developments such as the rise of consumerism and the Internet, the further splintering of media outlets and markets, the increasing sophistication of target audiences, and an emphasis on relationship marketing, public relations becomes an even more powerful tool in comparison to other marketing disciplines. Thomas Harris explains that:

> Because of its credibility, public relations is well positioned to address an ever increasingly diverse population, and is ideally suited to reach a much more sophisticated consumer.

Public relations in a regulatory environment

In the highly regulated pharmaceutical industry, public relations can help to provide support through the entire life cycle of a product, by first helping to develop the market through disease education and product awareness, and then by product launch and post-launch communications support. It can often establish awareness for brands quickly with professional and consumer audiences via dissemination in the mass media, with less regulatory encumbrance than other promotional vehicles.

In the USA and most other countries, companies are not allowed to promote new drugs prior to regulatory approval. In many European countries, even after marketing approval, laws prohibit promoting prescription drugs to consumers. Public relations, however, can use its liaisons with the media and other third parties in academia and advocacy groups to get the word out about a drug effectively – and legally.

The legal grounds are simple. In most countries, freedom of speech and freedom of the news media allow for the unfettered dissemination of medical or scientific information. Today the flow of information is instantaneous and pervasive on a global scale. Although regulatory authorities in different countries can prohibit traditional pre-approval promotion, that is, making claims in a promotional context about a drug's safety or efficacy prior to licensing, government regulation cannot override constitutional rights guaranteeing freedom of speech or freedom of the press. For example, the US Code of Federal Regulations contains a clause acknowledging the limits of its ban on pre-approval promotion:

> This provision is not intended to restrict the full exchange of scientific information concerning a drug, including dissemination of scientific findings in scientific or lay media.

Investor relations, a sister discipline of public relations, is another area where regulatory bodies have limited authority over pharmaceutical companies. Publicly held companies are required by law to disclose any materially significant information that may impact a company's stock. Therefore, significant milestones in a drug's development or pertinent information in peer-reviewed scientific publications can be a communications opportunity.

For both investor relations and public relations, the key to communicating within regulatory guidelines is striking a balance and releasing information that is genuinely newsworthy or materially significant. In a pre-approval context, it is acceptable to communicate accurate, balanced information describing a drug and its intended purpose in a non-promotional format (for example in a scientific or financial context). One must clearly indicate the investigational status of the drug and that it is awaiting regulatory approval. If the message appears overly promotional, even a news release will be seen as crossing the line by regulatory authorities. Once a drug is on the market, the key is to make sure that all the information is accurate, not misleading and contains fair balance, including information about potential side effects or safety issues.

Outside the USA, where the communications environment concerning drugs may be more restrictive (particularly in Europe), there is nonetheless an opportunity to get the word out through investor relations, work with third parties or the crafting of public relations materials and messages that will pass muster as scientific information that is newsworthy and in the public interest.

A case in point is the worldwide media coverage about Viagra. Well before the drug was approved in any market, an avalanche of medical news – and certainly an avalanche of public interest – took precedent over government purview.

The cascading effect of key influencers

Public relations is not just about getting the word out; it is about reaching the right audiences with the right messages and letting those audiences influence other audiences. The objective is usually to target key influencers – opinion-leaders, the media, government, industry analysts and so on – who can impact other audiences.

In recent years, key influencers in the financial arena have taken on increasing importance because of their ability to affect perceptions about companies and brands. Financial analysts, in particular, can have significant influence because they publish reports that cascade into other media. The most prominent analysts also regularly serve as quotable sources for business and science writers doing stories about promising new drugs. It is important, therefore, for investor relations and public relations to work closely together to manage the communications flow to the analysts who in turn influence the media.

One should also bear in mind that scientific-turned-financial information can generate awareness and interest for personal – as well as professional – reasons on the part of target audiences. Physicians, allied health professionals, pharmacists and others also happen to be investors. The old pharmaceutical industry adage, 'The best-read physician journal is *The Wall Street Journal*', has a lot of truth to it, particularly in these speculative times where everyone seems to be a stock picker or online trader.

The overall influence, and volatility, of the financial markets in recent years is another factor with which public relations must contend. Publicly held companies can be rewarded or punished depending on the performance of a few key brands. This includes pharmaceutical companies, which increasingly are drivers of the global economy and increasingly high profile compared to years past.

Before Celebrex hit the market as the first of the COX-2 drugs, it benefited from the support of numerous key influencers – not only science writers and medical reporters, but financial analysts, business reporters and others who made it the centerpiece of stories about Searle and its then parent company, Monsanto. The cascading effect of this coverage benefited Monsanto's stock and reached virtually every important target audience.

Conversely, the news in August 2000 that Prozac had lost a patent fight and might face generic competition two years sooner than expected sent Eli Lilly's stock down 30% in one day (*New York Times*, Section C, August 10, 2000). This may have been a dramatic overreaction, but it demonstrated that pharmaceutical companies – like Coca-Cola, IBM and Ford – increasingly *are* their brands. That is the double-edged sword of creating high-profile blockbuster drugs: medical news is business news and business news has a major impact on companies.

Public relations as a DTC tool

Although pharmaceutical companies historically have focused on the physician as the customer or decision-maker, in recent years companies increasingly have focused on reaching the end-user – the patient – as well. This makes good sense, as the patient ultimately makes the decision about seeking medical attention, responding to a physician's direction, filling a prescription, and remaining compliant on a therapeutic regimen. A patient who is informed and motivated is much more likely to seek and stay on a course of treatment than a passive, uninvolved patient.

Today's educated consumers are increasingly taking charge of their health and are going to physicians armed with information about illnesses and therapies gleaned from the media, the Internet or other sources. They are less inclined to be passive in the physician–patient relationship and are much more active in the management of their own health.

Studies have shown that physicians are influenced by patient demands, particularly in categories where:

■ the physician has flexibility on options and where patient compliance is important (for example osteoporosis, diabetes, epilepsy)

■ where symptomatic relief is important (for example arthritis, depression)

■ side effects are an issue (many drugs)

■ or where quality of life or lifestyle is important (for example overactive bladder, prostate enlargement, menopause, hair loss, impotence).

These so-called consumer-driven categories play to the strengths of public relations, which is an ideal tool for expanding the market by driving consumers to seek treatment.

Public relations also can be effective in reaching and influencing patient audiences as groups, in order to gain their advocacy in lobbying regulators, legislators and/or payers to support reimbursement for branded drugs and to combat unfriendly initiatives such as limited list formularies.

Direct-to-consumer (DTC) advertising of drugs in the USA has taken consumer communications to a new level in recent years. The use of DTC ads has helped popularize prescription drugs to the extent that they have become true consumer brands.

DTC advertising has not been without its issues, however. Heavy promotional expenditures have been blamed for the high price of branded drugs in the USA, and DTC advertising is the most visible example of such promotion. The effectiveness of DTC ads also can be questioned in those cases where the required fair balance disclaimers may create a more lasting image than the promotional message (the severe diarrhoea disclaimer for a heavily marketed obesity drug being a good example).

In Europe, the question of DTC advertising is still being debated. Whether Europe and the USA will converge on a DTC-friendly policy in the near future is uncertain, although in many other ways the trend towards global regulatory harmonization is moving toward unification.

Public relations offers many of the benefits of DTC advertising without some of the drawbacks. It educates and informs without calling attention to itself as a blatant promotional activity. It is usually less expensive than advertising. It offers balanced information but has fewer disclaimer requirements than advertising does. It is not limited to a 15- or 30-second spot on television, thus allowing for more in-depth explanation and education. It is also highly impactful, reaching its audience through the news media or other credible third parties.

This is not to suggest that DTC advertising should have less of a role in the marketing mix. A blend of public relations and DTC advertising can be highly effective, if both are utilized to do the things they do best: public relations educates regarding a disease category, and informs and influences regarding a brand; advertising reinforces brand awareness and does so with great control, reach and frequency.

The question of celebrity spokespersons

The role of celebrities in pharmaceutical marketing is an interesting one. Although somewhat controversial, they have become rather commonplace in the USA, with celebrities serving as patient spokespersons for public relations campaigns that evolve into advertising campaigns. Examples have included former presidential candidate Bob Dole pitching Viagra, and TV morning show personality Joan Lunden proclaiming the advantages of Clarityn.

These types of campaign are precluded in many other markets by the same regulatory issues that affect DTC advertising. However, celebrity campaigns cannot be ignored, given the pervasiveness of the global media, which easily crosses borders to reach audiences worldwide.

If appropriately used, celebrities can help to promote a pharmaceutical brand like many other kinds of brands, particularly if the celebrity is a patient who clearly has benefited from the medication. However, there are risks with using a celebrity (for example Marilyn Chambers, who advertised Ivory Snow and later became a porno star). There are also risks involved in a public relations campaign, which is by definition less controlled than advertising.

One of the first, and most controversial, celebrity campaigns on record was one that I happened to be involved with – the launch of a new arthritis drug, Voltaren, in the USA, in the late 1980s. Despite having been a blockbuster arthritis drug in the rest of the world for a number of years, Voltaren was slow in coming to the US market and was hampered with questions about safety. As a classic late entry into a crowded market, Voltaren faced an uphill battle against other widely prescribed non-steroidals such as Naprosyn, Motrin and Feldene.

However, because of its popularity outside the USA, Voltaren had a multitude of physicians and patients who swore by its effectiveness. And it benefited from entering a notoriously dissatisfied marketplace: the arthritis category, where quack remedies were rampant and where medications relieved pain and inflammation with only limited success. Therefore, the advance word or buzz on this new arthritis drug had considerable appeal to physicians and to millions of eager American patients.

The missing piece to the puzzle was identifying an American spokesperson who could speak on the benefits of Voltaren in a way that Americans understood and appreciated. As director of public relations at Ciba-Geigy, I was involved in identifying baseball hero Mickey Mantle, of the legendary New York Yankees, as a candidate who was widely known as having injured his knees early in his career and who was lionized for playing through pain for many years thereafter.

Mantle was close to 60 years old, and his injuries had progressed over the years to become an arthritic condition. He agreed to participate in the Phase III clinical trials for Voltaren in the USA. Over the course of the study, Mantle's symptoms and range of motion improved noticeably. He also began to enjoy an improved quality of life, and he agreed to be a spokesperson for Voltaren in connection with the product launch.

At a press conference announcing FDA approval, Mantle was the star of the show, along with company officials and physicians who explained the science and clinical experience of the drug. The media coverage was enormous, and patients began bombarding their physicians with inquiries about the new drug. Voltaren sales soared. Ciba-Geigy, meanwhile, was careful to pair Mantle with a physician in all media interviews to provide a fair balance and to make sure that the celebrity patient was not making claims for the product beyond his personal experience or outside the approved labelling.

Even so, when Mantle appeared on the number one morning TV show in America, *Today*, he could not resist saying that Voltaren was also good for hangovers. That statement caught the attention of the FDA, which determined that Mantle was indeed making claims outside the approved labelling. The FDA also took exception to the fact that a celebrity patient could cause such a sensation with an alleged 'me too' drug.

The FDA began an investigation that cast a harsh light on the company, and culminated in the removal of Mantle as a spokesperson and a moratorium on celebrity spokespersons. The heated climate surrounding celebrities subsided in subsequent years, allowing for the more recent public relations and advertising activities of Bob Dole, Joan Lunden and others.

The Voltaren episode is a reminder that public relations can produce both spectacular success and spectacular backlash, and the risks and benefits must be carefully weighed.

History and future

The role of public relations in pharmaceutical brand building has a strong history. Although Viagra may be the best-known example of a public relations-friendly brand, many others exist. They include Premarin, one of the first consumer-driven brands and still a powerful one, even though it has been off patent for years; Clarityn, the allergy drug that attracted much attention because of its non-sedating qualities; Prozac, the breakthrough SSRI (selective serotonin reuptake inhibitor) that offered fewer side effects than earlier anti-depressants; Fosamax, an advance in osteoporosis treatment; and Celebrex, the arthritis drug with a better gastrointestinal profile than standard NSAIDs.

Many of these drugs have attributes that have been readily understood by consumers, and have had the benefit of extensive educational campaigns laying the foundation for their arrival, and the support of medical opinion-leaders or other advocates backing them in public forums and the media. And they have all been successes, with substantial help from public relations.

Philip Kotler is right when he says that public relations can only go in one direction: up. The confluence of the information age, the power of the media, and the sophisticated customer have helped to bring public relations into the limelight as a valuable marketing tool. The role of the consumer will only grow stronger over time, as plugged-in patients use online message boards, personal websites and other avenues to, in effect, 'become their own media outlets' (*New York Times*, e-commerce, September 20, 2000).

On a global scale, as the pharmaceutical industry further extends its reach, the great efficiencies and the tremendous impact of global public relations programmes will become more apparent than ever before. Those companies that most effectively and wisely use public relations in their marketing mix will have a distinct strategic advantage over their counterparts in the new world order.

Reference

Code of Federal Regulations, Section 312,7 (a), US Government.

IV

Brand
Development

9 | Clinical development and branding

STUART COOPER Adelphi

The development of a brand and marketing strategy for new pharmaceutical products should not be the last item on the pre-launch agenda. Branding strategy should be embedded in the overall clinical development and commercialization processes.

This chapter reviews the need for a properly integrated brand strategy that can provide a sustainable proposition for each new pharmaceutical product – one capable of evolution as the products move from the laboratory bench and into mass markets.

Healthcare environment and trends

There are a number of vital forces in healthcare that drive global convergence (Figure 9.1). These include changes within the healthcare environment to focus on cost containment and resource utilization, an increasingly multifaceted communications network that recognizes no boundaries in expansion, and the rise of European and global developments such as the European Agency for the Evaluation of Medicinal Products (EMEA) and the International Committee for Harmonization that encourage effective rapid drug development. As the industry merges and restructures, a strong pipeline for longer term growth, scale and economic power becomes ever more important. Successful launches of billion dollar compounds are necessary just to remain competitive. Consistent best practice in preparing a new product is thus ever more important to ensure a successful and rapid launch.

The impact of *these requirements* and the new benchmarks for success can be clearly seen in the take-off curves of the drug launches of today, which are more rapid compared with those of the previous decade. In the context of their

Forces towards global convergence

■ Healthcare resource and cost management
  - Evidence-based medicine, clinical guidelines, formularies

■ Communication explosion ... without boundaries
  - Financial community, regulators, industry opinion leaders (IOLs), indexed literature, international meetings, continuing medical education (CME), direct to consumer, Internet, talk

■ Global drug development
  - Drive for international purity/fairness
  - 'Simultaneous' submissions
  - Fewer but larger, multicentre, multicountry pivotal studies

Hence trend towards global core positioning, pricing, promotion and branding

Figure 9.1 Forces towards global convergence

era, leading brands such as Prozac, Norvasc and Zoloft were highly successful. Today's product launches, however, have set new records in the speed of global take-off and in their trajectory towards peak sales. Zyprexa, Lipitor, Viagra and Celebrex all outperformed the mega-drugs of the 1980s five- to ten-fold. Achieving and sustaining this sort of success demands harnessing the forces of global convergence, via truly global branding from the earliest stages of development.

Role of global branding

Global branding is a key component and determinant of this convergence. It is, however, important to recognize that such branding encompasses much more than the visual and verbal elements of name and logo. It is also about the fundamentals of the product, that is, the product descriptors in the various domains of communication, and the way they express a consistent promise, tone and theme for the brand. These considerations themselves strongly influence the visual and verbal elements and need to be determined and evaluated before the more obvious developments can begin.

In the field of healthcare product marketing, this process of global branding should start early in the product development lifecycle. Ideally, it begins in Phase II clinical development. This allows the medical, scientific and lay community to appropriately discuss their needs as the product moves into Phase III. In this way, it is possible to seed the correct verbal elements and tone early, to support rather than fight against the overall brand message.

Brand messages must be expressed consistently and dynamically to the consumer. To be successful, the development of these messages should encapsulate scientific understanding while boosting public awareness of the product. This has become more important as direct-to-consumer (DTC) communication grows. In a programme measuring the impact of advertising on over 2000 US arthritis patients, 25% claimed to have seen the advertisement for a new anti-arthritic drug one year after the launch. Of this group, over 33% had requested the product as a result of the advertising (Adelphi, 1999/2000). Clearly, a strong and well-supported brand message is instrumental for capitalizing on such consumer behaviour to ensure long-term goodwill.

At the same time, a fact of the pharmaceutical industry, that of constant technological advancement against a background of inevitable patent expiry, must be heeded. Information will evolve (planned and unplanned) and new indications, formulations and doses will be developed. A durable brand message should thus include brand values that are capable of evolving rapidly within this environment.

Pharmaceutical branding – the talk

Today, the development of pharmaceutical products as brands is talked about more than ever before. There are increasing discussions and expressions of support for the development of global brands. We see more consistent visual branding in core campaigns and promotional materials. Managers of products have become creators and guardians of brands.

A good example of a global orientation in the above-the-line promotional media is that of Zyprexa. The visualization and brand messages for the Zyprexa advertisement (Plate 9.1) was truly global in terms of positioning, descriptors, promise and trade mark design. The purple theme and figures were universal, yet expressed in a visualization that was felt to be appropriate at individual country levels. Perhaps more impressively, the product positioning and promise were consistent across all major languages. For the German-speaking market, for example, 'Making Re-integration the Goal' is expressed as '*Re-integration als Ziel*'. 'For Routine Use' is conveyed more broadly and in a more consumer-focused way as '*Der Wegbegleiter*' – a concept with no literal English equivalent that communicates the message of 'Companion along the way' or 'Constant or reliable companion'.

Symbolism can also emphasize the leadership position of a company if nomenclatural coherence is not possible. Such was the case of Merck Sharp & Dohme's launch of their new angiotensin II antagonist product. Despite using differing brand names around the world, the AA symbol was clearly an emblem of global leadership in the field developed during the pre-launch period. It was then used globally as a central piece of the brand name, variously CozAAr or LorzAAr (Plate 9.2). The AA symbol was further utilized in the evolving range, including the combination products, such as LorzAAr Plus.

However, such examples of apparently seamless and consistent visuals in global brand launches only illustrate one aspect of truly global branding. True global branding requires that all aspects of a brand message, including its values and prospects, be reflected in every element of the brand's development and communication, even in the pre-launch period. This needs to encompass verbal, written and visual expression in all communication domains, be they scientifically based communication or promotional items. More often than not, messages used in the medical communication and pre-launch literature have not reflected the look and feel of the launch material. Similarly, well-planned, consistent pre-launch brand messages are frequently not built upon or used at all in the more visual promotional branding campaign.

Branding/key objectives

A key objective of developing branding messages early is to establish longevity. To achieve this, the name and its values must carry a promise, raise reasonable expectations, promise predictable results and confer (a measurable) value in their own right to all constituents. This reduces the hurdles and selling effort in the long term by creating more loyalty. This can be gauged by three parameters: higher first time use, less change from and more change to.

In the pharmaceutical industry, the period of patent protection limits the time of exposure of a product, increasing the need to maximize consumer awareness and interest in the product brand via DTC marketing. This urgency is exacerbated by the new systems of information dissemination and self-purchase of drugs, especially with the increasing use of the Internet. DTC marketing calls for a brand-focused strategy with core values that attend to consumer needs, building on scientific needs and knowledge while allowing room for product evolution.

Such a brand-focused strategy begins at the pre-launch phase. Key brand values must be developed alongside the product itself, so that they may guide the language used internally and externally, in print and in discussion. All publications for meetings, symposia, clinical trial protocols, expert meetings and advisory panels can subsequently reflect these values.

Developing brand values and vocabulary – the walk

The planning process for a brand's message and vocabulary ideally commences in Phase II. A solid grasp of the product profile and its science, together with specialist opinions of this product and competitors, both available and in the pipeline, is fundamental to this process. At this point, the market dynamics and relative positions of key products, the needs of customers – from patients to opinion-leaders and payers – should already be well understood. The success of a new product among customers is preceded by its successful adoption by the opinion-formers. The creation of a credible brand benefits greatly from marketing intelligence. Early consultation with advisory boards and opinion-leaders and market research will determine the scientific concepts that are of particular interest and debate in the therapeutic area under scrutiny.

The current status of the market and recent levels of innovation will guide analyses of how the market is segmented, and of the positions and perceptual values of existing brands (Figure 9.2). This process clarifies the specific and possibly unique place occupied by each brand in the customer's mind. Together

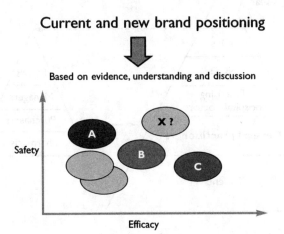

Figure 9.2 Current and new brand positioning

with a clear marketing and scientific assessment of the new product, a unique branding message and vocabulary of the new product can be formulated.

Thereafter, the twin customers of the brands, prescribers and patients will need to be researched to get under their skins. Their motivations, strength of feelings, disappointments and unmet needs must be defined. This process can further identify clear and important segments of the market and areas of need. It can also reveal any important unmet needs not currently occupied by an existing product. Customer research should also explore verbal and visual expressions of imagery, descriptors and product tone. The subsequent approach to brand design and execution and the clinical and outcomes research pathway makes the difference between a patient-driven product and one purely driven by technology. At the same time, it is important to bear in mind the differences between therapeutic fields in the balance between patient-driven and technically driven developments based on varying levels of innovation, complexity and current clinical need.

The translation and development of this scientific and market understanding into the appropriate brand vocabulary require experienced medical understanding. In order to be credible to the widest medical and regulatory audience (Figure 9.3), this vocabulary must lend itself to different forms of expression, each of which supports the core brand message to these different audiences while maintaining consistency. Such a brand vocabulary will support the brand in all its various domains: the drug class, type of product,

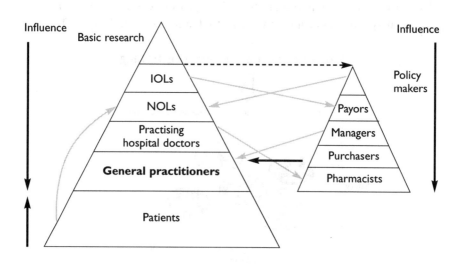

Figure 9.3 Customers and influencers

Plate 1.1
Potter's mark

Plate 1.2
Oculist's stamp

Plate 4.1 Nurofen pack

Plate 4.2 Voltaren Emulgel, Italian pack

Plate 6.1 Novartis consumer press advertisement

1

Plate 6.2 Pharmacia DTC

Plate 7.1 Viagra advertising

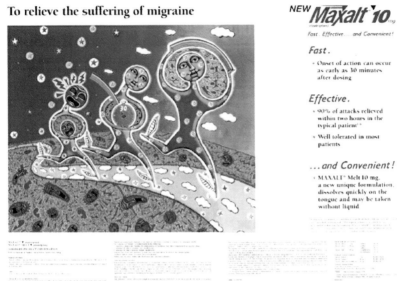

Plate 7.2 Maxalt advertising

Plate 9.1 Zyprexa advertisement

Plate 9.2
Global use of the 'AA' symbol in Merck Sharp & Dohme's advertising

Plate 11.1
Boots generic medicines range

Plate 11.2
Boots analgesics range

Plate 11.3 Boots symptom-specific range of analgesics

Plate 11.4 Boots Power Plus and Pain Relief Extra

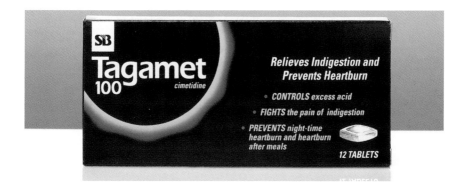

Plate 11.5 Tagamet after move to OTC

Plate 11.6 Zovirax

Plate 12.1 Eight typographic layouts

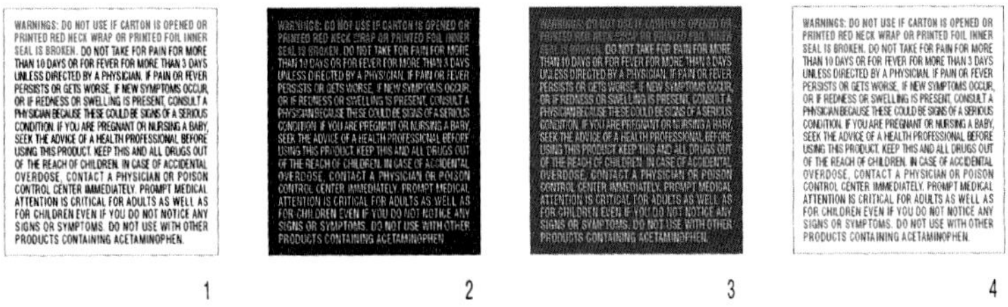

Plate 12.2 Four colour variations

Plate 12.3 Fast Cap

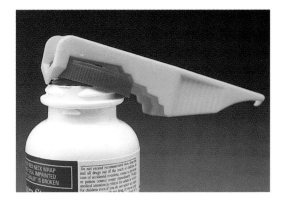

Plate 12.4 OpenAid

Plate 12.5
Some overwraps have
perforations and arrows
pointing to them that help in
removing the seals

VIII

 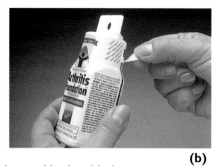

(a) (b)

Plate 12.6 Mechanisms that enable the elderly to
open and close packages with reasonable ease

Plate 12.7 Plastic screw cap with
deep indentations

Plate 16.1 Aviva

Plate 16.2 Red Bull

and disease area. At its most effective, it will be a driver of endpoints and studies of the product, and encompass the concerns of efficacy, safety and value. The brand vocabulary is not rigidly prescriptive, but should be flexible enough to be tailored to the appropriate audience in an appropriate format. By capturing the core values of the brand, the brand vocabulary can provide the building blocks to three aspects of a solid brand foundation: product promise and message, trade marks, symbols and logos.

Furthermore, the visual materials used to promote the product, from exhibition stands, patient education materials, to detail aids and brand advertising, should speak with the brand vocabulary and reflect the brand values. If these visual messages are supported by the research and brand-focused strategy initiated in Phase II, then the pre-launch and launch can address the whole community of customers, including those who consume and those who influence patient choice. This goal is a new benchmark for branding success in the pharmaceutical industry.

Conclusion

In the healthcare arena, the verbal elements of the brand describe as well as promise. Early in development, descriptive vocabulary has a definite role to play in enabling clear and accurate denotation of the product in scientific publications and meetings. It is, however, important that we do not stop here. The brand promise must be developed for succinct use in the wider marketing materials for promotion beyond the prescribers to the broad customer base.

The biggest challenge to the pharmaceutical business is possibly to make this type of branding happen consistently within pharmaceutical companies, organizations traditionally driven by product development along the parameters of scientific efficacy. This is no small task. It demands a true strategic commitment, with appropriate implementation and local flavouring, affiliate buy-in and understanding, encouragement, monitoring and policing. Effective internal communications, training and control processes must provide this support. Ultimately, the brand must be championed throughout the organization.

In summary, successful global branding in the pharmaceutical industry requires us to:

1. *Research:*
   ■ Identify customer needs
   ■ Differentiate
   ■ Establish rationale
   ■ Position.

2. *Integrate branding into the clinical development process:*
   - Employ research early to drive product development
   - Shore up credibility to ensure adoption.

3. *Understand the job of the brand:*
   - Use descriptors as part of the brand vocabulary

   - Use research results of the market to pitch the brand promise appropriately.

Reference

Adelphi Disease Specific Program: Arthritis 1999/2000.

10 Pharmaceutical brand name development

REBECCA ROBINS Interbrand

A good name is rather to be chosen than great riches. (Proverbs 22.1)

A good name can play a crucial role in building and maintaining customer loyalty and is therefore a very important element in contributing to the value and wealth creation of an Rx brand. In the course of this chapter, I will set out to establish why the brand name is such a critical part of the branding mix and will look at the legal, linguistic and regulatory issues that need to be considered when developing a brand name for a new drug. I will also be looking at how the changing dynamics both within and outside the industry, such as the emergence of direct-to-consumer (DTC) advertising and the rise of patient power, are impacting upon the choice of name for a new drug. What are the advantages and disadvantages of different types of name? What type of name would be most appropriate for your new drug? Finally, I will attempt to identify and rationalize some of the naming trends that have established themselves within the industry and venture into making some predictions for the future of pharmaceutical name development.

Importance of a name

One of the fundamental issues that needs to be addressed from the outset is why the brand name is such an important element of the brand. Clearly it is one element which will remain constant throughout the drug's lifetime. While such elements as packaging, price and promotions are all subject to change, the brand name is the one enduring means of identifying a product and subsequently plays a crucial role in building and maintaining consumer loyalty. With an increasing number of entrants to the market and therapy areas becoming ever more crowded, differentiation will be the key to success and a strong and distinctive brand name will be critical to enabling your drug to stand out from the crowd.

The global landscape

In the past, it has not been uncommon for a drug to be marketed under different names in different countries. However, companies are increasingly beginning to realize the benefits of developing a single brand internationally, as there are significant economies to be achieved through the promotion of one brand in all markets.

Of course, the task of developing a global trade mark within the pharmaceutical industry is not without its challenges. Not only does a name need to be linguistically acceptable and legally available as a trade mark in all markets in which the product is to be launched, it also needs to meet with the approval of the appropriate regulatory bodies.

The language barrier

Linguistic checks are of paramount importance to ensure that a name does not have any negative associations or serious pronunciation problems in the markets in which the product is to be launched. A name that is perfectly acceptable in English may prove to be highly amusing, or even disastrous, in other markets. The name Bonka, for example, is a perfectly innocuous name for a brand of coffee in the Spanish market, but one which would certainly be the subject of some amusement for the English speaking traveller! In other cases, however, failure to carry out appropriate linguistic screening on a name can be the downfall of a new product in a given market. A classic case is that of General Motors, who launched the Nova in Spain, without realizing that the translation of *no va* in Spanish is 'it doesn't go'! Needless to say the Nova failed to sell and the name was subsequently changed.

Pharmaceutical companies will invariably have an initial tier of markets across which a new product will be launched. However, it is vital to consider all potential markets of interest at the outset of the name development process, otherwise, you can almost guarantee that two years down the line, when you decide to launch, for example, in Japan, the name that has proved so successful in Europe and the USA turns out to mean something offensive in Japanese. Even in cases where a product may only be intended for use in one market, it is well worth carrying out some form of linguistic check across the major international languages. These checks should always be carried out prior to the trade mark searching programme, since the cost of trade mark screening is infinitely greater than that of linguistic screening.

The legal labyrinth

Critical to the creative challenge of developing a brand name for a pharmaceutical product is circumnavigating the tortuous path of trade mark searches. Trade mark registers are categorized into 42 classes and Class 5 (Pharmaceutical and medicinal products) is notoriously one of the most crowded. With over 40,000 trade marks registered in Class 5 in the UK alone, the challenge of securing the trade mark rights to a strong and distinctive brand name is becoming increasingly difficult.

Since the complexities of trade mark law are outlined so comprehensively in Chapters 13 and 14, I shall not attempt to venture further into the legal labyrinth at this point. However, later in the course of this chapter I will be examining how the crowded nature of the pharmaceutical trade mark class has impacted upon ways in which companies are approaching the name development process. I will be looking specifically at recent developments in pharmaceutical naming which exemplify how certain traditions have been broken with in order to maximize a company's chances of securing a brand name as a trade mark on a global basis.

Regulatory considerations

The development of a global brand name is further complicated in the pharmaceutical industry by the issue of regulatory approval. A name not only has to overcome the trade mark and linguistic hurdles that we have discussed, but it also needs to meet with the approval of the various regulatory bodies. Therefore, in order to increase the possibility of a name surviving both trade mark and regulatory approval, it is important to have an understanding of the regulatory framework for the development of a pharmaceutical brand name. The following guidelines have been developed by the European Agency for the Evaluation of Medicinal Products (EMEA).

■ Trade names (brand names) of medicinal products should not be liable to cause confusion in print, handwriting or speech with other trade names or with non-proprietary names

■ Trade names should not convey misleading therapeutic or pharmaceutical connotations

■ Trade names should not be misleading with respect to the composition of the product

■ The trade name of a product should avoid qualification by letters or a single detached letter and number

■ Trade names should not incorporate a generic stem or be similar to a generic name which has been adopted and published by the World Health Organization.

Creation of a brand name

Having established the legal, linguistic and regulatory framework within which the name for your product has to work, how do you go about the name development process? Given the difficulties of securing a brand name which is available as a trade mark and free from negative linguistic connotations in the relevant target markets, pharmaceutical companies are increasingly working with name development agencies to develop a brand name for a new product.

Before creative work can commence, however, it is vital to ensure that an appropriate naming strategy is established. In order to do this, a briefing workshop should be held with the agency and the key members of the project team involved with the name development. This project team should, at a minimum, include the following:

■ Marketing director
■ Product/brand manager
■ Clinical adviser
■ Trade mark attorney
■ Regulatory adviser.

The briefing workshop should encompass the following issues:

■ An attribute and benefit profile of the new product
■ The markets in which the product is to be launched
■ Key trends within the therapy area
■ The market dynamics
■ Competitor activity
■ The target audience(s).

Product profile

In order to establish such determinates as type and tone of name, it is important to gain a comprehensive insight into both the profile of the product and the dynamics of the therapy area in which it will be indicated. It is necessary to understand the product's attributes and benefits, its mode of action and how it will be positioned in the market. Of course, any claims that can be made about a drug are always dependent on clinical trial results, therefore an appropriate stage at which to commence the name development process would be during Phase II trials.

Competitor activity and market dynamics

In determining the naming strategy for a new drug, it is also crucial to consider competitor activity. What types of name are prevalent within the therapy area? What type of name should you adopt, therefore, in order for your product to stand out in the crowd? For example, if your product is truly revolutionary, it would be highly appropriate to signal this in the choice of a distinctive brand name which would be clearly differentiated from other names within the therapy area.

Target audience

The target audience plays a crucial role in identifying the most appropriate type of name for a new product. For example, a name for a highly specialized drug within a niche therapy area which is primarily targeted at hospital consultants is likely to be quite different, in terms of both content and tone, to a lifestyle drug with potential mass market appeal.

Traditionally, in the pharmaceutical industry, the core target audience for an Rx drug has been defined as the prescriber – be that the general practitioner, the pharmacist or the hospital consultant. However, the dynamics of the pharmaceutical industry are rapidly changing. With the rise of patient power and the advent of DTC advertising, the doctor–patient relationship is rapidly being redefined and, as patients become more health conscious and better informed, the brand name will need to have wider appeal beyond the realm of the prescribers. Healthcare issues, once the bastion of the doctor's waiting room, are now a staple of everyday life as people log onto health information websites and switch onto advertising campaigns.

Therefore, when developing names for Rx drugs, it is no longer simply the prescriber that needs to be considered. Pharmaceutical companies are increasingly taking this into consideration in their communications strategy and recognize that names need to appeal to a newly enfranchised patient base, have sufficient gravitas for hospital buying groups and, as general interest in health issues continues to escalate, also need to hold their own in face of the media.

The role of research in name development

In the same way that it is crucial to assess from a linguistic perspective what a brand name means in global terms, it is equally important to explore what connotations and implications it has among the target audience. However, researching names is not an easy exercise, which is one of the key reasons that name development should not only involve name creation specialists and linguists, but also brand researchers.

At Interbrand we have developed a research methodology for the evaluation of potential pharmaceutical brand names among the key external target audiences which we have called Pharmetrics. Pharmetrics provides us with the opportunity to put the candidate names in front of target market audiences (both patient and professional) in order to gauge and measure reactions across different nationalities according to the specific criteria which, through our experience, we know are important in the creation of successful brand names. The key criteria we use for evaluating names are as follows:

- *Impact:* how distinctive is the name?
- *Pronunciation:* how easy is it to say?
- *Scriptability:* how easy is it to write? (this applies to professionals only)
- *Confusion:* what likelihood of confusion is there with another drug?
- *Symbolism and communication:* what values and imagery is the name communicating?
- *Fit*: how well does the name fit with the proposition for the new drug?
- *Appeal:* what level of appeal does the brand name have?

Our methodology involves evaluating each name across a number of these criteria both before and after respondents are given the specific product profile. Research can be conducted on either a qualitative or quantitative basis, using the most appropriate methodology for the market and audiences involved.

The key aim of name research is to provide us with guidance rather than the definitive answer – to get a feel for which names appear to have more appeal and relevance than others in the eyes of the target audience. For example, respondents will typically gravitate towards names which are more descriptive or familiar. When evaluating the results of name research, therefore, it is crucial to take into consideration the broader strategic objectives of the project in order to arrive at an optimum conclusion and recommendation.

Two famous pharmaceutical brand names which have certainly managed to hold their own in face of prescribers, patients and the media are Viagra and Prozac. Indeed, such is the status achieved by the latter six-letter success story, that it has now come to embrace an entire generation and, in the public's eye at least, has become synonymous with the antidepressive therapy area.

If we put Viagra and Prozac under the nominal microscope for a moment, they provide us with some key criteria for developing powerful pharmaceutical brand names. As we have already established, on a fundamental level, a brand name must be available to register as a trade mark and free from negative linguistic connotations in the markets in which it will be made available. However, above and beyond this, a pharmaceutical brand name should also subscribe to the following criteria:

- Easy to pronounce
- Easy to write and read (to avoid prescription errors)
- Memorable and attractive to the target audience(s)
- Distinctive and differentiated from the competition.

Now that we have established the framework within which a pharmaceutical brand name needs to work, we should consider the different types of name that are available, looking closely at their respective advantages and disadvantages.

Types of name

If we continue to use the examples of Prozac and Viagra, we see that they are indicative of the *type* of name that has begun to proliferate within the pharmaceutical industry, namely the abstract brand name. As we have discussed, what type of name you choose will depend on a number of issues, such as the nature of the product, naming trends within the therapy area, the market dynamics and, indeed, the level of marketing spend that you have to put behind your new product. In considering which type of name would be most appropriate for your new drug, it is important to understand the advantages and disadvantages of the different types. Brand names can be broadly catego-

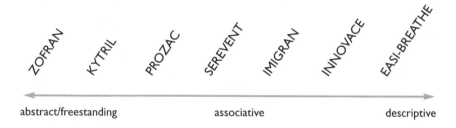

Figure 10.1 Naming spectrum

rized into three different types: descriptive, associative and abstract, examples of which are outlined in Figure 10.1.

Descriptive names communicate very clearly the nature of the product in question and are therefore very easy to understand. Innovace, while not *purely* descriptive, is a classic example of a very descriptive name for an innovative ACE inhibitor from Merck Sharp and Dohme.

However, although descriptive names are very direct and transparent in their communication, since they are descriptive only in one language, they do not tend to travel well on an international basis. Furthermore, they are difficult to protect as trade marks, since terminology which is generic to a given therapy area (such as ACE, for ACE inhibitor) cannot be monopolized by one trade mark owner.

Associative names are more flexible than descriptive names, as they are able to communicate some of the benefits or features of the product. The name Serevent, for example, is very clearly rooted in the drug's indication – the suffix 'vent' referencing an asthma treatment, while the prefix is coined from the word 'serenity', conveying the end benefit of relief.

An added benefit of associative names is that they tend to travel well internationally. Since the word parts which make up Serevent are both of Latinate origin, the meaning will be understood across a number of international markets. Associative names also make stronger trade marks since they are more distinctive than descriptive names.

As we move further along the naming spectrum towards *abstract names*, we see that the predominant factor is not so much one of content as of construct. Abstract names have no inherent meaning; they are, in essence, a collection of letters. In the case of brand names such as Zofran (Glaxo Wellcome) and Kytril (SmithKline Beecham), it is the tone and phonetic appeal of the letters that is the crux of communication.

Both Zofran and Kytril are brand names for anti-emetics, indicated for use predominantly in chemotherapy and radiotherapy. However, while both names are abstract, they could not be further apart in terms of the communications strategy behind the development of the names. In the case of Zofran, a brand name was required which would sound efficacious, while being soft and comforting in tone, whereas the approach for Kytril was quite different, with the focus on the communication of cutting-edge science and strength. Both names, however, are equally distinctive as they leverage a highly unusual combination of letters as a prefix and they demonstrate very clearly how the phonetic patterning and visual appeal of the letters is crucial in developing the appropriate tone for the brand name. Kytril achieves its impact through a hard-hitting combination of powerful consonants, whereas Zofran combines the dynamism of the letter Z with open vowels and softer consonants.

Companies are increasingly recognizing the benefits of abstract names, as we start to see more and more examples of this type of name come to market. Because abstract names have no core of meaning, they are less likely to cause offence across the various markets of interest and therefore have strong potential to travel well internationally. Due to their level of distinctiveness, abstract names also make very strong trade marks.

The attractiveness of the abstract is by no means something new. Back in 1888 George Eastman, the inventor of the photographic process, gave us an insight into the naming strategy behind the name Kodak:

> I knew a trade name must be short, vigorous, incapable of being misspelled to an extent that will destroy its identity and, in order to satisfy trade mark laws, must mean nothing. The letter 'K' had been a favourite with me – it seemed a strong, incisive sort of letter. Therefore the word I wanted had to start with 'K'. Then came the question of trying out a great number of combinations of letters that made words starting and ending with 'K'. The name KODAK is the result.

The dotcom dilemma

It is barely possible to move these days without being bombarded by yet another *dotcommercial*. However, we should not neglect the level of impact that the Internet is starting to exert, in naming terms, on the pharmaceutical industry. It is, of course, vital to register your corporate name as a domain name, but companies would increasingly be advised to register a drug name across all top-level domains (.co.uk, .com). If your drug does turn out to be the next blockbuster and is subsequently showered with media attention, the value of having secured your brand name as a dotcom will more than have been realized. Of course, hyperlinks can be embedded within the corporate website to enable your drug to be listed among the top 20 hits on an Internet search. However, with the rise of DTC advertising, as the end-user is prompted by a television advertisement to seek further information about a particular drug on the Internet, directing the consumer to your website and not that of a potentially unscrupulous third party will be crucial.

Conclusion

In the course of this chapter I hope that I have provided some insights into the importance of a brand name and the challenges surrounding the name development process for an Rx drug. As the dynamics of the industry continue to be redefined, with new channels of communication and an increasingly enfranchised patient base, the role of the brand name will become ever more important. Furthermore, alongside a pharmaceutical company's patents, copyrights and licensing agreements, the brand name is one of the most valuable assets. While the tangible life of a patent may be at best only 12 years (by the time a drug comes to market), the lifetime of a trade mark is indefinite, providing that trade mark continues to be used (correctly) and the registration renewed.

I would like to conclude this chapter with some insights into certain naming trends which have emerged within the pharmaceutical industry and from there will attempt to take a look into the crystal ball of the future of pharmaceutical naming.

In the late 1980s and early 1990s, the industry witnessed the meteoric rise of the letter Z, at the level of both product and corporate naming. A quick glance in the Monthly Index of Medical Specialities (MIMS) reveals no less than 48 names registered in the UK alone which begin with the letter Z (Table 10.1).

The letter Z is, of course, a very dynamic way of beginning a pharmaceutical brand name. It also has the benefit of looking and sounding both technical and scientific, therefore making it very appropriate for pharmaceutical products. In more recent years, however, the letter Z has been superseded by a favouritism for the letter X, as exemplified in such brands as Xanax, Xenical and Xepin. Of course, the letters Z and X both share the common denominator of looking unusual and sounding powerful and dynamic, and therefore, when used as prefixes, have the makings of a strong, distinctive brand name. It is, in fact, the need for differentiation that has been one of the key factors behind the predilection for certain letters, and these trends can be seen to have come about more by necessity than by design. The simple fact that the letters Z and X had in the past both been underutilized as prefixes has been as crucial a factor in their claim to pharmaceutical brand names as the level of their visual and phonetic impact.

TABLE 10.1		
Pharmaceutical brand names in the UK beginning with the letter 'Z'		
ZACIN	ZIAGEN	ZOLADEX
ZADITEN	ZIDOVAL	ZOLEPTIL
ZAMADOL	ZIMOVANE	ZOMACTON
ZANAFLEX	ZINACEF	ZOMAJET
ZANIDIP	ZINAMIDE	ZOMIG
ZANTAC	ZINCABAND	ZOMORPH
ZARONTIN	ZINERYT	ZONIVENT
ZAVEDOS	ZINGA	ZORAC
ZEASORB	ZINNAT	ZOTON
ZEFFIX	ZIPZOC	ZOVIRAX
ZELAPAR	ZIRTEK	ZUMENON
ZEMTARD	ZISPIN	ZYBAN
ZENAPAX	ZITA	ZYDOL
ZERIT	ZITHROMAX	ZYLORIC
ZESTORETIC	ZOCOR	ZYOMET
ZESTRIL	ZOFRAN	ZYPREXA

Source: Monthly Index of Medical Specialities, September 2000

We have also seen a distinct move away from Latin-based names, which had been traditionally the bastion of the industry, as they tended to have resonance with the prescriber base. Now that the prescriber–patient relationship is changing and consumers are taking more of an active interest in health issues, we have been experiencing a marked move towards names which are more end-user friendly in their appeal. For example, names which communicate the emotional benefits of the product, such as Relenza, or indeed abstract names which look and sound distinctive, such as Prozac.

We have even seen a few cases where real words have been used as brand names. These include Sonata, a drug to treat insomnia, and Muse, a drug to treat erectile dysfunction. While real word names offer an attractive proposition in terms of their uniqueness within the pharmaceutical namescape and the associated imagery they evoke, they should be considered with caution. It is important to remember that the brand name, while needing to appeal increasingly to the end-user, also needs to have a sense of gravitas and credibility with the medical profession. Therefore, for serious conditions and potentially life-threatening illnesses, a name based on an artistic or musical term would be best avoided. However, names which leverage a subtle play on a real word can be highly effective. The names Zestril and Allegra are classic examples of this strategy which takes the core of a real word and twists it to result in a name which is distinctive and emotive while at the same time retaining a sense of gravitas and credibility.

In looking to the future of pharmaceutical brand names, it is clear that we will increasingly experience a shift away from the doctor's language to the patient's language. The changing nature of the relationship between patient and physician is impacting on the way in which pharmaceutical companies communicate. Pharmaceutical brand names have truly come out of the closet and, as never before, are subject to public scrutiny. Therefore the development of a brand name will increasingly have to take into consideration how it will work in the context of such dynamics as DTC promotion. As trade mark classes and therapy areas become more crowded, companies will not only need to develop brand names which will differentiate their drug, but also which will have universal appeal across the prescriber–payer–patient relationship. It is no longer simply a case of daring to be different, but of defining the nature of that difference.

11 Brand packaging design

JEREMY SCHOLFIELD AND JULIAN THOMAS Interbrand

Introduction

A brand's packaging design can play an important role in projecting its personality. In the pharmaceutical industry the design of Rx packaging has been functional rather than decorative, and limited to the communication of essential information. But with the increase in brands moving from Rx to OTC, the design of brand packaging will take on a new importance.

The changing pharmacy environment

The pharmacy has become an extremely interesting retail space to observe recently. With the movement of so many products from Rx to OTC, POM (prescription-only medicine) to P (pharmacy), it has become as competitive and cut-throat as any supermarket shelf.

As new brands have entered the consumer domain they have been forced to get used to new rules of engagement. Their competitive set will have changed or, at the very least, their competitors will now be much closer to them. Suddenly they are rubbing shoulders with well-known brands that have years of media and advertising spend behind them and with livery that is instantly recognized and firmly fixed in the mind of the consumer. These brands will be imbued with values and meaning that inspire loyalty in consumers or even a sense of promise that is over and above the product's actual ability to deliver.

In all likelihood these new products will offer benefits and efficacy superior to the incumbents, but their existing Rx packaging will not be able to compete at the same sort of level. In the environment of the dispensary drawer or hospital shelf, the main drivers of the Rx packaging design would have been little more than the communication of the drug name and any essential or legal information. In all probability the pack format itself will have been a generic, easily accessible carton, tube, blister or bottle. The name of the product manufacturer or its medical definition may have been more important than the brand name itself. Hardly surprising, therefore, that the current pack will feel inadequate in this new environment.

Apart from the difference in the selling environment, the audience will have changed. The pharmacist, doctor and specialist will still be important, but now they may not be the primary target market. The consumers, with all their emotional mind-sets, are a completely different prospect.

The wariness of doctors and pharmacists of what they might perceive to be branding tricks and their preference, quite rightly, for proven evidence and statistics over illustration and graphics will have been a factor in dictating the nature of the brand identity and its packaging design to date. This will have created a pack that communicates all the rational reasons to purchase, but as all good marketers know, true brands need a combination of rational and emotional values attached to them if they are to appeal to more everyday consumers and fix themselves in their affections.

Their original audience will be an important link in the decision chain when it comes to purchase, but the identity must now extend the brand's appeal by adding a more emotive side to its character. In order to succeed the brand must appear effective, authoritative and professional but it will also need to have a good bedside manner in order to form a more personal and emotional relationship with the patient.

It could be argued that the move from Rx to OTC is the first step that some products take in the journey to becoming true brands.

Brand personality

Interestingly, however, the highly regulated, almost formulaic, appearance of Rx packaging has been a source of inspiration for OTC pack designers as they look to add clinical and authoritative visual clues for the consumer to recognize. The visual style of simplicity has become a strong signal for product efficacy. At Interbrand, when we developed the packaging for Boots own-brand range of basic medicines, we knew how powerful this could be. We recognized how important large amounts of white on the packaging would be in the communication of clinical and pharmaceutical values. The range covered a large number of medicine categories and the same principles were applied to the pack designs across all of them. On the analgesic range illustrated in Plate 11.2, the product information is arranged on the front of the pack to resemble prescription information on Rx labels. The effect is straightforward and uncomplicated. As so much emotional value is tied up already in the Boots' logo, that with this as the most prominent graphic on the pack we felt there was little need to add more emotional values. The overall effect is informative and reassuring. When the elements of the design are analysed, they give very similar signals to most Rx packaging (Plates 11.1 and 11.2).

Compare this range, however, to the added-value and symptom-specific ranges of higher specification analgesics that we also designed for Boots. The visual language is very different. More emotive imagery has been used to form a connection with the customer and the particular kind of pain they might be suffering. A metallic background is used on the symptom-specific packs to imply that these are products that have had some investment both in technological and financial terms. The added-value range uses colour and illustration to communicate the power of Pain Relief Plus and the speed to action of Pain Relief Extra. The Boots' values are still present in the designs and the information is clearly presented and straightforward in a similar way to the basic medicines range. However, the overall effect is very different; these ranges are more sophisticated and use graphic language not necessarily associated with the category. The packs tell stories and the ranges have distinct personalities (Plates 11.3 and 11.4).

In own-brand packaging the design challenge is made slightly easier as each range is supported and reinforced by the close presence of other own-brand ranges in the selling environment. For proprietary brands that more often than not stand on their own merit, receiving only limited support from the retailer, finding the right balance of elements for a product that is moving from Rx to OTC can be a difficult task. How much of the existing livery should be retained, and what additional signals should be added to the communication in order to create a truly distinctive personality in the market-place? These are the kinds of question that the brand team will be asking of themselves and probably their target consumers. What loyalty and equity does the existing packaging have? How is the brand positioned in the mind of the consumer?

When Tagamet made the move from Rx to OTC it chose to take a radical approach with the brand identity and pack design. Defying the conventions of the indigestion relief category and firmly distancing itself from its previous identity, it chose to communicate its difference and strength through powerful graphic devices. The resulting pack uses a confident logo – the background is dark and features an illustration of a solar eclipse (Plate 11.5). The pack is undoubtedly effective in its message and has distinct stand-out

on the shelf. However, according to the Pharmaceutical Association of Great
Britain, pharmacists around Britain were very unhappy with it. They found
the design too radical a move. In effect they found it too challenging and it
affected their choice of product when making recommendations to
customers. Getting the approval of the regulatory body is one thing, getting
the endorsement of pharmacists is another and in this case failure to do so
probably affected sales initially.

Conversely, a more evolutionary approach was taken with the cold sore
treatment Zovirax when it made the move from Rx to OTC. The design
changes were significant but not too challenging. The decision was taken to

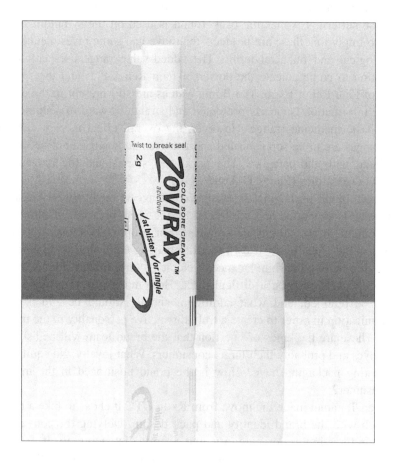

Figure 11.1 Zovirax pump dispenser

retain some of the equities of the Rx design, the strong use of blue being the key one. The resulting pack is still much more distinctive than its predecessor, the brand name is certainly stronger and the pack has better shelf shout to meet the needs of the OTC environment. For a product that had such a loyal following, and one that was unequalled in its arena, it probably was not a difficult decision to ensure that there were enough brand signals to reassure customers that this was essentially the same product they had been receiving on prescription (Plate 11.6).

Interestingly, when it was launched into OTC, Zovirax was offered in a dispensing pump as well as the existing tube. The cream could thus be dispensed accurately with minimum waste in a much more consumer-friendly way than squeezing a tube. In a market where legal restrictions can make it difficult to innovate graphically, considering how the brand personality can be communicated through the packaging format and functionality can be a good way around the difficulties (Figure 11.1).

Standing out from the crowd

When looking for the right ingredients for the brand identity and the packaging, it is also vital to consider the peculiar selling environment of the pharmacy itself and the way in which transactions take place. The product is often viewed at distances of over six or seven feet. The pack will be standing alongside other packs that are as determined to stand out as they are. Packaging is bright and loud with bold icons and graphics dominating in each brand's efforts to communicate their message. The result can be overpowering. Finding a way of cutting through this is one of the key challenges that the designer faces.

One way can be to use a calmer graphic approach. Simplicity and calm space can often be a great eye-catcher. For example, the Optrex packaging has a calm confidence and simplicity that stands out on shelf. Finding examples of a similar approach in pharmacy medicines is not an easy task, although the Strepsils packs are bold, clear and relatively uncluttered. I cannot not help feeling that this is an avenue that more brands could use to their advantage (Figure 11.2).

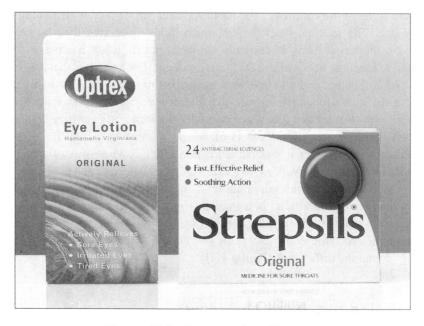

Figure 11.2 Optrex pack and Strepsils

The pack as source of information

The other factor that designers need to bear in mind is the way in which the packaging functions at point of sale. As well as selling the brand on shelf, quite often the pack will be used by the pharmacist as a visual aid when they are describing the product's features and benefits. They will use front of pack bullet points and back of pack text to remind themselves of the product's efficacy or to point out any of the side effects or restrictions on the use of the drug to the customer. With more and more drugs entering the OTC arena the pharmacist has become even more of a source of knowledge and guidance for the patient/customer. Their expertise is being utilized to its fullest as they are consulted on more and more areas of medicine. The intelligent arrangement of information can only be helpful as an aide-memoire and therefore in selling the product to the pharmacist and in turn to their customer. This is an often neglected part of the design which can make a big difference.

As well as the pharmacist there are other audiences, such as the elderly, who will appreciate the clear and legible arrangement of information on the back of pack. It is estimated that the population of adults aged over 65 in

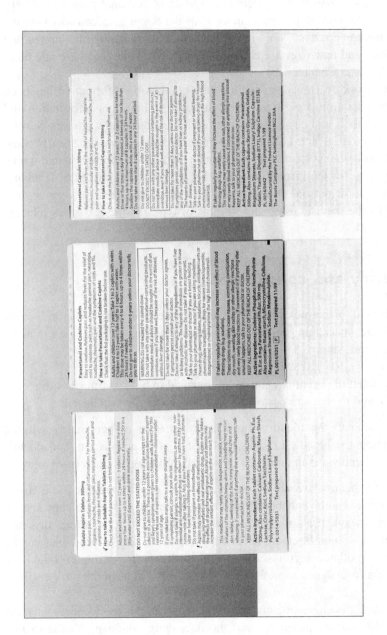

Soluble Aspirin Tablets 300mg

Relieves pain, reduces fever and inflammation. For headache, migraine, toothache, rheumatic pain, neuralgia, period pain and symptoms of colds and influenza.

✓ **How to take Soluble Aspirin Tablets 300mg**
Check that the foil packaging is not broken before each use.

Adults and children over 12 years: 1 - 3 tablets. Repeat the dose every hour, up to 4 times within 24 hours, if needed. Stir in a little water and disperse and drink immediately.

✗ **DO NOT EXCEED THE STATED DOSE**

Do not give to children under 12 years of age except on the advice of a doctor. There is a possible association between aspirin and Reye's syndrome when given to children with a fever. For this reason the use of aspirin is not recommended in children under 12 years of age.

If you take too many, talk to a doctor straight away.
If symptoms persist consult your doctor.
Do not take this product if you have: any of the ingredients, or any other non-steroidal anti-inflammatory drug as shown by asthma, itchy skin or runny nose after taking it. Also if you have, or have had, a stomach ulcer or have blood clotting disorders.

Do not take if pregnant or breastfeeding.
Aspirin may increase the effects of methotrexate, anticoagulant drugs, (eg warfarin) and oral antidiabetic drugs. Aspirin may reduce the effects of drugs for treating gout. Alcohol and steroids may increase the irritant effects of aspirin on the stomach lining.

This medicine may rarely cause indigestion, nausea, vomiting, irritation of the stomach lining, ulcers and bleeding may occur, skin rashes or asthma (wheezing), runny nose, tight chest and wheezing. If concerned or if anything else unusual happens talk to your pharmacist or doctor.

KEEP ALL MEDICINES OUT OF THE REACH OF CHILDREN.
Active Ingredient: Each tablet contains: Aspirin Ph. Eur. 300mg. Also contains: Calcium Carbonate, Maize Starch, Lactose, Citric Acid, Sodium Saccharin, Polyvinylpyrrolidone, Sodium Lauryl Sulphate.
PL 0014/5031   Text prepared 9/98

Paracetamol and Codeine Caplets

Easy to swallow. Relieves pain and reduces fever. For the relief of mild to moderate pain such as headache, period pain, neuralgia, toothache, rheumatic pain and the symptoms of colds and flu.

✓ **How to take Paracetamol and Codeine Caplets**
Check that the foil packaging is not broken before use.

Adults and children over 12 years: Take 1 to 2 caplets with water. Children 6 to 12 years: Take half to 1 caplet with water.
This dose may be taken every 4 to 6 hours, up to 4 times within 24 hours if needed.
✗ Do not give to children under 6 years unless your doctor tells you to do so.

WARNING: Do not exceed the stated dose.
Do not take with any other paracetamol-containing products. Immediate medical advice should be sought in the event of an overdose, even if you feel well, because of the risk of delayed, serious liver damage.

Do not take for more than 3 days unless your doctor agrees.
If symptoms persist consult your doctor.
Do not take if allergic to any of the ingredients or if you have liver or kidney problems. The hazards of overdose are greater in those with alcoholic liver disease. Do not take if you are pregnant.
Talk to your pharmacist or doctor if you are breastfeeding.
Talk to your pharmacist or doctor if you are taking mexiletine (heart drug), sleeping tablets, sedatives, tricyclic antidepressants or phenothiazine tranquillisers, drugs for nausea (metoclopramide, domperidone) or cholestyramine (for high blood cholesterol).

If taken regularly paracetamol may increase the effect of blood thinning drugs (eg. warfarin).
These tablets may rarely cause nausea, vomiting, constipation, dry mouth, sweating, skin rashes or other allergic reactions and very rarely blood reactions. If concerned or anything else unusual happens, talk to your pharmacist or doctor.

KEEP ALL MEDICINES OUT OF THE REACH OF CHILDREN.
Active Ingredients: Codeine Phosphate Hemihydrate Ph. Eur. 8mg, Paracetamol Ph. Eur. 500 mg.
Also contains: Maize starch, Microcrystalline Cellulose, Magnesium Stearate, Sodium Metabisulphite.
PL 0014/0251 [P]   Text prepared 11/99

Paracetamol Capsules 500mg

Relieves pain and fever. For the relief of headache, migraine, rheumatic/muscular and back pain, neuralgia, toothache, period pain and symptoms of colds and flu.

✓ **How to take Paracetamol Capsules 500mg**
Check that the foil packaging is not broken before use.

Adults and children over 12 years: 1 or 2 capsules to be taken three or four times a day if needed, at intervals of not less than 4 hours, up to a maximum of 8 capsules in 24 hours.
Swallow the capsules whole, with a drink of water.
✗ Do not take more than 8 capsules in any 24 hour period.

Do not give to children under 12 years.
DO NOT EXCEED THE STATED DOSE.
Do not take with any other paracetamol-containing products. Immediate medical advice should be sought in the event of an overdose, even if you feel well, because of the risk of delayed, serious liver damage.

Do not take for more than 3 days, unless your doctor agrees.
If symptoms persist, consult your doctor. Do not take if allergic to any of the ingredients, or if you have liver or kidney problems. The hazards of overdose are greater in those with alcoholic liver disease.
Talk to your pharmacist or doctor if pregnant or breast feeding. Talk to your pharmacist or doctor if you are taking drugs for nausea (metoclopramide, domperidone) or cholestyramine (for high blood cholesterol).

If taken regularly paracetamol may increase the effect of blood thinning drugs (e.g. warfarin).
This medicine may rarely cause a skin rash, other allergic reactions or very rarely blood reactions. If concerned or anything else unusual happens, talk to your pharmacist or doctor.

KEEP ALL MEDICINES OUT OF THE REACH OF CHILDREN.
Active Ingredient: Each capsule contains: Paracetamol 500mg. Also contains: Sodium Starch Glycollate, Gelatin, Magnesium Stearate, Sodium Lauryl Sulphate, Capsule: Gelatin, Titanium Dioxide (E171), Indigo Carmine (E132).
PL 0014/0442   Text prepared 1/99
Manufactured by the Product Licence holder
The Boots Company PLC Nottingham NG2 3AA

Figure 11.3 Back of Boots' packaging

England will increase 8.7% from 7.7 million in 1996 to 8.5 million in 2011 (Sub National Population Projections – Office of National Statistics, 1999). Therefore it is more important than ever for the designer to consider how the back of pack is arranged, how important information can be highlighted and which fonts and text sizes are chosen. (Herbert Myers covers these and other related issues in Chapter 12.)

In our work on Boots' medicines the organization information has been a key consideration. Coloured panels are used to highlight information and we used symbols and checklists to reinforce messages and warnings. Similar layouts were used across many different ranges, so that as they become familiar with the system, the pharmacist and the customer would know where to look for the information they need. Given the amount of legal and regulatory information required on the packs, the text is very legible because of the specific fonts, the weights of type and the text sizes selected (Figure 11.3).

Summary and conclusions

A number of principles should be taken into account, therefore, when designing new packaging for the OTC pharmacy if the brand is going to make the right impression:

- Ensure that the existing equities are retained to help pharmacists to recognize it and to reassure customers that the product is unchanged.

- Add value to the identity through the creation of personality without damaging the brand's existing relationship with pharmacists and doctors (who generally are unimpressed by what they see as commercial frivolity).

- Consider factors beyond the graphics for the identity and the pack. Brand personality can be enhanced by meeting the needs of the end consumer in different ways. If a pump dispenser can help a cold sore sufferer dispense the exact amount of cream needed for treatment, similar principles can be applied to other categories. An arthritis treatment, for example, could have a specially designed cap to help sufferers grip and open the pack easily.

The market is interesting enough at the moment, but one wonders what the future holds for the pharmacy and the packaging within it. As the market becomes ever more sophisticated and deregulated, will we see the emergence of marketing techniques that have so far been too challenging for the category? Could we see the emergence of brands with real attitude? Could the future yield the Pepperami of the analgesic sector, or the Tango of cough linctus? Will that attitude be reflected in the pack designs at a future date or will it be the preserve of advertising as it is at present? Will we see brands and packaging that are aimed at lifestyle rather than ailment and treatment? Certainly the Rx side is becoming more and more marketing led so it would seem to be a logical progression.

A note of caution, however. The regulatory bodies apart, designers must remain mindful of their responsibility to provide accurate and informative packaging as well as satisfying marketing objectives. Personality is one thing but there are ethics involved and this should not be achieved at the expense of truth. Whatever the future holds, I think the pharmacy will continue to make good watching for some time to come.

12 Packaging for the elderly

HERBERT M. MEYERS

With the human population increasing at an ever-accelerating rate, medical care is trying to keep pace and is making spectacular inroads in most modern countries. Responding to the needs of the ageing population, and taking advantage of the advanced art of computer technology, sophisticated research by pharmaceutical companies is producing an ever greater number of medicinal products packaged to provide everything from manufacturing efficiencies to consumer convenience.

In the meanwhile, world demographics are transforming the baby-boomer generation to one approaching their sixties. Branding and merchandizing of medicinal products are adjusting to conditions where the average life expectancy of men and women now reaches into the late seventies.

The relationship between the rapidly increasing need by the elderly for medical remedies to help them to cope with their advancing age and their ability to manage the packaging in which medicinal products are marketed therefore becomes an issue that deserves our discussion.

But first we need to examine what really defines an elderly human being. What identifies the lifestyle, interests, attitude, and behaviour of an elderly person? Young people may consider elderly equivalent to old. But an elderly view of self may be profoundly different. When we are 20 years old, 40 seems like an age we never want to reach. But when we reach 60, most of us like to think of ourselves as being young at heart and, assuming health is not a major problem, as mentally alert and physically capable as when we were in our twenties. To quote Mark Twain: 'Age is a thing of mind over matter. If you don't mind, it doesn't matter.'

Disregarding, for the moment, the older person's perception of self, we find that, from a demographic point of view, the definition of 'elderly' can vary according to location, local convention, governmental or organizational interpretation and a number of other factors.

Most significantly, the term 'elderly' defines a substantially larger segment of the world population today than it did 20 or more years ago. In Western Europe and Japan, one in five citizens will soon be over 65. In the UK, the percentage of people over 65 rose from 12% in 1965 to 18% in 1997 and is expected to increase to 21% of the population by 2025. The population in other European countries is expected to follow a similar curve.

In the USA, the trend of ageing forms a somewhat different, more diverse pattern. According to the Administration on Aging (AoA), a US federal government agency responsible for tracking statistical profiles of older Americans:

> the rate of aging has varied over the decades, primarily as a result of the fluctuation in the rate of decline in the birth rate; second, as a result of fluctuations in the rates and patterns of decline in age-specific death rates; and third, as a result of the shifts in the volume and age pattern of net immigration.

That pattern may change, however. The AoA concludes that 'the number of elderly and the rate of aging are expected to increase steeply' at about 2006, when the population of baby boomers will begin reaching the age of 60, and 2011 when many will reach 65. The American Census Bureau estimates that the number of Americans over the age 65 will soar 80%, to pass 100 million by the year 2025.

Indeed, the percentage of the ageing world population is increasing in mind-boggling proportions. Global projections suggest that between 1980 and 2020 the worldwide population of those over 60 will increase by over 240%.

Such rapid growth puts ever-increasing pressure on the ability to control the health of the world population, especially in Third World countries where health standards are often less developed, while people living in industrial countries are better able to take care of themselves. Changes in lifestyle, such as retirement at an earlier age and the growth of a wealthier population in the industrial world, accelerate the demand for health products. As manufacturers of branded and generic pharmaceuticals jockey for dominant marketing positions in the world of pharmaceuticals, more and more products become available both as prescribed by physicians and on the shelves of pharmacies, drug stores and various retail outlets.

With these developments, packaging, an integral component of marketing and distributing pharmaceutical products in the industrial world, takes centre stage.

Packaging of medicinal products

In view of the demographics described above, we can safely assume that an ever-increasing amount of drugs is needed by the elderly as age takes its toll on their health. All of these come in containers of one type or another – ranging from vials and ampoules, to blisters, bottles, cartons, tubes, jars and pouches.

Basically, packaging for medicinal products falls into two categories:

1. Packaging for prescription drugs, for example packaging for pharmaceuticals prescribed by a physician and obtained at a pharmacy (Rx).
2. Packaging for over-the-counter drugs (OTC), for example packaging for pharmaceutical products which can be acquired at a store without a physician's prescription.

Packaging serves the industry well in accommodating its ability to assemble, fill, control, protect, store and transport medicinal products. But how much attention does the pharmaceutical industry pay to its packaging in relation to age-related problems of consumers who depend increasingly on packaged drugs to help them cope with their advancing years?

And, considering the critical importance of proper use and administration of medicinal products by the elderly, to what extent do pharmaceutical manufacturers pay particular attention to the need for legibility and comprehension of labels and leaflets, and to the structural characteristics of the containers?

Conversely, how do the *elderly* view their ability – or inability – to manage containers for the medicinal products they use every day? Unfortunately, there is a gaping void between the methods used to package pharmaceuticals by most manufacturers of these products and the ability of the elderly to comprehend and handle them effectively. The US Federal Drug Administration (FDA) has received more than 6000 medication error reports since 1992 and 50% are related to confusion in the labelling or packaging of the drugs.

This chapter will try to throw some light on the interaction between three critical components in the distribution of packaged pharmaceutical products: the activities of manufacturers and distributors of packaged medicinal products; the guidelines for packaging by supervisory government agencies; and the ability of elderly consumers to deal with packaged medicines.

But for a discussion of packaging for the elderly to be relevant, it is necessary to examine first the *physiological* conditions which many, if not most, older consumers experience at age 60 and older.

Physiological difficulties of the elderly relating to packaging

It must be understood that the concerns the elderly have with packaging of pharmaceutical products include three physiological issues:

■ *visual issues:* reading and recognizing products effectively

■ *structural issues:* opening, dispensing and closing the product safely and correctly

■ *compliance issues:* taking the medicine correctly.

Visual issues of the elderly

When discussing the packaging of pharmaceutical products used frequently by the elderly, most people automatically conjure up thoughts relating to physical handicaps of the elderly, such as encountered when holding, opening, dispensing and closing containers.

While there is good reason for being concerned with the motor difficulties of elderly persons, less recognition is sometimes given to their visual limitations at age 60 and after. Visual deterioration among the elderly is a fact of life. By age 60, their abilities to focus, resolve images, distinguish among colours and adapt to different lighting conditions diminish rapidly. Subtle physiological changes often produce loss of visual clarity and sensitivity which will impair the elderly consumer's ability to perceive the graphic elements of a package clearly.

Many visual impairments affect light sensitivity. Increased opacity of the eye, including cataracts and clouding of the lens of the eye, reduces the amount of light that enters. This makes the contrast level of any visual element, such as medical information on a package or a pamphlet in the package, a critical issue. The greater the contrast between copy and background, or between two colours, the easier it is for the elderly to read and comprehend such information.

It is easy to understand that the ability – or inability – of the elderly consumer to read and comprehend important information, such as brand and product identification, usage and dosage declarations, identification of active substances, warnings and contraindications, is critical. Even though most elderly persons wear corrective lenses, they still find it difficult to read the fine print on many packages of pharmaceutical products, especially those panels that contain important information on dosage, usage and possible side effects.

Support systems, such as magnifying glasses and strong light are often needed in addition to their glasses to read the fine print on these panels. Elderly consumers are concerned about health and appreciate anything that helps them to comprehend usage information appropriate to their need. They want lettering to be large enough to read without a magnifier. Elderly consumers become frustrated with tiny and severely condensed typography on many pharmaceutical packages. They feel that marketers either do not care about their dysfunction or are trying to discourage reading certain information.

While frustration is an understandable reaction by the elderly to their difficulties in reading label text, to imply a conspiracy among pharmaceutical manufacturers is doing them an injustice. More often, difficult-to-read text is the result of an overreaction by the manufacturers to comply with governmental and organizational guidelines for mandatory copy. Such guidelines are sometimes vague and confusing. In trying to comply with these and fearing reprimands by governmental agencies if the guidelines are misinterpreted, manufacturers tend to take the safe road by packing onto the labels voluminous informational details, regardless of their usefulness to the consumer. Never mind that the often tiny label areas have no way of accommodating all this information in a readable condition. The upshot of this is copy so small and/or condensed that it is difficult to read even for someone with 20/20 vision. It becomes a case of maximum information at the expense of readability.

With this in mind, well before the readability issue of pharmaceutical labels was seriously addressed by either manufacturers or government offices, Gerstman+Meyers (now Interbrand), the international brand identity and design consulting firm, conducted a series of studies intended to provide a better understanding of the impact of pharmaceutical product packaging on the growing mature market. The study, which received wide interest in the press, was conducted among consumers aged 55 to 80.

To test the *extremes* of legibility and text comprehension, independent of existing organizational or governmental guidelines, respondents were shown back panel copy, typical of the labels on small packages for OTC pharmaceutical medicines. The treatment and layout of the copy on these hypothetical examples was modified in a variety of typographic styles, colours and arrangements.

The interviewees, who were shown eight typographic layouts (Plate 12.1) and four colour variations (Plate 12.2), responded favourably to:

■ *Option 3*, because its paragraphing helped them with legibility

■ *Option 5*, because the lines that divided the small text panels made it easier to comprehend the text of the three segments

■ *Option 7*, because the bold lettering drew their emphasis to important information, such as 'Warning' and 'Do not' copy.

Of four alternatives in text and background colours, the interviewees overwhelmingly preferred:

■ *Option 1*, because the black lettering with red highlights was found to be the most comfortable to read and comprehend.

The importance of expiry dates

Because of the concern for their health, elderly consumers are especially concerned with the legibility of expiry dates on pharmaceutical packages. They find the size of the date imprints often too small, distorted or hard to locate.

The importance of being able to clearly identify the expiry dates of drugs is emphasized by the fact that many elderly people tend to hoard drugs for lengthy amounts of time, either because they think that they may need them again at a later date, or simply because they forget that they have them. They thereby risk the possibility of inadvertently using drugs that have exceeded their expiry date and are no longer effective.

Different manufacturers use different methods of identifying the expiry dates on their containers. Most of them are printed, but debossed expiration dates are sometimes used on paperboard cartons. Thus, the legibility of these dates varies substantially. Some of the printed expiry dates are so light that they are barely legible or have accidentally shifted to a dark area of the package where they are hard to read. Older people find that they often have to twist and turn the package to find the expiry date. Some debossed dates are too shallow to decipher easily, especially under less than ideal light conditions. To overlook this issue or treat it with minimal attention can be a serious disservice to the elderly.

Colours and other visual issues

In addition to legibility concerns, visually impaired elderly consumers may have difficulty registering images clearly because, in today's market environment, there is a visual overload from the surrounding images, colours and shapes. The avalanche of images in the modern marketplace obscures the vision of the elderly and often confuses them. Since supermarkets and mass merchandise outlets are not likely to reduce the number of packages on their shelves, manufacturers and designers can help by understanding the visual impairments of older consumers and designing packages for maximum visual clarity.

Label colours take on special importance for elderly consumers. Colour coding of packages, or on portions of packages, is frequently utilized by manufacturers to differentiate between similar product varieties. This can be beneficial when colours on packages for pharmaceutical products communicate important cues to the elderly consumer, including alerting them to the possibility of picking up the wrong medicine. For example, colour coding can assist in differentiating between regular and maximum strength medicines, or call attention to different product forms, such as several varieties of cough syrup or antihistamines (Figure 12.1).

Unfortunately, this method of flagging product differences is not utilized often enough to best advantage. While manufacturers make good use of colours to differentiate between tablets and capsules of various medicinal products, in part on recommendation by the World Health Organization (WHO), pharmacists routinely repackage these in generic containers or cover original labels with generic ones with typed-in medical and other information.

Since it is not unusual for elderly people to use multiple drugs, or for different members of a family living under the same roof to use a variety of drugs, mix-ups are easy and do occur. Colour coding such labels suggests an opportunity to minimize the potential of mix-ups.

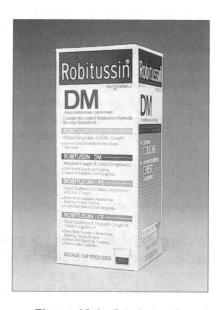

Figure 12.1 Cough syrup

On the other hand, colour coding of pharmaceutical packages that are frequently bought by the elderly has to be carefully considered as many older people have problems differentiating between certain colours. As mentioned earlier in this chapter, their ability to focus, resolve images, distinguish among colours and adapt to different lighting conditions diminishes with age. Increased opacity of the eye, including cataracts and clouding of the lens, reduces the amount of light that enters the eye.

In addition, yellowing of the eye may cause older consumers to feel that they are seeing through a yellow mist. Their eyes may receive less violet light. Because of this, older people may have difficulties discerning among such colours as blues, greens and violets. For example, if two product varieties are colour coded blue and green respectively, some older consumers may have difficulty differentiating between these, depending on the specific colour hues and the lighting conditions in the store. Differentiating between reds, oranges and certain yellows can be another problem more typical of the elderly than younger consumers.

Visual cues, such as icons, are another means of helping the elderly consumer to understand product usage and preparation and clarifying copy elements. Cues that effectively delineate, highlight or emphasize important information can facilitate readability without the necessity for enlarging the text with a magnifying glass. The back panel of the Pepcid AC package (Figure 12.2) is a good example of smart information on pharmaceutical pack-

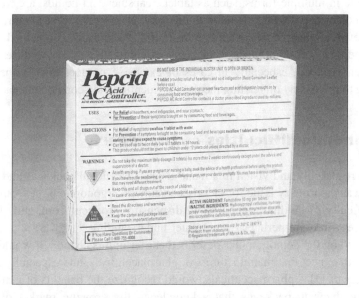

Figure 12.2 Back panel of the Pepcid AC package

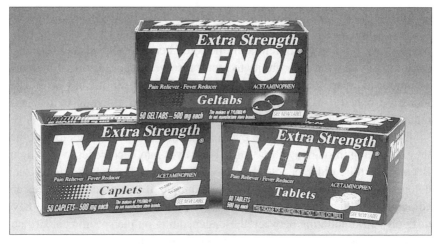

Figure 12.3 Products available in multiple forms,
such as tablets, capsules and liquids

aging. Icons can draw attention to important medical factors and graphically interpret the meaning of these, thus encouraging the consumer to pay extra attention and read the copy carefully.

Photographs or illustrations that identify products and product forms, suggest product flavours and define product usage are another means to which elderly consumers often react positively. Visual presentation of products that are available in multiple forms, such as tablets, capsules and liquids, are welcome aids to older people, helping them to differentiate between these (Figure 12.3). Whenever applicable, visually demonstrating the product contained in the package or the product function makes it easier for the elderly to differentiate between products, especially in cases of extensive product lines, rather than having to rely solely on reading the product identification copy on the packages.

Ergonomic difficulties of the elderly

While readability and visual treatment of pharmaceutical packages and labels are always a primary issue for elderly consumers, ergonomic issues – the ease or difficulty of holding, opening and dispensing products from, and closing, packages – require perhaps even greater understanding.

Based on the demographics described earlier in this chapter, it would seem logical to expect that manufacturers of pharmaceuticals, and especially manufacturers of OTC pharmaceuticals, would recognize the benefits of marketing their products in packages that acknowledge the growing market of older consumers. This suggests commercial advantages for marketers who take the initiative of shifting from stock containers to packages with features that benefit the elderly in coping with their physical limitations.

Unfortunately, this seems to take place in only the rarest instances. Most marketers of consumer products still believe that younger audiences are more important targets, that they purchase more products than elderly consumers and have more years ahead of them to remain loyal customers. Young brand managers responsible for pharmaceuticals are more comfortable addressing consumer segments of their own age. They continue to ignore the substantial elderly market, concentrating their efforts on the younger, 18–35 year-old consumer segment.

For example, focus groups and other types of consumer research used to obtain consumer feedback on new products or product improvements rarely include respondents over the age of 40, apparently on the assumption that anyone older is 'over the hill'. Not so, says *Modern Maturity* magazine, a publication of the American Association of Retired Persons, in a brochure discussing the lifestyles of today's elderly:

> Take off 15 years. At least. They look and act many years younger than their mothers and fathers at age fifty, sixty or seventy. Proper nutrition, a zest for fitness and a more active life-style have greatly extended the vital years.

But, even though today's 60-and-over consumers may feel young at heart, the fact is that, as they grow older, their ability to carry out the activities of daily living gradually decreases as their years increase. Grip strength in normal hands decreases steadily with age, reaching a point where it is only half that of their youth when they reach 70. Steadiness of hands becomes another difficulty for many elderly people, causing them to have perennial difficulties with many packages.

Complaints about structural aspects of pharmaceutical packaging are numerous among the elderly. They scoff at child-resistant caps that are also elderly resistant, 'push here' lids that refuse to yield and bottle seals that require knives or other tools to remove them. Equally disliked are jar lids that are difficult to grasp and turn, anti-tampering devices with undecipherable or confusing opening instructions and blister packages for tablets and pills that stubbornly resist attempts to dislodge the product.

At the same time, older people are very self-conscious about their problems. They are willing to cope with their difficulties but are grateful for packaging structures that make it easier to deal with them. Many are even willing to pay a little more for such features. But packages with features that are loudly promoted but do not seriously address their physical difficulties are regarded as gimmicky and not worth acquiring at additional cost. What the elderly are looking for are truly functional package components, especially those that help them to open and access their medicines.

Childproof versus elderly-resistant containers

What ignites the scorn of most elderly people more than any other packaging issue are tamper-evident and childproof packaging features. This is where a serious conflict crops up between those that are meant to protect and those that are geared to easy opening. Childproof closures naturally try to prevent children, curious as to what is in a package and innocent of the danger of drugs, from the mental or physical capacity of opening such containers. Many closures require pressing down hard or lining up elusive and often hard to see arrows, making them simultaneously childproof and elderly resistant.

Tylenol, the leading analgesic product in the USA, is one of several manufacturers that once marketed the so-called 'Fast Cap', which enabled the user to twist the cap more easily by inserting a pencil through the hole of the cap extension (Plate 12.3). Unfortunately, this package, so useful to elderly consumers, has been discontinued. Instead, several Tylenol package sizes are now available *without safety closures* but with a plastic 'OpenAid' gadget, provided by the McNeil Consumer Products Company without charge, to help in the removal of caps (Plate 12.4).

Elderly consumers are even more frustrated when they have to go through certain procedures every time the container needs to be opened. It is significant that the elderly differentiate the *initial* opening of a container from *subsequent* openings. Older people may be willing to put up with special efforts during initial opening if this means that the product is secure and tamper free. But they feel that subsequent openings and closings must be more easily achieved.

Moreover, opening problems are not confined to bottle caps. What can send an elderly consumer into a flurry are tamperproof and plastic overwraps applied to bottle finishes or around the entire package. While they appreciate the necessity of these protective methods, they feel that there is a need to strike a better balance between devices that prevent tampering and alert consumers to packages that may have been invaded, and seals that adhere to the packages so tightly that they require accessories to remove them. Some overwraps have perforations and arrows pointing to them that help in removing the seals (Plate 12.5), but there is a need for more of these on pharmaceutical packages.

Another packaging form that arouses the ire of the elderly are blisters for individual pills or tablets which stubbornly resist accessibility. The elderly do not object to blister packs per se. They understand their purpose in preventing tampering and access by children. But they feel that the sometimes overly complicated procedures for accessing the pills or tablets ignore the difficulties that these present to patients who are most in need of the products.

In summary, manufacturers and their package designers need to understand that packages for pharmaceutical products purchased extensively by elderly consumers require special sensitivity for and understanding of the needs of the elderly. Copy should be readable and comprehensible without the need of a magnifying glass. Text should be simple and brief. Colours must have maximum contrast. Icons can help in drawing attention to important health-related information. Expiration dates should be clearly legible and easy to find. Tamperproof and childproof packages should strike a balance between access prevention and the need of their major users – the elderly – to remove them.

Government guidelines

Most medicines for human use, whether prescribed by physicians or available at retail outlets without prescription, are subject to stringent regulations by specific departments of government agencies throughout the world.

To bridge the gap between the needs of consumers for pharmaceutical chemicals and the need to protect consumers from potential harm from these, an increasing number of guidelines and regulations are being launched by the governments of various countries. These range from monitoring the manufacture of existing medicines for human use and assessing the acceptability of newly developed pharmaceuticals to the compatibility of packages in which medicines are distributed.

In Europe, the Pharmaceutical Committee of the Council of European Communities issues and oversees Directives regarding the manufacture and distribution of proprietary medicinal products. In the USA this is the responsibility of the US Department of Health and Human Services of the FDA.

Not only are the medicines subject to close scrutiny by governmental administrations, but also various types of packaging materials, the chemicals of which could potentially interact with the chemical of the medicines inside them, are subject to stringent supervision by these governmental offices. In addition, to ensure legibility and comprehensibility, governmental documents specify a range of graphic design elements for packages and leaflets.

Although much too lengthy and complicated to serve the purpose of this chapter, a few excerpts from the guidelines issued by the US Department of Health and Human Services and the Pharmaceutical Committee of the Council of European Communities may help in understanding the complicated issues that are at stake.

US guidelines for packaging of pharmaceutical products

The numerous regulations that guide the physical characteristics of packages are there to protect the consumer from potential harm by ensuring the correct descriptions and identities of medicines, preventing false and misleading information, and to provide proper instructions and warnings.

In a lengthy and detailed document, *Guidance for Industry – Container Closure Systems for Packaging Human Drugs and Biologics*, the US Department of Health and Human Services addresses the issues of packaging from a chemistry and manufacturing perspective. The department differentiates between:

■ *Primary packaging:* packaging components that are or may be in direct contact with the dosage forms

■ *Secondary packaging:* packaging components that are not and will not be in direct contact with the dosage forms.

The *Guidance for Industry* specifies that manufacturers of packaging must submit to the respective government agencies detailed chemistry, manufacturing and control documents for every packaging component. The long list of packaging components ranges from ampoules, vials, bottles, tubes and cartons to inner seals, overseals, labels and administration accessories such as syringes, droppers and dosage spoons.

Specific design characteristics for packages for medicinal products, many relating to the needs and concerns of the elderly, refer to a variety of characteristics, including:

■ *Physical characteristics of packaging:* Dimensional criteria (shape, neck finish, wall thickness)

■ *Package suitability for intended use:* Product protection, safety and proper performance

■ *Performance:* Proper functioning of performance features and container closure system designed to improve patient compliance

■ *Protection:* Adequate protection from temperature, light, degradation, loss of solvent, oxygen, water vapours and contamination

■ *Safety:* Prevention of leaching and migration into the dosage that may be harmful to patient

■ *Containers for injectable products:* Accommodation of injectable medicine by providing single dose or multiple dose containers

■ *Containers for capsules and tablets:* Tight and well closed to avoid deterioration

■ *Child-resistant packaging:* Standards for opening and reclosing child-resistant packages.

In addition to existing guidelines for prescription drug packaging, the US Department of Health and Human Services is currently in the process of developing 'Guidelines for Industry' for all OTC packages sold in the USA. These are scheduled to be implemented by 16 May 2002. The guidelines will attempt to 'to make it easier for consumers to read and understand OTC drug product labeling and use of OTC drug products and use OTC drug products safely and effectively'.

The new US guidelines will specify a 'Standard Labeling Format' and include a 'Drug Facts' box. The long list of detailed specifications in the guidelines will include the following:

Headings, subheadings and text to be generally left-justified

Horizontal barlines and hairlines to separate headings and subheadings to contribute to overall organization of information

14 point Helvetica Bold Italic for titles, 8 point Helvetica Bold Italic for headlines, 6 point Bold for subheadings, and 6 point Helvetica Regular for text with 7 point leading

An arrow at the bottom of the first column, and the words 'Drug Facts, continued' at the top of the second column, if two columns of information are required within the Drug Facts box

Colour contrast to highlight Drug Facts information.

An alternative 'Modified Labeling Format' will provide instructions for labelling which cover 'more than 60% of the total surface area available to bear labeling'. Here 4½ point type will be permitted and the box can be omitted, as long as the Drug Facts copy is emphasized by colour contrast.

European guidelines for packaging of pharmaceutical products

The Council of European Communities also specifies physical and chemical characteristics for the packaging of medicinal products for human consumption, which are similar in many respects to those of the US FDA, but differ in some details. For example, according to Ellard's *Guide to the NHS and Medicines*, in the UK:

> bulk containers of products from which pharmacists have dispensed medicines into their own bottles or other containers are being phased out.

Instead:

> many medicines in the UK are supplied in patient packs – blisters or strip packaging for tablets and capsules, tubes for ointments or creams and bottles for syrups.

European law (EC Directive 92/27/EEC) requires that the graphics on labels, packages and leaflets must include specific information, including in part:

- *Name of the medicinal product* (invented name or common or scientific name) followed by common name, form, strength (baby, child or adult)

- *Common name* (international non-proprietary name recommended by WHO)

- *Strength of medicinal product* (content of active ingredient expressed qualitatively or quantitatively per dosage unit, per unit of volume or weight according to the dosage form)

- *Contents* by weight, volume or number of doses

- *Method of administration*

- *Special warnings* (to be stored out of reach of children, or medicinal concerns)

- *Special precautions* (storage/disposal)

- *Expiration dates* (month/year)

- *Batch number*

- *Manufacturer* (holder of authorization: name and address).

Of particular significance for the elderly is that the Council of European Communities identifies information that must be detailed in leaflets inserted in packages for pharmaceutical products. Specifications for leaflet copy cover a number of subjects, such as:

- Must include information about contraindications, precautions for use, interaction with other medicinal products and other special warnings.

■ Must identify the method and route of administration, frequency of administration, duration of treatment, risk of withdrawal effects and action to be taken in case of overdose.

■ Must describe undesirable effects that may occur, warn against using product after expiration date, warn against signs of deterioration and identify date of last revision of the leaflet.

■ Can be in several languages, providing all the information is the same in all languages.

Even more specific to issues of the elderly, the Pharmaceutical Committee of the European Commission has issued *A Guideline on the Readability of the Label and Package Leaflet of Medical Products for Human Use*, which spells out clearly what is required to make mandatory copy readable. While regulations may vary somewhat from country to country on the European continent, the guidelines issued by the European Commission are illuminating and suggested as guidelines not only for pharmaceutical packaging, but packaging and labels for all consumer products.

Some issues that the European Commission guidelines address are:

■ *Print size and type:* The particulars appearing on the label of all medical products should be printed in characters of at least 7 point Didot (or a size where the lower case 'x' is at least 1.4mm in height), leaving space between lines of at least 3mm. The type and print chosen should be such as to ensure maximum legibility. The particulars appearing in the leaflet should be printed in characters of at least 8 point Didot, leaving space between the lines of at least 3mm.

■ *Print colour:* Readability is not only determined by print size. Characters may be printed in colour allowing them to be clearly distinguished from the background. A different type or colour is one way of making headings clearly recognizable.

■ *Syntax:* As far as possible, overlong sentences (that is, more than 20 words) should be avoided. Moreover it is recommended that lines of length exceeding 70 characters are not used. Different fonts, upper and lower case, length of words, number of clauses per sentences can all influence readability.

■ A minimum number of words should be used in the bullet points. Abbreviations should be avoided.

Note that the guidelines by the Pharmaceutical Committee of the European Commission are more like suggested guidelines, leaving some creative flexibility to the designer. In contrast, the guidelines by the US FDA leave little, if any, opportunity for deviation.

Although the above excerpts represent only a small sample of the much more detailed directives of the Pharmaceutical Committee of The European Commission and the US Department of Health and Human Services, they identify clearly the need for addressing readability of small type on pharmaceutical labels and packages for the benefit of the elderly consumer. If conscientiously executed by drug marketers, these requirements will be a welcome benefit appreciated by the elderly.

Packaging features favoured by older consumers

Compared to the no-nonsense approach to packaging for prescription medicines, which is subject to stringent jurisdiction by governmental agencies in various countries, the slightly more lenient restrictions for OTC medicines offer pharmaceutical manufacturers the opportunity for developing packaging with visual and ergonomic features especially beneficial for the elderly.

Many ergonomic and ocular problems experienced by the elderly could be eliminated, or at least lessened, by packaging features that enhance the administration of medicines, and although some of these features have already been outlined in this chapter, it is appropriate to make a brief summary, as well as pointing out some that were not mentioned previously.

Ergonomic features

While the chemical composition of medicines often dictates packaging materials, elderly consumers prefer, whenever possible, plastic containers over glass since they are lighter to lift, carry and handle, and less likely to break.

A primary issue for the elderly is opening packages of medicinal products. They prefer mechanisms that are easy to handle and do not require supplemental opening devices.

Elderly consumers appreciate the need for safety devices to ensure that the package contents have not been tampered with and are fresh and sanitary. This is consistent with the group's concern for their health and healthy lifestyle. However, this goal must be balanced with mechanisms that enable the elderly to open and close the packages with reasonable ease (Plate 12.6).

In addition to opening, the ability to close the package efficiently is important in the mature market. As the elderly may not use up the product quickly, they want the package to preserve product freshness until all the contents are used.

When pharmaceutical products utilize bottles with plastic screw caps, the elderly invariably prefer those with deep indentations (Plate 12.7) that provide a better grip. Of special interest are such rare features as cap extensions that provide better leverage.

Also liked by the elderly are bottles with flip-top caps that can be opened and closed easily, even with one hand (Figure 12.4).

Older consumers are extremely value conscious. They want the containers to easily dispense all the contents in order to avoid waste. High and square shoulders on jars containing creams or ointments can make total product removal difficult.

Convenience features such as portion-packs are often valued by older people. They welcome these packages, even if they have to pay a slightly higher price, because they conveniently provide just the right amount of medicine and preserve the freshness of the products.

However, older consumers are not likely to switch brands as a result of package preference alone. Packaging must offer significant improvement over current alternatives for the elderly to appreciate its value and influence their

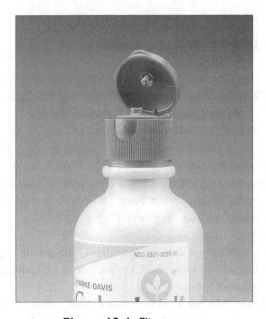

Figure 12.4 Flip-top caps

purchase decision. Older people differentiate between packages that solve real problems and those that are just promotional novelties, the latter being not worth the additional cost.

Ocular features

Elderly consumers want packages that communicate and provide information clearly, and label and pamphlet text to be large enough to read without the need of a magnifier. To the extent allowed by the regulatory requirements of governmental guidelines, older people appreciate text that enhances readability through the use of highlighted words, delineation and paragraphing. They prefer usage copy to be in sharp contrast with the background, such as black or dark colours against white. Shiny backgrounds, such as foil labels, make legibility difficult and should be avoided by all means on packages for pharmaceutical products used by the elderly.

Icons or graphics can be especially helpful cues for the elderly consumer. These assist in drawing their attention to important functional and usage information and even in remembering the brand names of prescription and OTC products, differentiating these from other, similar products. Colour coding can help in differentiating between similar products and product forms, as long as the colours are sufficiently contrasting to avoid confusion.

Performance features and accessories

Among performance features that elderly consumers consider important are those that make it easier for them to control product flow and those that help them with medicinal compliance. Davis Garner, Chairman of the Healthcare Compliance Packaging Council in Washington, DC says that:

> well-designed packages can help patients to keep track of doses taken, can be made to carry treatment instructions, and often make it easy to use and follow instructions properly. While patients forget about 50% of the doctor's or pharmacist's instructions, the package stays with them as a reminder.

Bottles that control dosage flow, pre-filled syringes, dosage spoons and measuring cups are among those package performance features that can help to administer medicines accurately.

Most pharmacies offer medical accessories that, although not packages in the traditional sense, are helpful to the elderly. Among the most popular are

Figure 12.5 Pill organizers

pill organizers that are designed to help users to remember to take the correct medicine at the right time (Figure 12.5). These little containers for pills and tablets are small enough to fit into a coat pocket or purse and feature compartments with markings and Braille identifying week, day or even time of day.

Innovations

Based on what can be learned with the older consumer in mind, there is no question that there are numerous opportunities for packaging concepts that can ameliorate many of the ocular and ergonomic impairments of the elderly.

With this in mind, the temptation of experimenting with design concepts, that could accomplish some of these objectives by providing important benefits to the elderly, is hard to resist. Shown here are a few examples meant to suggest breakthrough packaging that would benefit not only the mature consumer, but would be just as beneficial to consumers of *any* age:

Figure 12.6:   Pull-apart extensions and zipper-like closing feature on plastic pouches.

Figure 12.7: Bottle cap featuring a recess that, by inserting a pencil, provides better torsion to twist the cap open.

Figure 12.8: Cap extensions to facilitate better torsion in opening and closing.

Figure 12.9: Pencil-shaped dispenser that is inconspicuous and easy to carry and that releases tablets or capsules one at a time by pushing a button, similar to the mechanism of an automatic pencil.

Figure 12.10: Pill dispenser, functioning similarly to a stapler, with LED read-out to help with medicine administration schedule.

Figure 12.6 Plastic pouches

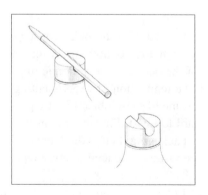

Figure 12.7 Recessed bottle cap

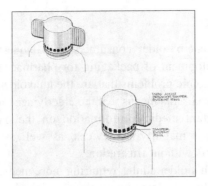

Figure 12.8 Cap extensions

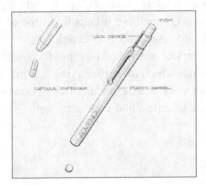

Figure 12.9 Pencil-shaped dispenser

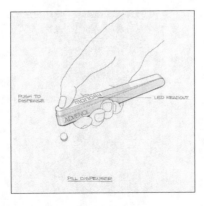

Figure 12.10 Pill dispenser

Conclusions

The growing segment of older consumers will unquestionably continue to impact on the development of packaging for pharmaceutical products. Both the visual and ergonomic problems that are the unavoidable by-product of old age must be addressed. This means that the elderly need to be able to read and comprehend important medical information on the packages and leaflets without the need for magnifying devices, as well as to open, close and dispense the products without frustration.

While it is true that older adults, requiring more medical care than younger people, would benefit most from innovations designed to alleviate their packaging complaints, everyone, regardless of age, could benefit from packaging that communicates clearly and is comfortable to use. Especially in categories of seemingly similar equivalent products, one brand might be able to carve a niche for itself vis-à-vis competitive brands by virtue of the superior communication and functionality assets of its packaging.

In that way, marketers of pharmaceutical products will contribute medicinal products for better health which offer packaging features that are likely to gain the enthusiasm of not only that segment of the population identified as the elderly but create *ageless* appeal and popularity among consumers of all ages.

Trade Mark and Regulatory Issues

13 Regulatory issues and generic names

ALISON AZULAY Markforce Associates

At a time when thousands of trade mark applications and registrations[1] for pharmaceuticals populate the world's trade mark registers, it is becoming increasingly difficult to create, clear and protect pharmaceutical marks on a global basis. Here we will explore the regulatory issues and legal aspects which impact on the creation of pharmaceutical brands as well as the criteria for trade mark searching and protection for pharmaceutical brands. We will then turn our attention to ways of maintaining the brand well after registration and the use of trade mark notices and symbols. We will also touch upon domain names.

An application for marketing authorization is made in the early stages of the life of a new compound, and, when and if granted, supports the safety and efficacy of the new drug. The regulatory authorities in the countries of interest are responsible for considering and granting the licences.

The regulatory authorities of various countries all share the same goal of granting marketing authorization in respect of a safe and efficient product. These authorities, however, operate independently and may regard different aspects of a product's profile (including its packaging or labelling) as being paramount. We will now take a look at some of the regulatory institutions and their practices in order to understand how they impact on the creation and protection of a global trade mark.

European Union

The regulatory authorities responsible for granting marketing authorization throughout the EU are national authorities and the European Agency for the Evaluation of Medicinal Products (EMEA).

Mutual recognition versus the centralized procedure and the single trade mark

In the EU there are two routes for applying for drug marketing authorization. These are mutual recognition and the centralized procedure.

Mutual recognition: Under the mutual recognition system of regulatory approval, an application to market a particular drug is filed with the regulatory authority in a chosen member state. The grant of a single initial authorization from a 'reference member state' can then be extended to other member states by mutual recognition after those countries have had an opportunity to consider an assessment report. One advantage of this system is that it is possible, if desired, to adopt a different trade mark for the product in different countries.

The centralized procedure: Under the centralized procedure which came into force by a Regulation on 1 January 1995,[2] a single marketing application is filed with the EMEA for a licence which covers the whole of the EU. This procedure is subject to the *single trade mark* requirement. It requires that an identical trade mark is cleared in each of the 13[3] trade mark registers of the member states of the EU. There are no express grounds in the Regulation for this requirement. The impact of the single trade mark requirement is that the trade mark searching process is far more expensive and timely than if mutual recognition is adopted. A global trade mark (identical throughout the world) is always commercially desirable since it facilitates, among other things, marketing activity, distribution, print and packaging and has obvious cost advantages. Nevertheless, global marks are often extremely difficult to clear, and frequently companies must tolerate some variations in their marks in certain countries. Under the centralized procedure, however, no variation in the mark is permissible among the member states, except in the circumstances described below.

In July 1998, the European Commission published a Communication setting out the circumstances in which an exception would be granted to the single trade mark requirement. This specifies that where the proposed trade mark:

> has been cancelled, opposed or objected to under trade mark law in a Member State, the Commission will address the issue in order not to disadvantage patients and their access to the medicinal product.

The marketing authorization holder would have to show that despite its attempts to overcome the difficulties, the trade mark is unavailable for use in a particular member state. In exceptional circumstances the Commission may authorize the use of a different trade mark in that member state. Nevertheless, in circumstances where the Commission permits the exception the marketing company would have to agree not to use the two marks in order to partition the European market. Only once since the centralized procedure was introduced in 1995 has the Commission granted the exemption. This was to Hoechst Marion Roussel, who had been granted a European marketing authorization for their anticoagulant under the trade mark Refludan, but had failed to obtain registration in Spain. The Commission allowed them to use the mark Refludin in Spain on the condition that Hoechst Marion Roussel provided an undertaking not to use the existence of the two marks to prevent repackaging or relabelling of parallel imports from Spain. This exemption was permitted after the authorization had been granted. In fact, they had already started marketing the drug in Spain.

It is not clear whether, had Hoechst Marion Roussel approached the Commission prior to the granting of the licence (and launch of the product under the two marks in the EU), such an exemption would have been made. The exemption would seem to apply to the facts of the case. The product was for use in hospitals, and, in view of the pricing policies at the time, parallel importation of the product was unlikely. Even if an approach to the Commission prior to the granting of the authorization were permissible, an approach at such a late stage could result in a delay for the launch.

At the time of filing the regulatory submission – generally approximately one year prior to launch – a declaration is made in the application stating that the designated trade mark is free for use and registration throughout the EU. If a clear statement cannot be made in the regulatory submissions, then a licence for the designated mark is unlikely to be forthcoming. Of course, the product could be marketed under the generic name, but this turns to a question of profits and ownership after patent expiry.

Despite continued lobbying by pharmaceutical companies to the Commission, the single trade mark requirement remains. Currently awaited is the decision of the European Court of Justice (ECJ) Court of First Instance in a case brought on 8 May 2000 by a subsidiary of Boehringer Ingelheim, Dr Karl Thomae GmbH, requesting the Court to annul a decision of the EMEA in which it refused marketing authority for variant trade marks under the centralized procedure.[4] The facts of the case are outlined below.

The plaintiff was granted marketing authorization valid throughout the EU under the trade mark Daquiran for its pramipexole medicinal product for the treatment of Parkinson's disease. It was soon apparent that Daquiran was not available for the German market in view of a conflicting mark Taxilan of BykGulden Lomberg Chemische Fabrik GmbH, whose trade mark Taxilan is in respect of a medicinal product for the treatment of diseases of the central nervous system.

As a result, the plaintiff had to change its trade mark in Germany. The plaintiff applied to the EMEA to obtain a modification of the name of its product to Firol in respect of the German market. At the same time, given that in Denmark, Sweden and Finland the trade mark Daquiran had not yet been registered, the plaintiff decided that it would be preferable to use the already registered and available trade mark Sipnok in those countries. Therefore, the application for variation included a request to change the single trade name Daquiran to the trade marks Daquiran, Firol and Sipnok. The EMEA refused the application on the grounds that the marketing authorization under the centralized procedure requires authorization of a single trade mark. The application to vary should include a new trade mark to cover all of the EU member states.

The European Federation of Pharmaceutical Industries and Associations (EFPIA) is an association which represents the interests of some 18 (15 of which are European) national pharmaceutical industry associations and (to be added by EFPIA) individual pharmaceutical companies. EFPIA have filed an Application to Intervene in support of the claim of Dr Karl Thomae GmbH on the grounds that the Court should annul the decision of the EMEA.

The outcome of the present case is eagerly awaited and is likely to have an effect on the economic and legal position of pharmaceutical companies.

Pending a positive decision by the ECJ Court of First Instance in the case of Dr Karl Thomae GmbH, it is, therefore, necessary to commence the searching process as early as possible, preferably a minimum of four years prior to launch where the centralized procedure is used. This may be as early as Phase III clinical trials. This would provide a more comfortable period for strategic planning for searching and protection. Frequently, such a period of time is not available. When searching commences, if a decision has not been taken as to the regulatory route (centralized procedure or mutual recognition), then it should be assumed that the centralized procedure will be used.

The single trade mark requirement under the centralized procedure requires that thorough and detailed clearance searches are carried out in relation to each of the proposed marks in each of the EU countries. In addition, Norway, Iceland and Liechtenstein may also be relevant since they have been identified to join the centralized procedure. Other countries soon to join the EU should be given equal attention in the searching and filing programme short of being unprepared. Countries which may shortly join the EU are Cyprus, the Czech Republic, Estonia, Hungary, Poland and Slovenia. The centralized procedure requires additional time and expertise in the trade mark clearance and protection process. It increases considerably the overall expense in protecting the global name.

Mutual recognition versus centralized procedure

A new product which is accepted in the UK under the system of mutual recognition may face objections in other countries in the EU. The result is that authorization and, therefore, marketing may be delayed. Hence, the advantage of the centralized procedure.

On the other hand, if difficulties in clearing marks are experienced in one member state, it is a comfort if the global mark can be substituted with a back-up mark in that member state. As discussed earlier in the chapter, it is not as simple as this with the centralized procedure.

EMEA – criteria for evaluating proprietary names

When creating and searching trade marks for pharmaceutical products it is necessary to be aware of the pitfalls that may await at the regulatory authority. Let us take a look at some aspects of proprietary names (trade marks) which have provoked comment or objections by the EMEA in the past. These are summarized below.

- The trade name of a veterinary or medicinal product should not be liable to cause confusion in print, handwriting or speech with the trade name of an existing veterinary medicinal product.

- The trade name of a veterinary or medicinal product should not be liable to cause confusion in print, handwriting or speech with an established non-proprietary name (see the section Generic names, later in this chapter) relating to a different active ingredient. Objection to trade marks based on risk of confusion as described above is the most frequent basis for objection. This has been applied in relation to risk of confusion with the trade name products authorized outside the EU. The test generally applied by the EMEA is that *if there is a minimum of three distinguishing letters, it is unlikely that it will be considered that there is a risk of confusion in writing.* The three-letter rule originates from Austria, where it was one of the tests used by the Austrian Trade Mark Registry in the examination process. The EMEA have adopted the test from the Austrian Registry, but it is controversial. Many pharmaceutical companies have complained about it on the grounds that even though marks may contain three identical letters, the marks differ when taken in their entirety. No other trade mark office or regulatory agency employs this mechanical rule.

■ The mark for a medicinal product should not convey misleading therapeutic or pharmaceutical connotations. For example, laudatory claims, such as super, efficient, miracle and eco, will be rejected.

■ The trade name of a veterinary or medicinal product should not be misleading with respect to the composition of the product.

■ The trade mark for a product should avoid qualification by letters where possible.

■ Qualification of a name by a single detached letter and by numbers is unacceptable.

■ The trade name should comply with World Health Organization (WHO) guidance. In summary, it should not incorporate a generic stem or be similar to a generic name which has been adopted and published by WHO. Checks should also be made against British Approved Names (BANs), United States Approved Names (USANs), International Non-proprietary Names (INNs), and where possible against Japanese Approved Names (JANs), Dénomination Commune Français (DCFs) (generic names in France) and Denominazione Comune Italiana (DCIt) (for Italy).

The EMEA is not concerned as to whether the mark will or may constitute an infringement of another party's trade mark rights, although the EMEA may refuse a mark on the basis of a third party mark if it is liable to cause confusion or a risk to safety.

USA

The Food and Drug Administration

The Food and Drug Administration (FDA) is responsible for drug marketing authorizations in the USA. The FDA is by far the strictest of authorities and its policies and decisions can influence other bodies.

Pharmaceutical companies should submit the proposed trade marks to the FDA for evaluation as soon as possible. The most common current practice is to submit the proposed marks to the FDA after the end of Phase II clinical trials. It is now possible, however, to submit a proposed mark during Phase II trials, provided draft labelling is available.

Following recent changes in the FDA evaluation process, proprietary names receive two evaluations:

1. A detailed evaluation; and

2. A second evaluation approximately 90 days prior to the New Drug Application approval. This evaluation concentrates on FDA product approvals during the interval between the first and current evaluation. The second review is to confirm that the mark under consideration is not phonetically or visually similar to trade marks recently approved by the FDA.

FDA detailed evaluation

Pharmaceutical companies may submit up to two potential trade marks for evaluation, presented in order of preference. Only if the first name is found unacceptable will the second name be considered. The risk assessment as to phonetic and other safety issues compares the proposed mark with products available only in the USA.

Unlike the EMEA, which requires a declaration that the mark is free for use and registration throughout the EU to accompany a regulatory filing, the FDA risk assessment of the trade mark is independent of any decision by the US Patent and Trade Mark Office (PTO) to accept the mark for registration. The FDA risk assessment focuses on the clinical context in which the product is used, such as dosage and route of administration.

Let us take a look at some of the criteria used by the FDA for assessing the safety of a proprietary name. The emphasis is to avoid the risk of medication errors resulting from visually or phonetically identical or similar names:

■ *Handwriting analysis studies:* A group of FDA volunteers who are generally physicians, pharmacists, nurses and other healthcare professionals will conduct handwritten tests in respect of retail and hospital prescriptions. The tests will include the proprietary name as well as other information, such as dose, regimen and route of administration, to simulate written prescriptions in a retail and hospital setting and to check for the potential for medication errors in each.

■ *Verbal analysis studies:* Another group of FDA volunteers will listen to a tape-recorded order for the new product using the proposed name, to simulate a verbal dispensing order in clinical settings where potential errors due to phonetic similarities can be discovered.

■ *Expert group:* The FDA's Office of Post-marketing Drug Risk Assessment expert group, staffed by medication error staff and a representative from the Division of Drug Marketing, Advertising and Communication, exchange opinions on safety and other nomenclature issues based on professional experiences, and review criteria for name suitability.

■ *Computer-assisted analysis:* computer software with an associated drug name dictionary can provide information such as names of applications undergoing FDA product review in order to more accurately detect orthographic (spelling) or phonetic similarities in proprietary names. The FDA is currently working to develop this component of its review process.

The FDA review process focuses on identifying the potential for medication errors. Thus, although both the FDA and the US PTO seek to prevent the adoption or registration of pharmaceutical trade marks that might cause consumer confusion, these two agencies employ different analytical tools in making this determination and may award different priority status to names being reviewed simultaneously by both agencies.

Latin America

Latin American countries also have specific regulatory requirements, which impact on the trade mark searching and filing programme. In certain Latin American countries evidence of the trade mark registration certificate and in others, evidence of the trade mark application must be filed with the regulatory submissions. Table 13.1 details the requirements (at the time of writing). As a result of these requirements in certain Latin American countries, a trade mark application needs to be filed or even registered very early in the process. Sometimes the trade mark registration is required as early as one year prior to launch. In addition, registration in Latin America can be slow. The process in these territories requires early attention, if relevant.

TABLE 13.1		
Regulatory requirements for trade marks in Latin America at the time of submission and prior to approval		
Country	Requirement for submission of product	Requirement for approval
Costa Rica	Trade mark certificate	–
Dominican Republic	Trade mark certificate	–
El Salvador	–	–
Guatemala	Proof of application	Proof of application
Honduras	Proof of application	Trade mark certificate
Nicaragua	Proof of application	Trade mark certificate
Panama	–	–

It should be taken into account that there can be a tension between the goals of developing and clearing trade marks at a sufficiently early stage in order to achieve the earliest possible regulatory submission date, and the desire to develop trade marks that relate to a product's attributes. Because it is now possible to submit names to the FDA during Phase II trials, name creation may be likely to commence very early in Phase II. Often, information about dosing regimens, dosing forms and distinctions between the new product and others in its class are not clearly understood at this phase. Careful consideration should be given to the trade-offs between waiting for more certain information about a product and obtaining the earliest possible filing priority and regulatory submission dates when deciding when to commence name creation for a new pharmaceutical.

Multiple trade marks

The FDA, EMEA and national European regulatory authorities do not generally permit multiple trade marks in respect of a substance with more than one therapeutic indication. This is not necessarily the case in all other regulatory agencies.

By way of example, in the USA, Glaxo Wellcome's product for the treatment of HIV and hepatitis B is known as Epivir for the treatment of HIV and Epivir HBV for the treatment of hepatitis B. In many other markets, this product is known as Zeffix for the treatment of hepatitis B. In the USA, however, the FDA discourages the use of a truly different trade mark for each indication. Likewise, in the UK Abbott Laboratories' product with the generic name terazosin is used to treat hypertension under the trade mark Hytrin and benign prostate hyperplasia under the trade mark Hytrin BPH.

Recently, the FDA have approved Eli Lilly's antidepressant, fluoxetine, under the trade mark Sarafem for the additional indication of premenstrual dysphoric disorder (PMDD). This drug is best known as Prozac. The new brand name is being used to reduce confusion as to the differences between depression and PMDD. The separate name was requested for the new indication to avoid the mental illness stigma associated with Prozac. It is unlikely that this decision signifies a move by the FDA in its attitude against permitting multiple trade names for a substance having more than one therapeutic indication. However, the decision does indicate that the FDA may be willing to consider an additional trade mark for a new indication of an existing drug on a case-by-case basis, weighing the relative advantages and risks of having either a single trade mark or multiple trade marks for the same drug.

Generic names

Unlike other products, a pharmaceutical is not only referred to by a trade mark, but also by a generic name. The generic name is a single name of worldwide acceptability for each active substance that is to be marketed as a pharmaceutical. WHO works closely with the national nomenclature committees to this end. From a practical point of view, the generic name is required at the time of regulatory submissions.

In contrast to the trade mark, the generic name is not the property of the company which discovers or develops the new compound. Nevertheless, third parties are not free to use the generic name for an identical product until after patent expiry for risk of being sued for patent infringement. Once a generic name has been published, any company or party can use the generic name for the purposes of identifying the product or compound. For instance, a third party may use a generic name in research or other publications to refer to a specific product or compound. The generic name is commonly referred to as a *non-proprietary name*.

Timing and development of a generic name

It is recommended that the generic name process is commenced as early as possible and is underway by the commencement of Phase II clinical trials. The process is timely. It is obviously preferable to commence the generic name development when the project is more secure, for instance at Phase III, but the risk is that the launch may be have to be postponed due to the absence of an approved non-proprietary name.

The stem

The generic name consists of a stem and variant. The stem designates the group of pharmacologically related substances. Frequently, a new compound will take a stem which has been allocated by WHO for a specific family of compounds or substances. If a compound has a new mechanism of action, chemical structure and therapeutic indication, a fresh stem is required. The new stem is generally allocated by the nomenclature commission in the country where the compound originates, with approval, amendment or refusal by WHO. If a product originates in the USA, then the United States Adopted Names Council is generally approached for the new stem. It will in turn be forwarded to WHO for approval.

TABLE 13.2	
Examples of non-proprietary stems for pharmaceutical substances	
Stem (English)	Pharmacological family
-ac	Anti-inflammatory agents of the ibufenac group
-adol -adol-	Analgesics
-ast	Antiasthmatic, antiallergic substances not acting primarily as antihistaminics
-astine	Antihistaminics
bol	Steriods, anabolic
-cain-	Antifibrillant substances with local anaesthetic activity
-caine	Local anaesthetics
-cillin	Antibiotics, derivatives of 6-aminopenicillanic acid
cort	Corticosteroids, except prednisolone derivatives
-coxib	Cox-2 inhibitor
gest	Steriods, progestogens
io-	Iodine-containing contrast media
-mycin	Antibiotics, produced by streptomyces strains
-nidazole	Antiprotozoal substances, metronidazole derivatives
-profen	Anti-inflammatory substances, ibuprofen derivatives
-tidine	Histamine H_2-receptor antagonists
-trexate	Folic acid antagonists

Examples of stems are provided in Table 13.2. As a general rule the stem will fall at the end of the non-proprietary name. There are exceptions where a stem may be used anywhere in the name. In the table, stems prefixed by a hyphen fall at the end of the generic name.

The variant

The variant is created by the person or company first discovering or developing the new compound. This will often be the research team in view of their understanding of the chemical and pharmacological characteristics of the new compound. However, it appears that frequently the entire project team are becoming involved at this stage.

Submission of the proposed generic names is made to the naming authority in the country of origination of the compound. For example, in the USA the proposed generic name would be submitted to the United States Adopted Names Council. Specific information including the mechanism of action, chemical structure and therapeutic indication of the new product, as well as the compound number, first and second choice proposed non-proprietary names and the name and address of the manufacturer should be provided on the relevant form, which should be sent with the relevant fee to the United States Adopted Names Council. The proposed names are then examined and a name is selected and accepted by the national nomenclature body (or amended, substituted, refused) in accordance with the procedure for the selection of recommended INNs for pharmaceutical substances and the general principals for guidance in devising INNs. The proposed name will then be submitted to WHO for approval. The name must be agreed by all members of the WHO Expert Panel on the International Pharmacopoeia and Pharmaceutical Preparations. This is the body designated to select non-proprietary names. Once agreed, the name is published for the first time as a *proposed INN*. A four-month period is provided during which time any person can forward comments or lodge a formal objection to a name. An objection may be on grounds of similarity with a trade mark or otherwise. If no objections are raised during the relevant period, the name will be published for a second time as a *recommended INN*. The status of a recommended INN signifies the acceptance by WHO of the generic name. An INN should not be used, for example in research papers or in pre-launch material, until it has been published as a recommended INN.

Publication of a proposed and recommended INN takes place twice a year. This adds to the timetable of the process, because even if the generic names are proposed to the relevant national nomenclature body early, consideration at national level may take several months and there may be a further delay before they are considered and published by WHO.

WHO has published guidelines for non-proprietary names for pharmaceutical substances. These are divided by WHO into primary and secondary principles and are discussed below.

Primary principles

▪ An INN should be distinctive in sound and spelling

▪ It should not be inconveniently long

■ It should not be liable to cause confusion with names in common use

■ Anatomical, physiological, pathological or therapeutic suggestions should be avoided.

Secondary principles

Secondary principles are those which may assist in implementing the primary principles. These are provided below:

■ The relevant stem should be used. These frequently fall at the end of the generic name

■ The use of an isolated letter or number should be avoided

■ Hyphenated construction should be avoided

■ For reasons of pronounciation of the INN, the spelling of words may require adjustment as follows:

Use F instead of PH
Use T instead of TH
Use E instead of AE or OE
Use I instead of Y
The letters H and K should be avoided

■ In devising the INN, or even the stem, of the first substance in a new pharmacological group, consideration should be given to the possibility of devising suitable INNs for related substances belonging to the new group

■ INNs for acids – one-word names are preferred; their salts should be named without modifying the acid name, for example 'oxacillin' and 'oxacillin sodium', 'ibufenac' and 'ibufenac sodium'

■ INNs for substances which are used as salts should in general apply to the active base or the active acid. Names for different salts or esters of the same active substance should differ only in respect of the name of the inactive acid or the inactive base

■ For quaternary ammonium substances, the cation and anion should be named appropriately as separate components of a quaternary substance and not in the amine-salt style.

Names which follow these principles are likely to receive preferential consideration by WHO.

The process

Large companies will generally have in place a strategy and team for developing and clearing generic names/variants. It is recommended that the team create approximately 20 potential candidates at the outset. Whether the names are developed by research chemists or the project team, they will require clearance searching prior to submitting to the relevant nomenclature authority. Clearance is discussed in more detail in the next chapter in relation to trade marks. For the purposes of this section, suffice it to stress that the generic name must not be identical or similar to an INN, BAN, USAN, JAN, DCF, DCIt or a trade mark.

Notes

1   All trade marks referenced in this chapter are registered trade marks of the respective pharmaceutical companies.

2   Council Regulation No 2309/93.

3   Austria   Benelux   Denmark
     Finland   France   Germany
     Greece   Ireland   Italy
     Portugal   Spain   Sweden
     UK

     Belgium, the Netherlands and Luxembourg share a single trade mark register – the Benelux Register.

4   Dr Karl Thomae GmbH *v.* The Commission of the European Communities (Case T-123/00).

14 How to achieve global trade mark protection[1]

ALISON AZULAY Markforce Associates

There are a number of ways of securing a global mark. One option would be to develop a strategy in order to meet the above aims in the timelines and circumstances provided in relation to a specific project. The strategy is likely to vary for each project and should be monitored throughout so that adjustments can be made as necessary.

Our aim is to provide a strategy to clear and protect:

- a global main mark, a licensing mark and a back-up mark for the product
- identical trade marks throughout the EU in accordance with the centralized procedure and single trade mark policy (if relevant)
- a trade mark which will retain its value long after patent expiry subject to correct usage and marketing.

It is also necessary to provide:

- a clearance report for the main mark at the time of regulatory submissions – marketing authorisation authority and new drug approval (MAA and NDA) which may be approximately one year to 18 months prior to launch

The above criteria may vary from project to project.

Trade mark creation guidelines – a legal perspective

The guidelines set out below should be considered in conjunction with the creative rules discussed in Chapter 10 by Rebecca Robins.

Consideration should be given to the following when creating a trade mark for a new pharmaceutical product:

1. The trade mark should be consistent with the legal trade mark rules. Briefly, the mark must be capable of being a trade mark. Among other things, the mark must be inherently registrable. This requires that the mark is sufficiently distinctive to be registrable as a trade mark (it must not be merely descriptive or laudatory) and must not offend against any of the provisions for registrability as set out by the relevant trade mark laws (for example, in the UK, the Trade Marks Act 1994). Second, the mark must not conflict with any prior marks, which may prevent use or registration of the proposed mark. It is important to take care that the proposed marks are not identical, similar to or convey the idea of a competitor's mark. The legal tests are discussed in greater detail in the next section.

2. The mark should be easily recognizable so that it is the trade mark which is remembered and used rather than the generic name. At this stage it is important to take note of the generic name and the stem, which may be apparent even if it has not yet been accepted by the World Health Organization (WHO).

3. The trade mark should also be scriptable, that is, easy for practitioners to write, pronounce and spell. Consideration of handwriting convenience and spelling are important in assisting doctors in jurisdictions that rely primarily on written prescriptions to use the mark correctly. Again, note should be taken of competitor marks in this respect.

4. The trade mark should anticipate regulatory objections. European Agency for the Evaluation of Medicinal Products (EMEA) and Food and Drug Administration (FDA) criteria should be considered (discussed in Chapter 13).

5. The mark should not provide obvious links to the non-proprietary name. For example, there should be no use of the stem, the variable part or the prefix or suffix of the generic name. It is often tempting when creating the new mark to include a reference to the stem or the generic name, because the benefit from a marketing perspective is that a doctor, patient or pharmacist is likely to associate the trade mark with the generic name and perhaps favour the memorable brand. The downside to this approach is that if the generic name is included or referred to in the trade mark, the trade mark rights in such a mark are unlikely to be sufficiently strong to prevent a third party from using a similar mark or one incorporating the common feature of the generic. For example, Minocin and Minocin MR are the UK registered trade marks of Lederle Parenterals Inc. for which the

generic name is minocycline. The common feature 'mino' may be used by a third party in relation to a minocycline product and because this refers to the pharmacological family it will be difficult to prevent its use.

6. The mark should be acceptable in all relevant languages. A mark may be meaningless in one language, but have serious implications for the product in another. The name Dribbly was created in Sweden for lemonade, where it had no meaning. Luckily the product was never launched in the UK where the name conveyed that the drink 'dribbles'! Negatab should be avoided as a pharmaceutical name in the UK, since it portrays that it has 'negative' characteristics. Rana was identified as a pharmaceutical mark until linguistic tests reported that its meaning in Spanish was 'frog'. In Japan the trade mark Skinabebe was the name given to an ointment for children. The substantial financial loss and embarrassment to a company if negative meanings are not identified prior to launch truly merit the cost of carrying out linguistic testing. Trade mark searches carried out by local trade mark attorneys are also likely to identify such horrors.

7. The mark should be easy to pronounce. Attention should be give to language issues. For example 'th' is difficult to pronounce in certain languages; a 'j' is pronounced 'h' in Spanish, presenting irregularities not only in Spain, but also in other Spanish-speaking territories such as Latin America.

Multiple trade marks

The issue of multiple trade marks in respect of a substance having more than one therapeutic indication is discussed in the previous chapter with regard to regulatory practice. When creating a trade name for a new substance, it should be taken into account that in most circumstances the FDA, EMEA and national European Union (EU) regulatory authorities will be reluctant to grant marketing authorization for multiple trade marks. For commercial reasons, different trade names may be desirable for the different indication. Careful consideration is required before pursuing this end in view of current practice and the risk of delaying the product launch.

Trade mark assignment

If a trade mark is created by a branding agency, it is necessary to ensure that the trade mark is transferred to the proprietor of the product by means of a formal assignment. The trade mark application should be registered in the name of the true proprietor. This will ensure that any infringement actions can be brought without delay and without the risk that ownership will be contested.

Trade mark filings

National rights

Trade mark rights are national rights. Generally, an application can be made to the national trade mark registry in the country of interest.

Community trade marks

In addition to national filings it is also possible to file a Community Trade Mark (CTM) application. This is a single trade mark application, which covers all 15 member states of the EU. A CTM is a unitary right, and if the mark is not available in one or more countries of the EU, the CTM application will fail. Assuming the CTM does not meet with objections, there are substantial cost (and administrative) savings compared to filing 13 national applications (although there are currently 15 member countries, three of these – Belgium, the Netherlands and Luxembourg – share a single trade mark register: the Benelux Register), because for the CTM there is only one filing fee, one registration fee and one renewal fee.

International trade marks

It is also possible to file national applications under the system of the Madrid Protocol or the Madrid Agreement. The international registration system does not provide a single registration covering multiple countries, but does provide a mechanism for filing 'requests for extension of protection' into multiple countries based on a single filing with the World Intellectual Property Organization (WIPO). Applications can be filed by an applicant who has a 'real and effective commercial or industrial establishment' or by someone who is a national of or domiciled in a country which has acceded to the Agreement or the Protocol. An applicant for international registration must have one or more existing registrations in the country of origin before he or she can file under the international system. Under the Protocol it is sufficient to have an application (rather than a registration) in the country of origin. The original application or registration is known as the base application or registration.

Countries which are members of the Agreement or Protocol can be designated as national applications in the international application. Priority may be claimed from the filing date of the base application or registration provided that the later application(s) are filed within six months of the filing date of the earlier application and that the countries are members of the Paris Convention. A list of countries which are members of the Paris Convention can be found in Appendix B, at the end of this chapter.

The UK is a member of the Protocol but not the Agreement. At the present time, the USA is considering joining the Protocol. The Protocol has several advantages over the Agreement. Filing applications under the international system may have cost-saving implications and in certain circumstances can be quicker than filing national applications. The international system should be considered in the context of a specific project in order to ascertain its suitability.

Classification of trade marks

Classification of trade marks requires comment, because it identifies the goods and services which the searches and the trade mark applications should cover.

Trade marks are classified into 42 classes depending on the nature of the goods or services on which the marks are to be used. This is known as the International Classification of Goods and Services.[2] A search should be carried out at a minimum in the relevant classes specific to the product or service so that conflicting marks covering identical or similar goods or services can be caught. Pharmaceuticals fall within Class 5 and this is the key class for searching and protecting pharmaceuticals. Depending on the nature of the product or related services, other classes may be relevant when searching pharmaceutical products. Similar marks in respect of similar goods may be filed or protected in the classes referred to below, which may present an obstacle to the use or registration of the proposed mark. Therefore, an assessment needs to be made as to whether searching for identical or similar goods in these classes is required. The following classes may be relevant: a pharmaceutical device such as an inhaler for asthma (Class 10); if the device is electrical (Class 9); chemicals and similar substances, which in certain countries may present an obstacle to use and registration of a pharmaceutical product (Class 1); cosmetics, toiletries, non-medicated soap, dentifrices, essential oils and similar products (Class 3); medical services (Class 42).

The compound/project – a checklist

Before we look at the strategy and process for clearance and filing we need to gather information regarding the new compound and the project as a whole. The following details are required:

- Who should be identified as the applicant of the trade mark? It is necessary to ascertain who owns the compound and who has rights in it. For example:
  - The company who discovered or is developing the compound.
  - Has the compound been assigned? It would be prudent to see a copy of the assignment.
  - The licensee. A copy of the licence is required in order to confirm its duration and the rights transferred. Does the agreement transfer rights in the trade mark, device mark, logo, copyright and other rights that may need to be addressed?
  - Is there a joint venture agreement? If so, how are the trade mark rights and other rights treated? Again, the agreement needs to be considered.
- Description of the compound, its therapeutic area, mode of action, method of application (intravenous, tablet, capsule and so on).
- Distinctive features, such as colour, colour combination, distinctive shape of tablet or bottle, a device (for example an inhaler), which may require protection as trade mark, design or, in the USA, copyright registration. It may also be necessary to clear and protect other features of the product.
- A list of countries of interest and estimated timings for regulatory submissions and launch in each of these territories. This should assist with phasing the searching and protection.
- The number and nature of the required marks. For example, the project will require a main mark and back-up mark. Are licensing marks needed and, if so, how many?
- Banked marks. Does the client have any banked marks that could be considered for this project?
- Budget/financial constraints.
- List of competitors and their trade marks (if available), launch dates and an estimated lead time.

■ The client's or company's (owner's or licensee's) relationship with other pharmaceutical companies. This may provide assistance in clearing marks and deciding whether negotiations or settlements are an option.

■ Generic name/stem. Has a generic name/stem been allocated for the compound? (see previous chapter).

The above information is used throughout the process and is necessary for it to run as smoothly and effectively as possible. We will turn now to rules relating to trade mark creation and searching.

Trade mark searching and filing

Preliminary

Responsibility for the global searching and filing can fall either to in-house intellectual property or external trade mark specialists, who are often attorneys or solicitors. For ease of reference, this person is referred to in this chapter as the 'attorney'. The attorney should manage centrally the searching and filing programmes, because the majority of the searches and trade mark filings are carried out on a national basis by qualified trade mark attorneys in the country of interest. The results need to be collated and reported so that a decision as to whether a mark is sufficiently clear to progress to the next stage can be taken. Another responsibility of the attorney is to ensure active and frequent communication with an identified contact(s) of the project team, the client. The global searching programme is timely, changeover in staff or attitude is possible and early notification of any changes is required.

Trade mark searches are unlikely to result in a clear global mark free from obstacles and ready for registration. This is partly due to the number of products and applications for registration in relation to pharmaceutical products. The search results require detailed analysis and a risk assessment regarding the possibility of infringement and refusal of registration. Frequently, further enquiries, investigations, searches and negotiations with third parties are required (see the section regarding 'Negotiations and settlements'). While a trade mark attorney should provide a concise report as to the risks revealed by the search, other factors are likely to be influential, and the decision generally turns to a commercial one on the part of the pharmaceutical company. For example, a company's relationship with the owner of the conflicting mark may be crucial as to whether co-existence is granted.

Why search?

Searches are carried out in order to ensure that there are no identical or similar trade marks in respect of identical, similar and in certain circumstances non-similar goods or services on the relevant registers or in use which may present a risk of infringement or bar to registration of the proposed mark. In countries that recognize common law trade mark rights, such as the USA, a search is also an important tool for identifying potential senior users of similar trade marks who may or may not have registered their trade mark rights. Searches of some trade mark registers will identify non-proprietary names approved by the appropriate national nomenclature authority and/or WHO.

A company names index search should be included with the search in countries where available in order to detect an identical or similar company name. Such a name may present an obstacle to use if it relates to a pharmaceutical company or one with related or overlapping interests.

Pharmaceutical marks require extra care when searching. Apart from conflicting marks, there is the need to avoid the risk of danger to the public as a result of confusion by the patient, pharmacist, doctor or other provider of the medicine. Confusion may result from identical or similar marks for identical, similar or non-similar goods either visually, phonetically, conceptually or in handwriting. A detailed description of the product is necessary when searching including the therapeutic area, mode of action and method of application (that is, intravenous, tablet, cream or a combination and so on), as well as the dispensing environment (for example, hospital, retail pharmacy and so on).

Filing under the CTM system does not negate the need to carry out separate national searches in each of the 15 member states of the EU. It is also necessary to search the CTM register in order to ensure that there are no conflicting marks which would prevent the use or registration of the proposed mark in each of the member states. Likewise, filing under the international system such as the Madrid Agreement or Protocol to that Agreement will not avoid the need to search nationally.

Countries of interest/launch timings

The countries of interest and estimated regulatory submission (generally MAA/NDA) and launch dates should be available at the outset. These should be used to develop the searching and filing strategy, which may consist of two or more stages. We will refer to these stages as Stage I and Stage II. The estimated launch times which need to be met are dependent on the estimated submission dates. These may alter during the process and, therefore, it is important that any chages are conveyed to the attorney.

The countries of interest for a global project will often form different phases for launch. For example, approval and launch in the EU and the USA may be estimated for the second quarter of 2004, whereas approval and launch in South East Asia may be estimated for the second half of 2005. Therefore, phasing the searching and filing process should be possible. This may also make the process more cost effective.

Stage I searching and filing

As an example, let us look at the countries that might be included in the first stage:

■ The first stage of searching and filing will necessarily cover the whole of the EU if the centralized procedure is adopted due to the single trade mark requirement.

The USA is currently one of the largest, and consequently most crowded, registers. As such, the USA can be one of the most difficult countries in which to clear a mark and should be included in any first stage searching.

■ Other countries which are identified for early launch.

■ Switzerland and Norway are not part of the EU and if of interest for early launch may be included at this stage.

■ Countries of interest that have been identified as soon to join the EU. These are currently Cyprus, the Czech Republic, Estonia, Hungary, Poland and Slovenia.

■ Countries which are notorious for parallel importation and counterfeiting practices. In some countries, rights can be used to prevent parallel importation by a third party. This is not the case for parallel importation within the EU due to the principle of free movement of goods.

■ Latin American countries in which proof of a trade mark registration or application must be filed at the relevant time during regulatory submissions (Table 13.1).

Stage II searching and filing

The countries that are likely to be included in the second phase are those in which regulatory approval has been postponed or which have been designated for late launch.

A commercial decision may be taken not to search in territories where marketing is likely to be minimal despite the commercial risks involved.

Searching process

Decisions should be taken as to the management, the relevant countries for each stage of searching depending on the estimated regulatory and launch times, the classification requirements at the commencement of Phase III clinical trials or earlier depending on the estimated launch dates.

The proposed marks – as created in accordance with the legal rules discussed above and the creative ideas (see Chapter 10) – are submitted to the attorney.

With the aim of clearing a main mark or first choice mark, a back-up mark and a licensing mark, it is recommended that a list of at least 100 candidates is submitted to the attorney. The marks should be presented in groups of ten, each group listed in order of preference, Group 1 being the list of first choice marks, Group 2 the second choice marks and so on. This 'grouping' exercise may assist from both a cost and speed point of view.

The main mark may require approval by specific directors or the board. A shortlist of names should be approved at the appropriate level required at the agreed stage in the process. Once the global mark has been cleared there is unlikely to be time to recommence the searching process, if the mark is no longer desirable.

A schedule monitoring the success of the searches should be maintained. The project team leader or client should be updated at regular intervals as to the status of the searching, and any comments acknowledged with appropriate action. This may involve deleting mark(s) from the list of potential candidates if, say, linguistic or market testing (see below) has proved negative.

As the searches produce positive results, the process of filing applications will start. Initially, this may take place in tandem with the searching process. It may also enable an early filing in territories of commercial importance.

At the early stages in the filing process it is important to bear in mind that priority claims require filing within six months of the original filing.

In view of the number of marks on the registers in Class 5, resulting in the likelihood of conflict, it is possible that more candidates will be required for searching in addition to the first list. The likelihood increases if the centralized procedure is adopted due to the necessity of the single trade mark.

Summary of searching strategy

1st stage pre-screen searches

A number of rough and ready pre-screen searches are carried out in stages. These searches are fairly quick considering the number of marks being searched. The pre-screen searches are by no means conclusive, but are likely to identify at an early stage a number of the proposed marks which face conflicts. This avoids the expense of carrying out full availability searches in relation to these marks. In this way, marketing or project teams can be notified of potential candidates that are unavailable as early as possible, providing the opportunity, if time permits, to create further marks if desirable.

Pre-screen searches may consist of the following:

■ *Phase I:* Quick hand check to delete candidates which fall foul of the requirements identified under the heading 'Trade mark creation guidelines – a legal perspective' at points 1–7 at the beginning of this chapter.

■ *Phase II:* Quick hand checks of the latest publications of British Approved Name (BAN), United States Approved Name (USAN) and International Non-proprietory Name (INN) listings in order to eliminate the proposed marks which conflict with a generic name or stem.

■ *Phase III:* Online searches of trade mark registers of interest in order to identify identical or closely similar marks. The registers searched at this stage can be varied to meet the specific needs of the project. The EU national registers and CTM register should be included if the centralized procedure is to be used. The US register is also typically included. If a decision has not been taken as to the regulatory route that will be used, it is necessary to search on the assumption that the centralized procedure will be used. The advantage of including the international register at this stage is that it may catch marks which have been filed or registered in a variety of registers. Searches of the registers of countries of prime interest should be included at this stage if time and budget permit, since unavailable candidates can be located and deleted from the search early on in the process, thus saving time and money.

■ *Phase IV:* The surviving marks may be searched on the online database of pharmaceuticals in use. Money, but probably not time, may be saved by searching for the marks in the most up-to-date Pharmaceutical Trade Mark Directory.[3] The Directory is, therefore, useful where a few marks require investigation.

It is desirable for a minimum of 20 candidates to survive the pre-screening searches. If fewer than 20 survive it is likely that the project or creative team will be required to create more candidates.

2nd stage

The candidates which survive the pre-screening searches are presented to the client who is required to identify 20 marks which will undergo full availability searches.

3rd stage

Full availability searches may be carried out in the CTM register and the 13 national registers of the EU member states, as well as the register of the US Patent and Trade Mark Office (PTO) and any other significant markets. Because the USA recognizes common law rights, a full search, which will include common law references, is particularly important.

Depending on time and budget it may be preferable to search in two phases in groups of ten marks.

4th stage

Once approved the clear marks are the subject of new trade mark applications, which should if possible be filed in a country which is a member of the Paris Convention so that a later identical application filed within six months of the first application in a Paris Convention country can claim the priority filing date of the first application.

Priority filings under the Paris Convention, provide a further six months period before a decision needs to be taken as to the chosen mark(s). At this stage, particularly if timing is limited, attention should be given to filings in countries where marketing is intended, but which are not members of the Paris Convention. This is because there is a risk that a third party may register an identical or similar mark with a filing date prior to the client's mark which could defeat the use and registration of the chosen mark in the relevant country. The non-Convention country of most importance seems to be Taiwan, but there are others. A list of members of the Paris Convention is given in Appendix B at the end of this chapter.

Trade mark applications in other countries may be given priority even though the territories are not marked for early launch. These are as follows:

■ Countries of commercial importance but not a member of the Paris Convention

- Territories where counterfeiting or parallel importation is common

- Territories which require proof of application or registration at some stage during the regulatory procedure for marketing authorization (for example Latin America, discussed in Chapter 13).

5th stage

The surviving marks proceed to full availability searches in the territories designated for first phase launch.

6th stage

The surviving marks are forwarded to the client for approval.

7th stage

The surviving marks should be approved by the client, including any directors or the board if applicable, prior to proceeding to full availability searches in the remaining territories of interest.

Generic names and searching

WHO listings for INNs and national nomenclature listings for BANs and USANs should be considered. These are generally identified in the trade mark searches. Japanese Approved Names (JANs), Dénomination Commune Français (DCFs) and Denominazione Comune Italiana (DCIts) should also be considered and searched, if possible.

Negotiations and settlements

As previously mentioned, it is unlikely for a global search to identify a totally free candidate. The risk assessment may identify potentially conflicting marks and further clearance work may negate or reveal that the risk is commercially feasible. This may involve an investigation into the exact use of the product used under the conflicting mark, whether the mark is in fact in use, and whether potential options would be to seek a co-existence agreement with the owner of the conflicting mark, an assignment or file a cancellation action.

If the conflicting mark is for another pharmaceutical, information is required as to the therapeutic area, the mode of action, method of application (intravenous, tablet, cream), whether use is restricted to humans or veterinary use. It is also helpful to ascertain whether the identical conflict exists in other countries so that they can be dealt with together, if relevant.

An investigation may need to be carried out in order to ascertain the above information, including the degree of use (in turnover or profit) and the length of use in each of the relevant territories, the nature of the proprietor of the conflicting mark and whether there is a commercial relationship between the parties, since this may assist in negotiations. Investigations may reveal that the conflicting mark has not been used for a period of time.

It may be that the mark is not in use in some or all of the territories. Each jurisdiction has a 'use period' after which time a mark, which has not been in use for the duration of that period, may be vulnerable to cancellation on grounds of non-use. For example, in the UK a mark which has not been used for a continuous period of five years from the date that registration was granted (as opposed to the filing date) may be vulnerable to a cancellation action. Many countries follow the five-year period, but by no means all. In the USA, for example, a presumption of abandonment arises after three consecutive years of non-use. There are also discrepancies as to whether time starts to run from the date of filing the application or the date the mark is entered on the register. The situation should be verified in each case. If a mark is vulnerable to cancellation on grounds of non-use, this may facilitate negotiations for a co-existence agreement or for an assignment, so that cancellation is not the only option.

Assuming that the conflicting mark is not vulnerable to a cancellation action, the options are:

■ To assess whether the information gathered in the investigation is sufficient to argue that the marks are not in fact in conflict in view of all the circumstances. The registries vary in strictness in approach. If a co-existence agreement would not present a risk to the public or of infringement, it would be worth filing submissions with the relevant registry in an attempt to overcome the objection.

■ To approach the other party for a co-existence agreement on the basis that the marks do not present a risk of confusion or a danger to the public.

■ Some registries require that a letter of consent is filed at the registry in order to overcome conflicts. This can be dealt with at the same time as requesting the co-existence agreement.

■ If investigations reveal that worldwide sales and turnover relating to the product under the conflicting mark are minimal, even though the mark is in use, the proprietor may be willing to assign the mark (with or without the product). The cost for the assignment of such a mark will depend on several things including the value of the trade mark to the present proprietor, and the degree and scope of the registrations. The potential seller in this situation may be in a position to name his price. There may be regulatory reasons why such a mark cannot be used in relation to a different product, but the transfer of the name may enable the blocked application to proceed. Assignments can be drafted by intellectual property attorneys and may need to be recorded at the relevant trade mark registries within a specific time period in certain countries.

If the trade mark is vulnerable to cancellation on grounds of non-use, the above options would be available in addition to filing a cancellation action. An assignment of a mark which is vulnerable to cancellation should be at a nominal value to reflect the fact. A cancellation action could take anything from a few months to several years if the proprietor defends the action.

Whether or not a conflicting mark is in use at the time of the negotiation, a co-existence agreement would not be appropriate where it would result in a risk of confusion or a danger to the public at the time the agreement is made or in the future. In such a situation, the proposed mark should not be used.

Negotiations should commence as early as possible at the searching stage and a decision taken that, despite the conflict, the proposed mark should be pursued. This is because negotiations can take a matter of weeks or many months since they are dependent on the cooperation of the third party proprietor. If there is a commercial relationship between the parties, it is recommended that the approach is made by the prospective proprietor since this provides a more amicable basis for the negotiation and may receive a quicker response.

Market testing

Deciding when best to carry out market testing is a chicken and egg situation. It is a commercial decision, and one often taken by the client. It must be appreciated that if the testing is undertaken during the early stages of the searching process, a mark which receives a positive market test result may not survive the searches. In contrast, a mark which survives the preliminary searches and perhaps some of the full availability searches may meet negative results in the market testing. In theory, market testing early in the process is recommended. This should provide as much time as is available to carry out searches on fresh marks due to negative market testing results. In practice, there is seldom the luxury of time or budget to find the perfect mark due to imminent launch dates and the requirement of the centralized procedure, if relevant.

Market testing, as its name implies, tests potential names in real life situations, which include speech and handwriting, among patients, general practitioners, consultants, nurses, specialists and carers. The tests are designed in order to ascertain the suitability of a proposed mark for a particular product.

Market testing can be carried out by market testing companies specializing in pharmaceuticals, specialists within brand agencies or in-house by the pharmaceutical company.

Banked marks

It is always useful to ascertain whether there are any banked marks available for the project. Banked marks may be required if the timelines are tight or if objections are met at a late stage, for example, during opposition. It is important that banked marks are checked as to their status (registered or pending) in all countries of interest. If not, new filings may be required. In addition, an audit should be carried out in order to ascertain whether the banked marks are vulnerable to a cancellation action on grounds of non-use in any of the countries of interest (see earlier). If so, clearance searches may be required to ensure that no conflicting rights have been used or registered, which may be used to defeat the vulnerable mark. Provided that the search is clear (or once any obstacles have been dealt with) and if the vulnerable mark is not intended for immediate use, a fresh application should be filed in the relevant territory in order to recommence the 'use' period.

Filing the application

The filing date is crucial. In many countries, trade mark rights start to run from the date of filing the application (as opposed to the date that registration is granted), provided that the mark is registered. It is from the filing date that trade marks are judged against each other with regard to who has the earliest right (the prior right).

The trade mark applications are filed at local trade mark registries. These are government organizations and in certain territories can be extremely slow to operate; the average pendency of a trade mark application in many countries is 12–18 months, but some countries can take up to four years or more to process an application. Apart from monitoring the applications and reminding the registries via local attorneys, generally there is no means of accelerating the process.

Further filings in additional countries may be required in accordance with the filing programme. A check needs to be made for any changes to the countries of interest and the regulatory submission/launch dates, since this may result in amendments to the filing programme.

The client should be notified at regular intervals of the status of the marks and may be required to assist with negotiations to overcome unforeseen obstacles or to provide evidence in support of the registration.

Examination of the trade mark application

After trade mark applications are filed, they will be examined by the local registries. The tests adopted on examination of a trade mark application will depend on the law of the country in question. In the majority of countries examination will fall into two catagories:

- whether the mark is inherently registrable

- whether the mark conflicts with any third party identical or similar trade marks.

In the EU, harmonization of trade mark laws of the member states was intended by the First Council Directive of 21 December 1988 to approximate the laws of the member states relating to Trade Marks (89/104/EEC). Member states have amended their trade mark laws to adopt some or all of the requirements of the Directive. In practice, trade mark law is not identical in all member states. However, as the body of case law provided by the European Court of Justice (ECJ) increases, the differences may diminish. As a result, local advice is still required from local attorneys.

The tests on examination of the trade mark application also impact on the trade mark searching. The tests will be elaborated upon here with reference to the trade mark laws in the UK and the USA, which are set out in the Trade Mark Act 1994 (the Act) and the Lanham Trade Mark Act of 1946 (as amended) 15 USC respectively. The tests in many other countries maybe similar, but local advice should always be sought.

The UK law sets out what can constitute a trade mark and then states grounds of refusal. The grounds of refusal are split into two categories, absolute grounds of refusal on grounds of inherent registrability, and the relative grounds for refusal which are on the grounds of conflicting prior marks.

Examination – what is a trade mark?

The Act sets out what can be a trade mark as follows:

> a 'trade mark' means any sign capable of being represented graphically which is capable of distinguishing goods or services of one undertaking from those of other undertakings. A trade mark may, in particular, consist of words (including personal names), designs, letters, numerals or the shape of goods, or their packaging. (S1(1))

This definition is similar to that in the Lanham Act:

> the term 'trade mark' includes any word, name, symbol, or device, or any combination thereof:
>
> (1) used by a person, or
> (2) which a person has a bona fide intention to use in commerce and applies to register on the principal register established by this Act,
> (3) to identify and distinguish his or her goods, including a unique product, from those manufactured or sold by others and to indicate the source of the goods, even if that source is unknown. (15 USC Section 1127)

Therefore, a trade mark must identify a product or service as coming from a particular source and no other. It is not necessary that the mark identifies the name of the source (that is, the name of the proprietor or company). Not only words, but also designs, shape of goods or their packaging can be trade marks. In the USA colours, sounds, scents and other non-traditional indicia of origin or source can qualify for protection as trade marks. The lists provided under both the statutory provisions above are not exhaustive. In fact, anything capable of distinguishing goods or services of one producer from those of other producers should be capable of being a trade mark.

Examination – absolute grounds of refusal

The absolute grounds of refusal are grounds which may present a basis for refusal at the examination stage. These grounds are as follows:

- the mark must not be contrary to the principle of what is a trade mark as set out in S1(1) of the Act (above)

- the mark must not be devoid of any distinctive character

- the mark must not be descriptive or otherwise refer to the characteristics of the goods

- the mark must not be a sign which is customary in the trade

- certain shapes will be refused

- the mark must not be contrary to public policy or be of such a nature as to deceive the public

- the mark must not be prohibited by law which would include certain emblems or words such as 'Red Cross'

- the mark must not be registered in bad faith.

The list of absolute grounds provided by the Act is non-exhaustive. There may be other reasons for refusal.

Examination – relative grounds of refusal

A mark will be refused registration if due to an 'earlier mark' (see below) the following apply:

- an identical mark in relation to identical goods or services

- an identical or similar mark in relation to identical or similar goods or services and there is a risk of confusion

- an identical or similar mark in relation to non-similar goods or services, and where use without due cause takes unfair advantage of the earlier mark or is detrimental to the distinctive character or repute of the earlier trade mark. The earlier mark will only be protected if it has a reputation in the UK.

Examination – definition of 'earlier mark'

'Earlier mark' is defined by the Act at S6, which states that an 'earlier mark' includes:

- A registered UK trade mark

- International trade marks or CTMs which benefit from earlier priority dates than the mark applied for

- Pending applications for such marks, which would benefit from an earlier priority date if accepted on the relevant register

- Registrations which have lapsed up to one year earlier, unless there was no use of such marks for the two years prior to the expiry of the registration

■ Unregistered trade marks which are well known within the meaning of the Paris Convention (defined in S56 of the Act). These marks may be unregistered in any relevant jurisdiction, but can be protected as an earlier right if the reputation extends to the UK even though no goodwill as such exists here.

Under Article 6bis of the Paris Convention (S56(1) TMA94), a mark can be 'well known' in the UK 'whether or not that person carries on business or has any goodwill in the United Kingdom', provided it is a mark of a person who is a national of a Convention country or established in a Convention country. Therefore, marks can be well known in the UK even if they have not been used in the UK or if they have been used in the UK but not to the extent as to establish goodwill.

Examination process – USA

The examination process in the USA is similar. Each application is first reviewed by an Examining Attorney at the US PTO. The Examining Attorney will make sure that the application is in order with regard to formalities, such as the use of international classes, the specificity of the identification of goods and so on and will also examine the application to ensure that the mark is registrable (that is, it does not create a likelihood of confusion with any pre-existing registration and is not merely descriptive, misdescriptive, scandalous or otherwise excluded from registration under the Lanham Act).

Depending on the nature of the issue involved, the Examining Attorney may contact an applicant informally, by telephone, to seek to resolve minor concerns by an 'Examiner's Amendment' (an amendment to the application that is entered by the Examining Attorney with the consent of the applicant) or the Examining Attorney may issue a written 'Office Action' that requires a written response within six months.

Assuming that any issues raised by the Examining Attorney can be successfully resolved, the application will be published for opposition in the *Official Gazette* of the PTO. Publication in the *Official Gazette* commences a 30-day opposition period in which third parties who may be damaged by the issuance of a registration may either oppose the application or request additional time in which to do so.

Objections, negotiations and settlements

Objections may be raised by the UK Registry or the US PTO during the examination process on any of the above or related grounds. The situation will be similar in other jurisdictions. The objections must be overcome prior to moving onto the next stage. It may be possible to overcome objections by filing submissions, arguments responding to the objections or by filing evidence of distinctiveness in relation to the subject mark. Additionally, providing a narrower identification of goods or services can sometimes remove an objection raised by the UK Registry or the US PTO. Conflicting third party marks which cannot be dealt with in this way may need to be addressed in the following ways:

■ Carrying out an investigation to acquire further information regarding the conflict which would support an argument that the mark is not in fact in conflict or a risk to the public

■ Negotiating a co-existence agreement with the proprietor of the conflicting mark (this can be particularly useful in the USA, if properly drafted, since the US PTO is instructed to give deference to agreements between competitors regarding the absence of any danger for consumer confusion by co-existing marks)

■ Assignment of the conflicting mark

■ Cancellation of the conflicting mark.

These have been discussed in the earlier section 'Negotiations and settlements'.

Publication

Provided that all the objections and conflicts are overcome, the mark will be advertised in the relevant publication in order to notify third parties of the accepted mark for opposition purposes during the relevant period. The opposition period in the UK and in many other territories, but by no means all, is three months from the date of publication. The opposition period in the USA is 30 days from the date of publication, although additional extensions are available. In the majority of territories, the opposition period cannot be extended. There are exceptions and, in some countries, a mark is published for opposition purposes after registration is granted. Provided that no oppositions are filed the mark is registered.

If oppositions are filed, registration will be refused if the opposition is successful. Alternatively, registration may be delayed for several months or years where the process and/or negotiations are timely. Timelines are often tight when seeking a global mark and, therefore, it may not be practical to wait for the final decision. Settlement negotiations should be opened wherever they would be a reasonable option. This may also be dependent on relationships with the other party. Where negotiations are not possible, there may be the opportunity to bring a counterattack for non-use of the opposing mark, although if the opponent has been well advised, such an action is unlikely to be available. As a last resort it may be necessary to consider use of the back-up mark.

Registration and maintenance

Registration generally follows publication or settlement of any oppositions. Thereafter, the registration needs to be maintained by payment of the registration fees and renewal fees.

It is also necessary to ensure that third party use of the registered trade mark is monitored, and that the trade mark is used in the correct manner.

Policing the trade marks

It is necessary to ensure that the trade marks are actively policed in the territories of interest as soon as the new marks are identified and new trade mark applications are filed. This can easily be done by using a trade mark watching service which will provide notification of conflicting marks, generally when they are published for opposition purposes. Large companies or those with contacts in other countries will also rely on their employees or contacts to notify them of conflicting marks, parallel imports and repackaged products. In order to maintain a strong and valuable trade mark these matters need addressing without delay either by filing oppositions, bringing infringement actions or actions against counterfeiters or parallel importers where available.

Non-use of the trade mark

A mark may become vulnerable to cancellation following a specified period of non-use in a relevant country. This was discussed in the section 'Settlements and negotiations'. There are exceptions to the rule of cancellation on grounds of non-use for the specified period. In a number of territories, it is accepted that non-use of a trade mark due to delay in granting the marketing authorization may not give rise to a cancellation action. However, non-use due to delay in marketing plans is not excepted use. The exception applies in the UK, the USA and many other countries, but may not apply in all territories of interest.

Pharmaceutical trade mark usage

It is recommended and, indeed, required by the regulatory authorities in some countries, that a trade mark for a pharmaceutical product should be used in conjunction with the accepted generic name of the product. The trade mark should also be used together with a description of the therapeutic indication and mode of application (IV or tablet and so on). For example, 'Trade mark (generic name), oral tablet for use in the treatment of cardiovascular diseases'.

Trade mark notices

The ™ sign should be used in superscript immediately after the trade mark. The ™ notice can be used whether a mark is registered or not, it is irrelevant whether the mark is the subject of a trade mark application.

The ® symbol can only be used if a trade mark is actually registered. It may be illegal and even constitute a criminal offence in certain countries to use the symbol ® if the mark is not, in fact, registered in that country.

Where a proprietor uses a trade mark throughout the world and on products which may move from one country to another through distribution channels or as a result of parallel importation, a trade mark correctly marked ® may end up in a country where registration has not been granted, possibly constituting an illegal act. In circumstances where the mark is used globally it is recommended that ™ is used in all cases, except where ® is legally required.

Certain countries (such as the USA and Canada) legally require that a registered trade mark must be labelled as being so registered in some way or another, usually by the ® symbol, in order for the trade mark owner to collect damages in an infringement action. A search is required to confirm that the mark is registered prior to using the symbol. Also, in view of the fact that products trade marked with the symbol ® could find themselves in other countries (where the trade mark is not in fact registered), it may be preferable to use the symbol ™ instead of ®, together with a visible footnote on the packaging confirming the country in which the trade mark is registered. For example, the ™ symbol would be used with the trade mark with the footnote:

'UVW™ of Company X is registered in [US Patent and Trade Mark Office] or [Canada]'.

It is recommended that the proprietor of the trade mark is identified in a prominent position on the packaging, insert, container or other material. Again, a footnote can be inserted on the packaging in a prominent position to the effect that 'ABC™ is a trade mark of Company X'.

Rebranding

It is necessary to be aware of any deliberated changes in the use of the mark(s) or brand identity so that these rights can be protected as early as possible. Products may undergo global rebranding programmes and new trade marks (including logos and packaging or shapes) may need to be considered.

Domain names

It is recommended that domain names are registered for important brands. The '.com' is the most internationally sought. However, it may cause commercial issues if a third party were to register and use the identical mark in a '.co.uk' website or other country domain. Therefore the client should make a commercial decision as to the country or other domain names of commercial importance.

It is not sufficient to rely on domain name registrations alone. The ownership of a domain name does not provide equivalent rights to that of a trade mark. However, in many territories a trade mark registration will be sufficient to defeat an identical domain name. This should be considered when seeking country domain names.

Notes

1   All trade marks referenced in this chapter are registered trade marks of the respective pharmaceutical companies.

2   A copy is available from the World Intellectual Property Organization (WIPO).

3   Pharmaceutical Trade Mark Directory (IMS AG, Dorfplatz 4, 6300 Cham, Switzerland).

APPENDIX A
List of Parties to the Madrid Agreement and Madrid Protocol

Status on August 8, 2000

State	Madrid Agreement	Madrid Protocol
Albania	✓	–
Algeria	✓	–
Antigua and Barbuda	–	✓
Armenia	✓	✓
Austria	✓	✓
Azerbaijan	✓	–
Belarus	✓	–
Belgium	✓	✓
Bhutan	✓	✓
Bosnia and Herzegovina	✓	–
Bulgaria	✓	–
China	✓	✓
Croatia	✓	–
Cuba	✓	✓
Czech Republic	✓	✓
Democratic People's Republic of Korea	✓	✓
Denmark	–	✓
Egypt	✓	–
Estonia	–	✓
Finland	–	✓
France	✓	✓
Georgia	–	✓
Germany	✓	✓
Greece	–	✓
Hungary	✓	✓
Iceland	–	✓
Italy	✓	✓
Japan	–	✓
Kazakhstan	✓	–
Kenya	✓	✓
Kyrgyzstan	✓	–
Latvia	✓	✓
Lesotho	✓	✓
Liberia	✓	–
Liechtenstein	✓	✓
Lithuania	–	✓
Luxembourg	✓	✓

State	Madrid Agreement	Madrid Protocol
Monaco	✓	✓
Mongolia	✓	–
Morocco	✓	✓
Mozambique	✓	✓
Netherlands	✓	✓
Norway	–	✓
Poland	✓	✓
Portugal	✓	✓
Republic of Moldova	✓	✓
Romania	✓	✓
Russian Federation	✓	✓
San Marino	✓	–
Sierra Leone	✓	✓
Singapore	–	✓
Slovakia	✓	✓
Slovenia	✓	✓
Spain	✓	✓
Sudan	✓	–
Swaziland	✓	✓
Sweden	–	✓
Switzerland	✓	✓
Tajikistan	✓	–
The former Yugoslav Republic of Macedonia	✓	–
Turkey	–	✓
Turkmenistan	–	✓
Ukraine	✓	–
United Kingdom	–	✓
Uzbekistan	✓	–
Vietnam	✓	–
Yugoslavia	✓	✓
(Total: 67 States)		(48)

APPENDIX B

List of Parties to the Paris Convention for the Protection of Industrial Property

Status on July 15, 2000

State			
Albania	Côte d'Ivoire	Indonesia	New Zealand
Algeria	Croatia	Iran (Islamic Republic of)	Nicaragua
Antigua and Barbuda	Cuba	Iraq	Niger
Argentina	Cyprus	Ireland	Nigeria
Armenia	Czech Republic	Israel	Norway
Australia	Democratic People's Republic of Korea	Italy	Oman
Austria	Democratic Republic of the Congo	Jamaica	Panama
Azerbaijan	Denmark	Japan	Papua New Guinea
Bahamas	Dominica	Jordan	Paraguay
Bahrain	Dominican Republic	Kazakhstan	Peru
Bangladesh	Equador	Kenya	Philippines
Barbados	Egypt	Kyrgystan	Poland
Belarus	El Salvador	Lao People's Democratic Republic	Portugal
Belgium	Equatorial Guinea	Latvia	Qatar
Belize	Estonia	Lebanon	Republic of Korea
Benin	Finland	Lesotho	Republic of Moldova
Bhutan	France	Liberia	Romania
Bolivia	Gabon	Libyan Arab Jamahiriva	Russian Federation
Bosnia and Herzegovina	Gambia	Liechtenstein	Rwanda
Botswana	Georgia	Lithuania	Saint Kitts and Nevis
Brazil	Germany	Luxembourg	Saint Lucia
Bulgaria	Ghana	Madagascar	Saint Vincent and the Grenadines
Burkina Faso	Greece	Malawi	San Marino
Burundi	Grenada	Malaysia	Sao Tome and Principe
Cambodia	Guatemala	Mali	Senegal
Cameroon	Guinea	Malta	Sierra Leone
Canada	Guinea-Bissau	Mauritania	Singapore
Central African Republic	Guyana	Mauritius	Slovakia
Chad	Haiti	Mexico	Slovenia
Chile	Holy See	Monaco	South Africa
China	Honduras	Mongolia	Spain
Colombia	Hungary	Morocco	Sri Lanka
Congo	Iceland	Mozambique	Sudan
Costa Rica	India	Netherlands	Suriname

State			
Swaziland	Togo	United Arab Emirates	Venezuela
Sweden	Trinidad and Tobago	United Kingdom	Vietnam
Switzerland	Tunisia	United Republic of Tanzania	Yugoslavia
Syrian Arab Republic	Turkey		Zambia
Tajikistan	Turkmenistan	United States of America	Zimbabwe
The former Yugoslav Republic of Macedonia	Uganda	Uruguay	
	Ukraine	Uzbekistan	

15 The government view

RICHARD MARSH AND GARETH EVANS
Government Policy Consultants

It is widely accepted that most countries faced with increasing demands, rising costs and limited resources are acutely concerned with the performance of their health systems. The need to design a health system that durably meets both economic and social goals is not new. Beveridge envisaged a comprehensive health system for the UK half a century ago, and the resulting National Health Service remains the UK model today. In government, both political parties have sought to retain the original principles and origins of the NHS and both are committed to doing so in the future. Maintaining a health-care service free at the point of delivery to the general public has tended to come before ensuring that the correct balance of provision and levels of reimbursement are attained.

The present UK Labour government has brought in a number of new policies aimed at ensuring what Alan Milburn, the current Health Secretary, calls the 'sustainability'[1] of the NHS. To some extent Labour health policy can be seen as the continuation of policies developed under the previous Conservative administration, including evidence-based medicine and the health and economic evaluation of pharmaceuticals. Labour have gone further, however, in terms of defining standards of service that the NHS ought to provide and establishing central mechanisms for ensuring and coercing delivery.

A central tenet of Labour Party politics and policy is that there should be equity of access to and provision of care throughout the NHS. The current Labour government lays particular emphasis on national standards of care, with the aim of ensuring that the public receives the same standard of treatment whoever they are and wherever they happen to live. The assault on the so-called postcode prescribing of prescription medicines is part of this approach.

Policies introduced to ensure the establishment and delivery of national standards include the National Institute for Clinical Excellence (NICE), national service frameworks and the Commission for Health Improvement. The NHS national plan, published in July 2000, announced the creation of an NHS Modernisation Agency, a new arm of the Department of Health designed to spread best practice and implement standards throughout the NHS.

Critics of this approach are sceptical towards whether the aim of improving standards can be achieved through a policy of central push as the government envisages. Supporters of the previous government's GP fundholding initiative, for example, argue that that model drew strength from practitioners being able to develop innovative ideas themselves, outside the constraints of detailed national rules. But the scheme foundered on the allegation that it was creating a two-tier National Health Service and the present government abolished it. Achieving the right balance between local initiative and national control remains, however, a live issue and the government has acknowledged as much by talking about the concept of earned autonomy in the national plan. A growing proportion of the funding available for the health service will be conditional on the NHS locally matching up against the new national standards.

The vast majority of the NHS budget – around 95% – is provided direct from the taxpayer. Most of the money is distributed to health authorities who allocate it for the provision of a range of healthcare services. In addition, this government has created what it calls a modernization fund, in effect money that it held back centrally, creating a budget from which particularly favoured initiatives can be funded. This manner of funding and allocation can and does give rise to the accusation that the NHS is politicized or that priorities are set according to the particular political imperatives of the party in power. The Labour government fell foul of this accusation in respect of its policy towards waiting lists. The simple target of cutting waiting lists, with which Labour had made political capital in opposition, was widely felt within the NHS to lead to a distortion of clinical priorities, with patients with less urgent, but simpler, operations receiving preferential treatment. The government has now quietly shifted its focus from waiting lists to waiting times, although critics continue to allege that this leads to the achievement of simplistic targets ahead of real clinical priorities.

The UK's system is thus significantly different from that in other European countries in relying so heavily on taxpayer funding. One of the consequences of this has been that for many years the UK has lagged behind other countries comparable in size and national income in terms of the level of funding dedicated to healthcare. Taxpayers have proven to be less elastic than other sources of funding such as health insurance.

In January 2000, the Prime Minister Tony Blair committed his government to increasing spending on the NHS to the European average of healthcare funding as a proportion of gross domestic product (GDP) over the next five years. The sums announced in the budget in March 2000 will take the UK towards that destination, although whether it will arrive is a matter of some debate. The opposition Conservative Party, meanwhile, argue that it is only by relying on increasing amounts of privately arranged funding that the UK can hope to attain levels of spending on healthcare common in other European countries.

The government sees its additional allocation of finance to the NHS in historic terms and the year-on-year increases now committed for the next few years are certainly higher than the health service has been used to over its 52-year history. There have been some isolated years of particularly high spending increases (and no years at all of actual cuts in the NHS budget), but these have not been sustained. The government sees the sustained nature of the proposed funding to be as significant as the amounts themselves.

Such a commitment in funding must, according to the government, be met by an equally historic commitment on the part of the NHS to reform. The government's dissatisfaction with the NHS, and hence the impetus for reform, is based upon the following perceptions of weakness in the system:

■ The NHS is too slow at adapting to change and at adopting new and better methods of working. One of the main tasks for the Modernisation Agency will be to spread best practice.

■ Working practices in the NHS are too inflexible. The government sees this challenge as a battle against the forces of conservatism, felt to be ingrained within the medical profession in particular.

■ The NHS is insufficiently responsive to the needs of patients. The Health Secretary has talked of the NHS becoming a 'patient-centred service sector industry'.[2]

In terms of clinical priorities, the government has focused above all on cancer, with coronary heart disease a close second. In both cases, ministers have pledged to improve survival rates to levels common elsewhere in Europe over the next ten years. The focus on these areas is a response to the fact that the UK lags well behind in terms of both treatment and outcomes. Yet some predictions suggest that the key growth areas in terms of treatment demand over the next few years will be elsewhere, such as rheumatology, musculoskeletal and respiratory disease, with oncology and cardiovascular in particular further down the list. Potentially therefore, the NHS will find itself resourced to deal with priorities different from those that are actually creating mounting demand on the system.

The government's approach towards pharmaceuticals

For as long as the NHS has been in existence, successive governments have been concerned about the growth, both current and potential, in the drugs bill. To some extent this can be attributed to the fact that the drugs bill is easy to measure and track, easier than most other elements of healthcare expenditure. The demand-led nature of expenditure on medicines is of special concern to the Treasury. Through the introduction of unified healthcare budgets to be administered ultimately through primary care trusts, the Treasury has secured its long-pursued ambition of cash limiting spending on prescription medicines, albeit within a wider overall budget.

The current Health Secretary, Alan Milburn, has set out to take a different approach towards spending on medicines. He has argued on several occasions that the drugs bill should not be viewed as a burden or a drain on the NHS budget, but potentially as a measure of the health service's investment in treatment. Mr Milburn, so far as his public pronouncements have been concerned, has given the impression of being more relaxed than his predecessors about potential growth in expenditure on prescription medicines.

Welcome though such sentiments may be, few in the pharmaceutical industry have been moved by them to uninhibited celebration. The reality is that policies are still operating with the objective of controlling demand for prescription medicines within the NHS. And NICE in particular has proven to be a source of controversy.

NICE came into existence on 1 April 1999. It covers England and Wales only, although a body with a similar role, the Scottish Health Technology Assessment Board, is being set up north of the border. NICE is a special health authority, which means that it is part of the NHS and is accountable to the Secretary of State for Health and the National Assembly for Wales, who appoint its chairman and senior officers. The role of NICE, according to the government, is to give 'new coherence and prominence to information about clinical and cost-effectiveness'.[3] NICE has either overtaken the funding and functions of the following Department of Health programmes or has a clear role in relation to them:

■ The National Prescribing Centre appraisals and bulletins

■ PRODIGY (computer-based prescribing guidelines for general practitioners)

■ The National Centre for Clinical Audit

■ *The Prescriber's Journal*

▪ The National Guidelines Programme and Professional Audit Programme, and Effectiveness Bulletins.

NICE appraises new and existing medical technologies (medicines and devices) based upon their clinical and cost-effectiveness and makes recommendations on their use throughout the NHS. It also produces guidelines relating to the management of specific clinical conditions. The selection of technologies for NICE to look at, and guideline areas, is made by the government, not by NICE itself. The NHS is not obliged legally to follow NICE's recommendations, although there is a policy and political assumption that it will do so. This assumption will be reinforced by the enforcement activities of the Commission for Health Improvement. The climate created is that any parts of the NHS, or even individual doctors, who do not follow NICE guidance will be required to give an account of their reasons to the centre.

The early work of NICE has caused considerable controversy within the pharmaceutical industry. A number of the Institute's decisions appear to be motivated by an overall desire to moderate or reduce costs. Much of the problem revolves around NICE's remit to assess the 'cost-effectiveness' of different medical technologies. This is a vague and unspecific term that can be interpreted in a number of different ways. Nor does the policy framework that encases NICE address the fact that cost-effectiveness is meaningful only in comparative terms. This lack of policy definition creates an environment in which there is widespread suspicion around what NICE is really about.

Alan Milburn sees NICE as the quid pro quo of his open-minded approach to drug expenditure. In his model, NICE serves to sift out the medicines or medical technologies that provide added value for the NHS from those that do not and to channel NHS spending in the direction of effective treatments. Equally importantly, NICE is supposed to generate a national approach ending the current situation where a particular medicine might be available in one health authority area but not another. The government is also making additional funds available to health authorities to enable them to implement NICE recommendations that have cost implications. Such money is not, however, ring-fenced and there is no guarantee that it will be spent for the purpose of implementing NICE guidance.

The industry meanwhile sees the dangers in NICE developing as a regulatory fourth hurdle. It is perceived that, far from encouraging faster access to new and innovative medicines, as the government has claimed, NICE will erect a further barrier to access. This has implications not just for patients but also for the attractiveness of the UK as a location for investment by the pharmaceutical industry.

If things continue as they are expected to, there is a likelihood that NICE will set a precedent and model for similar systems in other countries. It is clear that NICE itself has ambitions to be adopted as a model in other countries. A further possibility is that the NICE-type appraisal of cost-effectiveness may develop as a regulatory requirement, alongside the existing criteria of safety, quality and efficacy. For the UK this would be a major and unprecedented step. At the moment the separation between product licensing on the basis of safety, quality and efficacy and cost-effectiveness assessment is enforced in primary legislation. NICE, as it is currently constructed, without legal powers over reimbursement, has allowed this separation to be maintained. This is not to say, however, that this tradition of separation, which is indeed long and strong, could not be undermined in the future, especially if this is a direction taken in European regulations.

The pricing of branded medicines for sale to the NHS is regulated in the UK through the Pharmaceutical Price Regulation Scheme (PPRS). This scheme has been in existence in various forms for over 40 years and upheld by governments of both political parties. It is a voluntary scheme (though now with statutory backing) renegotiated between the Department of Health and the Association of the British Pharmaceutical Industry (ABPI) representing the industry every five years. The last renegotiation took place in 1999 and the current scheme is due to run until 2004, with a mid-term review in 2002.

Despite its name, the PPRS does not regulate prices, or at least not directly. Under the PPRS, companies are free to set the prices of new medicines at launch. The proviso is that they do so within an overall framework that limits the profit they can make from sales of their branded portfolio to the NHS to levels set by the Department of Health. Allowances are made within the scheme for spending on research and development and for sales and promotion activity. The sales and promotion allowance, in particular, has tended to become the target of a government squeeze on each occasion that the PPRS is renegotiated.

The benefit claimed for the PPRS is that it allows companies considerable freedom in setting their own prices while also ensuring reasonable prices for the NHS. The emphasis is on reasonable rather than on minimum prices because the government accepts that companies should be encouraged to invest in R&D. As noted above, it is less positive towards expenditure on promotion. There is, nevertheless, a widespread feeling among manufacturers that the scheme is unduly restrictive and produces an undue balance of advantage with the purchaser. Whatever strengths should be given to the different sides of the argument, the operation of the PPRS is held by its advocates in both government and industry to have contributed substantially to the high level of pharmaceutical investment in the UK.

During the renegotiation of the PPRS in 1999, the argument was advanced by the industry side that greater reliance should be placed on market mechanisms to secure the proper balance between an industry incentivized to invest and reasonable prices for the NHS. Many in the UK government and beyond are suspicious of this approach, not least because experience in the USA suggests that it leads to higher prices. The government has agreed, however, to explore jointly with the industry the dynamics of the pharmaceutical market in the UK, with a view potentially to some deregulation of price controls. A joint ABPI/Department of Health project is undertaking this work, with a view to informing the mid-term review of the PPRS in 2002.

One factor to take into consideration is the especially high level of generic prescribing in the UK. The government has ambitions to take this even higher and has set a target of achieving a 72% rate of prescriptions written generically. It has, however, ruled out generic substitution by pharmacists. This policy is not designed to be specifically opposed to branded medicines. Rather the government sees it as an opportunity to create what it calls 'headroom for innovation', in other words saving money in the drugs budget, where cheaper non-branded medicines are available, that can then be invested in new innovative products.

Parallel trade has long been a concern in the UK, with substantial penetration of parallel imports severely undermining the competitiveness of the industry. The Department of Health has for some time now been sympathetic to the problem of parallel trade, although its proffered solutions are not necessarily welcome to the industry. The fundamental problem stems from the fact that neither of the ingredients that combine to create the problem of parallel trade – the free movement of goods across the EU and pharmaceutical price controls in different countries – are directly in the power of the UK government to influence.

Policy at EU level

Whatever the merits or demerits of the system in the UK, the fact is that pharmaceutical reimbursement schemes in continental Europe tend to be more restrictive than in Britain. The rest of Europe adheres to the general rule of promoting a system wherein pharmaceutical companies negotiate yearly contracts directly with government instead of through trade associations, thus leaving little or no margin for ensuring a better return should a medicinal product do particularly well. This is in direct contrast to the UK model.

Differences between countries also exist with regard to how reimbursement schemes are managed at a consumer level. Each country sets the price and level of reimbursement of the medicinal product. The percentage of reimbursement depends on the rules in force in that country.

Quite unlike the USA, under the conditions of established EU law, healthcare provision and reimbursement are governed and legislated at individual European member state level. This implies that each of the 15 countries within the EU is solely responsible and accountable for its own healthcare policy. The European Commission attempts periodically to extend its competence into the health field and has had some recent success by being given the right to intervene in matters relating to public health which it will no doubt seek to interpret as widely as possible.

As noted above, among EU member states, the UK is the only one which, to meet healthcare costs, relies almost exclusively on funds collected through direct or indirect taxation. The other EU countries encourage a co-payment system in addition to public funding. This means that a more comprehensive bilateral coverage is available to almost everyone. Although the cost to the individual, and his or her employer, is much higher in terms of revenue tax, both medical and dental healthcare are reimbursed by the state and by a private insurer.

Since the signing of the Treaty of Amsterdam, even though the responsibility for healthcare provision and accountability is still left up to each nation state, an established, all-encompassing legislative structure has been put into place. In particular, as regards legal developments in EU health, Article 152 of the Amsterdam Treaty stipulates that 'a high level of health protection shall be ensured in the definition and implementation of all Community policies and activities', that actions shall not only aim at 'improving health and prevent diseases', but shall likewise aim at 'obviating sources of danger to human health'. This legal backdrop, coupled with the political imperative that the European Commission gives to health as one of its key priorities, influences the way in which countries decide and implement health policy.

The European Commission adopted on 16 May 2000 its 'Communication on the Community's health strategy' (COM 2000/285). The new public health action programme, which is expected to run for six years will have a total budget of €300 million. The new programme has three core objectives:

- First, a comprehensive health information system will be developed, targeted at the general public, health professionals and other stakeholders, and health authorities. This will provide reliable and up-to-date information on key health-related topics using the Internet with links to national websites.

- Second, there will be mechanisms to respond to major health threats including a rapid reaction capability. This will ensure that the Community can respond effectively to potentially serious threats both from major diseases and emerging risks which cannot be effectively tackled by member states on their own.

■ Finally, the programme will address health determinants, in other words the underlying factors which affect people's health. Main priorities will include seeking to reduce the high levels of premature deaths and illness in the EU from major diseases, such as cancer and cardiovascular diseases, as well as mental illness. This will be achieved by focusing on key lifestyle factors, such as smoking, alcohol, nutrition, physical activity and drug abuse, as well as major socio-economic and environmental factors.

In addition to best practice, the Commission wants to introduce economic mechanisms such as cost comparisons and benchmarking. Given the sovereignty that each country holds over its healthcare system, many elements of the programme are likely to be unpopular with the member states.

Encouraging the use of innovative technology, such as the Internet, is also very much part of the Commission's strategy. Within the e-Europe action plan adopted at the last European Council in Lisbon in June 2000, the EU heads of government and state put forward three objectives to be reached before 2002:

■ a cheaper, faster and more secure Internet

■ investment in people and skills

■ stimulation of the use of the Internet.

On this basis, ten priority areas for action have been defined. One of the most important of these is the Health Online initiative. The prime objective of the Health Online action is to develop an infrastructure of user-friendly, validated and interoperable systems for health education, disease prevention and medical care. Many of the tools for the building of such an infrastructure exist. However, the Commission perceives that efforts are needed at member state level to move towards the implementation of the infrastructure in a coherent way which enables them to use technology to achieve their health objectives. The Commission has identified four key challenges necessary for the full exploitation of the Health Online initiative:

■ Identifying and disseminating best practice. There is also a growing anticipation that European benchmarking criteria will need to be developed.

■ The need to ensure that European citizens have the resources they need to be able to assess the quality and authenticity of the vast amount of health-related information on the Internet.

■ Public expenditure on health telematics tools and devices is a significant item in health budgets. Yet currently very little independent technology assessment exists to guide the purchaser's decision making. Similarly, medical practitioners need access to up-to-date, networked public health data guidelines in order to assist their disease management decision making.

■ Europe currently holds a strong position in the nascent e-health industry, which represents approximately 6% of the IT market. Yet particular uncertainty persists in the health telematics-related industry about responsibility and data protection, the legality of providing online medical opinions, as well as online pharmaceutical information and product supply.

Review of EU pharmaceutical regulation

A review of the EU rules governing the pharmaceutical industry is due in 2001, including the way that new drugs are registered by the European regulatory body responsible for issuing Community-wide approval of new medicines, the European Agency for the Evaluation of Medicinal Products (EMEA). Part of the impending review will also include how the centralized and decentralized authorization procedures have operated since the establishment of the EMEA in 1995. Among the industry's key goals in the forthcoming review is the maintenance of a registration system that allows manufacturers to choose between EU and national procedures.

In view of the enlargement of the EU and global competition, the pharmaceutical industry wants to make sure that regulatory procedures actually function as they are designed to and that, for example, member states allow mutual recognition of national authorizations and rigorously apply industrial and intellectual property protection.

Restatement of fundamentals of US healthcare model

The US healthcare system is unique among wealthy industrialized countries in the extent of its reliance on the private sector for the financing, purchasing and delivery of healthcare services. Public expenditures – through federal, state and local governments – total 45% of overall health spending, primarily for purchasing health services for specific populations (for example the elderly, disabled, veterans and the poor). The large majority of US residents receives health insurance benefits through their employers and accesses services delivered by the private sector.

However, almost 44 million people are not covered by any continuous public or private health insurance scheme and have limited access to private medical resources. They receive care through publicly operated clinics and hospitals or pay out of pocket for services to private providers, or go without.

At 13.5%, the USA devotes a higher percentage of its GDP to healthcare than any other country. This percentage has remained essentially flat since 1992, which is attributable to the strong US economy, the Balanced Budget Act of 1997, and the dramatic shift away from indemnity insurance into managed care plans. Although annual per capita health expenditures in 1998 were still well above those of other OECD (Organization for Economic Co-operation and Development) countries, they are growing at a much slower rate than in the past.

Some health maintenance organizations (HMOs), however, serve as both purchasers (pooling the risk) and providers of care; 89% of employees are now enrolled in plans with some form of managed care. Provision of health services is predominantly through private providers, including hospitals, integrated healthcare organizations (which link physicians, hospitals and other providers) and physicians. The USA has a higher ratio of specialists to primary care physicians than most OECD countries. With the rapid spread of managed care, the demand for primary care providers has grown.

Indemnity insurance

Under traditional indemnity insurance, the money follows the patient. Patients select healthcare providers and visit them as they choose. Providers then bill the private insurer or public payer and are reimbursed on a fee-for-service or per-case basis. Most indemnity plans attempt to limit demand through financial barriers to the patient, such as deductibles and co-insurance, rather than constraints on the provider. Many also require the patient to pay the provider directly and seek reimbursement from the insurer, often with payments less than charges. This form of insurance is rapidly disappearing.

Managed care

In traditional managed care plans (for example HMOs), the money follows the 'member', whether ill or not. Although there are many definitions of 'managed care', generally the term describes a continuum of arrangements that integrate the financing and delivery of healthcare. Purchasers contract with (or 'own') selected providers to deliver a defined set of services at an agreed per-capita or per-service price. In practice, managed care encompasses a wide range of arrangements, some of which resemble discounted fee-for-service (for example preferred provider organizations, in which the member receives better benefits with lower co-payments by using contracted providers rather than non-preferred providers) and others (for example some HMOs) using capitation and gatekeepers – primary care physicians serving as patients' initial contacts for medical care and referrals – to manage patient care and authorize referrals.

Most managed care organizations offer a wide array of benefit designs that include HMO products, preferred provider organizations, and direct access products that allow patients to self-refer to specialists. This variety of arrangements and payment mechanisms makes it difficult to draw conclusions about the effectiveness of managed care.

Strengths and weaknesses

It goes without saying that those Americans who can indeed afford it are privy to one of the world's most dynamic and state-of-the-art systems for healthcare provision. Both American and European pharmaceutical companies have a large presence on the US market owing to the huge financial gains to be had in a country where free pricing is a fact of life.

However, a number of elements are contributing to make US citizens much less proud of the effects that a system based on pharmaceutical free pricing and legalized direct-to-consumer (DTC) advertising, in the media and on the Internet, can have on the end price to be paid.

Although prescription products are made more readily available in the USA than in more conservative European countries, the rising costs being passed onto the American consumer are beginning to affect public opinion.

Key developments (parallel trade risk)

Most recently, media attention on North American examples of pharmaceutical pricing policy has turned to America's other partners in the North American Free Trade Agreement (NAFTA) zone – Canada and Mexico. Patient and pressure group action is mounting and US government representatives are considering putting into effect legislation that would effectively legalize parallel trade of prescription medicines emanating from Mexico and Canada into the USA.

If this campaign is indeed successful, the outcome could very well mirror the current controversial situation in the EU, where the principles of free movement of goods within a single market prevail. Needless to say this would have serious implications for industry and would entail a major shake up for the US regulatory body, the Food and Drug Administration (FDA).

DTC advertising

Existing European legislation (Directive 92/28/EEC) means that, to all intents and purposes, DTC advertising of prescription only medicines in Europe is prohibited. However, since 1998, European Commission officials have been publicly stating that in view of the rapid development of the Internet, legislation should be brought up to date to reflect the current situation. This view is also gaining ground in the UK.

The European Commission has established a Pharmaceutical Committee Working Party on advertising and e-commerce. This committee prepared a questionnaire in order to get an overview on the current situation and the expectations of the different interested parties on these issues and to evaluate different options. The Commission believes, however, that the answer must be found on a global scale.

The Commission is also becoming increasingly aware of the potential for the EU to continue losing e-business to the USA, and generally takes the view that control should be regulated at international level. Commission officials have also contributed to a WHO working group examining DTC advertising on the Internet.

Council Directive 92/25/EEC of 31 March 1992 laid down the common rules relating to the advertising and wholesale distribution of medicinal products for human use. In general, all advertising relating to a medicinal product is forbidden if it has not been granted marketing authorization either centrally (through the EMEA) or at decentralized, nation state, level. The information contained in a company's submission must be compatible with the information listed in the summary of the product's characteristics, must encourage the rational administration of the product and must not be misleading.

The conditions for approval in the submission process can have a substantial impact on the success of a company's business as they set out the different circumstances under which pharmaceuticals can be promoted and advertised to the general public. Furthermore, they set out a series of prohibitions to advertise, for example, when pharmaceutical access is restricted by the product being available only on medical prescription.

To date, a resounding call for change in legislation has been proactively driven by the European Federation of Pharmaceutical Industries and Associations (EFPIA) in Brussels, which represents the pharmaceutical trade associations at national level across the EU and other member companies of diverse nationalities. Progress on attaining a Europe-wide agreement will no doubt take time as each individual member state has its own set of different guidelines and legislative measures for pricing and reimbursement. It will therefore be some time before a unilateral decision is taken on the controversial issue of DTC advertising of prescription-only medicines. A further factor here will be the interrelationship of views and approaches between the European Commission and the member states. Since the member states are themselves responsible for funding healthcare in their own countries, they feel that they have the greatest stake in the debate about whether or not to allow DTC advertising to proceed.

Concluding thoughts

At no other time has the pharmaceutical industry approached such a level of consolidation, not only in the various mergers and acquisitions that have taken place, but also in the current trends towards globalization and centralization. Therefore, at a time when pharmaceutical companies are realizing the value of developing global brands and are beginning to adopt centralized procedures for the marketing of drugs, forces such as DTC advertising and NICE can be seen to be pulling against the tide of globalization and unification.

Europe is currently in a catch-up situation to the USA as it attempts to grapple with the issue of DTC advertising. Until this is resolved, the current divide that has been created between the USA and Europe continues to grow. Equally, will NICE present as many barriers as opportunities? Will it act as a role model for other countries, or will it pose restrictions and barriers at both a national and international level? If the parameters of the existing regulatory framework result in patients being denied access to certain medicines, does such an environment risk alienating potential investment in the UK by the pharmaceutical industry? Only time will tell how these issues are resolved, but this is certainly a space worth watching.

Notes

1   Speech to Clinical Excellence 1999, 8 December 1999.
2   Speech to the Association of the British Pharmaceutical Industry annual dinner, April 2000.
3   *The New NHS: Modern, Dependable*, December 1997.

VI

The Expanding Healthcare Market

16 | Nutraceuticals

HUGO EHRNREICH Datamonitor Consumer Markets Practice Area

Introduction

Ever since the emergence of terms such as 'nutraceuticals', 'food as medicine' and 'functional foods', the food and pharmaceutical industries have been mesmerized by the promise of lucrative premium branded revenues on the boundary between their respective industries. However, finding the right formula for turning this vision into reality is proving a difficult task. Indeed, although individual cases of success such as Yakult can be found, the results from the bulk of the first major initiatives in this sector have been ambiguous at best. A series of high-profile initiatives, such as Raisio/McNeil's Benecol range of cholestrol-lowering products, have either failed to meet investors' initial (high) expectations or, like the Kellogg Company's Ensemble range, have been withdrawn following a lack of consumer interest.

One thing has, therefore, become clear in recent years, overnight success is unlikely in the nutraceuticals arena. Successful development of this new area will require a much clearer identification of consumers' wider needs. These must be matched by much more precise targeting of individual opportunities around clearly defined consumer occasions, combined with significant investments in clinical research and consumer education. Even so, the nutraceuticals opportunity is far from clear.

Defining the nutraceuticals environment

With the wealth of terms in use, the first problem facing the nutraceuticals area is a definitional one. Although their focus might differ slightly, most of these terms aim to describe the same basic idea – the creation of *'food plus'*.

Specifically, food and drinks products have new or extra levels of ingredients that already occur naturally in the product. Examples range from the inclusion of cholesterol-reducing stanol esters in Benecol margarine to boosting the calcium levels in dairy products aimed at the high-risk osteoporosis group.

One issue complicates the situation, however. In the pharmaceutical industry in particular the term 'nutraceuticals' is often used to describe the active ingredient used in the 'food plus' rather than the 'food plus' end product itself. This approach also means that dietary supplements are often included within the nutraceuticals definition, referring to over-the-counter (OTC) vitamin and mineral supplements (VMS) and herbal supplements. This chapter will use the term nutraceuticals to refer to the 'food plus' end product itself, rather than the generic active ingredient that is used in it. Dietary supplements as described above will be mentioned separately.

There are two reasons for this approach. On the one hand, the fact that the opportunity for active ingredients is derived directly from the success in stimulating end-consumer demand for food plus products implies the desirability of an end-consumer trend focus. On the other hand, this approach more accurately captures the essence of this new opportunity. Of course the opportunity to increase the supply of certain active ingredients to the food manufacturing sector is attractive in its own right. However, the key question facing most pharmaceuticals companies is whether there is an opportunity to actually open up a lucrative new source of OTC branded end-consumer revenues on the blurred boundary between the traditional food and pharmaceutical industries (Figure 16.1).

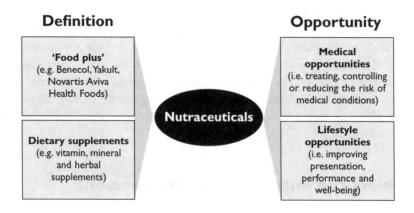

Figure 16.1 Nutraceuticals opportunities

The different opportunities – medical versus lifestyle

An analysis of consumer trends paints an encouraging picture, with a strong and growing consumer interest in the concept of *self-medication*: consumers playing a more active role in maintaining their health. Indeed, in an increasingly individually empowered society, rapidly rising awareness and basic knowledge of health issues are creating a growing desire for control over areas ranging from daily nutrient intake to performance enhancement and cholesterol level regulation. Steadily increasing life expectancy, concerns about future healthcare provision and costs, and the growing awareness among most consumers that this requires them to take better care of their health is adding further momentum to this trend. Outside the food and drinks industry, indicators ranging from the growth in the number of gym memberships to the decline in the number of smokers confirm this trend. Finally, the demographic momentum of an ageing (over 50 years of age) population is set to increase the levels of interest in addressing age-related illnesses and medical risk factors, ranging from osteoporosis to heart disease.

Together, these developments imply a strong potential for products that provide consumers with more control of their health. 'Health' is a very general term, however. The key to assessing the opportunities for nutraceuticals lies in identifying which specific health-related issues consumers are interested in addressing. Two key areas can be identified in this context:

■ *Medical applications* – concerned with treating, controlling or reducing the risk of important medical conditions such as high cholesterol, diabetes, heart disease and cancer.

■ *Lifestyle applications* – concerned with softer, lifestyle-related issues such as improving physical presentation and enhancing physical and psychological performance and well-being.

Medical opportunities – prevention versus treatment

One of the most apparent application areas for nutraceuticals relates to the maintenance of disease-free good health. In this context, a number of alternatives can be identified:

■ *Treatment* – products that act as pharmaceuticals, moderating or curing the effects of specific medical conditions (for example the role of calcium-enriched products in addressing osteoporosis in older women, and Benecol's role in reducing cholesterol levels).

■ *Prevention* – products that aim to reduce the risk of a particular medical condition (for example the role of antioxidants in helping to prevent cancer, and the role of Omega-3 polyunsaturated fatty acids in preventing heart attacks).

■ *Maintenance* – products that help the body to maintain itself by helping to achieve the appropriate intake of vitamins, minerals, fibre, sugars, fats and other beneficial nutrients (for example dietary supplements and vitamin and mineral enriched products), as well as providing other benefits (for example the role of Yakult in maintaining a healthy digestive system).

The boundaries between prevention, treatment and maintenance of good health are blurred in many cases and these three alternatives are therefore not meant to be mutually exclusive. Indeed, there is an obvious link between diet and the maintenance of general good health and the prevention and even treatment of many diseases (Figure 16.2).

However, from the point of view of making and supporting specific health claims for nutraceuticals products, it is highly relevant to consider the positioning on this axis between the *active* treatment of a specific health problem

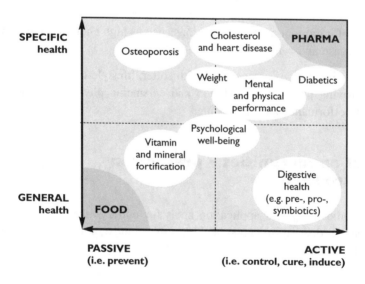

Figure 16.2 Applications for nutraceuticals

and the *passive* maintenance of good health. Specifically, in terms of clinical trial sample size, timescale and control over external factors it is relatively easier to prove convincingly that consumption of a certain product is effective in treating a clearly diagnosed disease than it is to show that it lowers the risk of contracting an as yet undiagnosed disease in the future. As a result, it is likely to be much easier to make a strong marketing claim for products that treat a clearly observable medical condition. Raisio, for example, has been able to obtain regulatory approval for the claim that their Benecol product 'actually helps lower cholesterol'. Nestlé, on the other hand, had to be content with the highly general claim on its LC1 range of probiotic dairy products: 'a companion to good health that makes you look and feel good everyday.'

Medical opportunities – choosing the right condition

In addition to the type of health claim, it is also crucial that the right medical condition is chosen. In this context there are important differences between the end-user food and drinks and pharmaceutical markets. In general terms, the pharmaceutical industry focuses on providing a solution to a well-defined problem – a clearly defined medical condition of which consumers are highly aware either because of self-diagnosis or diagnosis by a physician. In the nutraceuticals arena, awareness among the potential consumer audience cannot always be assumed automatically, even for well-documented medical conditions.

The issue of high cholesterol is a good example. With an estimated 45–70% of the populations in countries such as France, Germany, the UK and the USA suffering from high or borderline cholesterol levels, there is a clear medical need to control the problem. However, high cholesterol is not commonly screened for in the general population. As a result, although public information campaigns might have generated high levels of general awareness among the population, the level of urgency felt by most individuals is probably insufficient to justify paying a significant premium for products that address this problem. In addition, the danger exists that consumers who have been made hypochondriac by these health warnings, but do not actually suffer from the specific medical condition, use the product. At best this could seriously undermine the credibility of the product. At worst it could lead to actual adverse effects among these non-intended users of the product. In all cases, there is a real danger of a consumer backlash against the product.

Therefore, OTC or self-help, rather than prescribed, products enjoy sustainable success in generating premium revenues from targeting specific medical conditions. This requires a combination of the following factors:

■ *A clearly defined consumer group with sufficient levels of concern* –
Awareness of a particular medical condition is not sufficient. What is
crucial here is identifying those medical conditions for which levels of
concern among the general population are sufficiently high to justify a
significant price premium and/or induce a change in consumption habits.
Related to this is the need to target a clearly defined consumer group, often
based around specific life-stages (for example children, pregnant women,
menopausal women and older men).

■ *The possibility of (self-) diagnosis and/or measurable results* – What is
crucial here is identifying either or both of two alternatives: a clearly
defined group of well-informed sufferers of the specific medical condition,
supported by professional medical advice (for example menopausal
women receiving regular advice from their physician); or a more general
problem which consumers are able to diagnose themselves (for example
digestive discomfort). Particularly in the latter case, where an external
force such as a physician's advice does not stimulate continued use, it is
crucial that consumers can observe the results of taking the nutraceutical
for themselves.

Lifestyle opportunities – 'social drugs'

The narrow definition of the self-medication concept discussed above offers
attractive opportunities for medical applications, ranging from the treatment
of high cholesterol to constipation. A much wider set of opportunities can be
identified for products with a lower level of functionality, however, in the area
of lifestyle or social applications. Three areas are of particular interest:

■ *Physical presentation* – in an increasingly visually oriented society, aimed
at optimizing physical presentation, ranging from oral and dental care (for
example breath freshening, tooth decay prevention, teeth whitening) to
weight control.

■ *Performance* – aimed at boosting mental and physical performance in
everyday situations, socially and at work. Examples range from the need
for extra stamina and energy during a night of dancing in a nightclub (for
example Red Bull soft drink) to the need for extra concentration and alert-
ness during a university examination or a high-pressure day in the office
(for example Dextro Energy confectionery).

■ *General well-being* – aimed at consumers' relatively unfocused desire to
'live a healthy lifestyle' and manage their overall mental and physical

health. In this context there is a clear overlap with the general maintenance issue discussed in the medical opportunities section. In addition, however, it refers to 'mood foods', that aim to address issues ranging from low-level depression to the need to unwind or relax. Alcohol and cigarettes are perhaps the most well-known examples, but more recent ones include products containing St John's wort, a herbal ingredient known for its anti-depressant qualities.

Although the specific health message is weaker, these lifestyle issues often exert a much stronger positive emotional or aspirational appeal on consumers on a daily basis. Indeed, there are strong parallels here with the point made earlier about the level of concern required to demand a price premium. On a daily basis mainstream consumers without any serious medical conditions are often likely to be more concerned with lifestyle-related issues than with health issues with which they are not confronted on a daily basis. Related to this is the fact that the demanding consumer of the 21st century increasingly expects instant gratification. This implies that 'magic bullet'-type nutraceuticals are likely to be better received than those that require months and years of disci-pline with difficult-to-measure results. Unlike most medical conditions, lifestyle problems offer the opportunity to provide these types of one-off quick fix. In addition, the fact that the areas that are being addressed are often more superficial and cosmetic, for example boosting energy levels versus treating life-threatening heart disease, implies that the message is often perceived as more positive and less threatening.

As a result, this type of application offers manufacturers a more powerful platform for consumer brand building than the more scientific or medical one. In addition, this type of weaker functionality has a close fit with current consumer concerns, particularly in Europe but rising in the USA, with regard to the increasingly artificial nature of modern life, driven by issues ranging from food scares to increasing urban pollution and genetic modification. The resulting interest in more natural products combines with the self-medication concept to build a strong momentum for products that incorporate natural and herbal ingredients and are perceived to work in harmony with the body or nature.

Exploiting the opportunity – the key success factors

Having discussed the two key areas of opportunity in the nutraceutical area – medical and lifestyle – and having highlighted some of the issues involved in identifying the individual opportunities, one crucial question remains unresolved. What is the successful model for exploiting the functional food opportunity? The industry has long speculated about the potential synergies of combining the food processing and branding skills of a major food manufacturer with the healthcare expertise of the pharmaceutical sector. With the announced formation of a US joint venture to develop and distribute functional food products in February 2000, Novartis' Consumer Health business unit and the Quaker Oats Company have taken the first step towards putting this idea to the test. While Quaker pioneered the issue of making health claims in food with its oats products and has extensive experience in the energy drink category (Gatorade), the 1999 launch of the Aviva Life Foods line of products claiming heart, digestion and bone benefits has given Novartis invaluable experience in the marketplace. Although it is too early to reach any conclusions about the success of this approach, the rationale behind this initiative is sound.

Indeed, such a combination between pharmaceutical and food companies potentially reconciles two basic issues that need to be addressed before the nutraceuticals concept can be converted effectively into sustained purchasing behaviour:

- *Clinical discipline* – the need for claims to have solid clinical support. This is to prevent further erosion of consumer confidence in the functional food concept as a result of unfocused fortification and advertising of overambitious claims.

- *Holistic consumer marketing* – the need for consumer-driven market development. To effectively target a non-patient consumer audience it will be essential to pick up the soft signals from the market and incorporate functional aspects into wider, lifestyle-oriented consumer solutions.

Nutraceuticals – combining the pharma and food skill-set

Each of these two areas requires a different skill-set. The corporate culture that breeds pharmaceutical excellence and clinical trial discipline will not necessarily breed an environment conducive to proactive trend spotting and effective DTC marketing disciplines. The reason for this is that each sector focuses on resolving a very different issue. In the pharmaceutical sector, the need (that is, the medical condition) is very clearly defined in the minds of the consumers, accompanied by a sense of urgency. In other words, pharmaceutical companies generally focus on finding a complex solution to a well-defined and urgent problem. It is therefore not surprising that marketing activities focus more on pushing the product into the channel (that is, prescribing physicians) than creating a demand pull from the end-user.

The situation in the food industry is very different. The key issue for food manufacturers is generally to discover a consumer problem that needs to be solved. Compared to the pharmaceutical industry, these needs are generally not essential or very urgent and are often difficult to define even by consumers themselves. This necessitates an ability to pick up the soft signals from the marketplace and translate these into specific product parameters. In addition, although marketing activities aimed at the channel (the retailers) are important, the key to success is to create end-consumer demand for the product in the first place. This necessitates an ability to communicate effectively with consumers.

Clinical discipline – better support for health claims

Although food manufacturers have these essential marketing skills, they often miss the type of strategic long-term commitment to the search, identification and clinical testing of ingredients for which the pharmaceutical industry is known. The testing required to meet traditional safety guidelines in the food industry is not enough to achieve success in the nutraceuticals arena. One of the most important changes in the functional food market has been this realization by major food manufacturers: that there are no shortcuts to sustainable development of the opportunities it offers.

Contrary to popular opinion, however, the primary reason for the need for a greater focus on clinical trials is not a lack of regulatory clarity. In most cases where companies have run into problems with products' claims, regulatory ambiguity has not been at fault. Instead, failure has been due mainly to a lack of discipline in providing sufficient evidence before making health claims and in putting a solid case before the consumer and its representatives, the local regulatory authorities. These are at the core of gaining approval in the pharmaceutical industry. Moreover, it is not likely that the regulatory environments in Europe and the USA will change significantly in the short term. Although the European Commission has launched an ambitious new food safety programme that includes sections on fortified foods, the short-term focus of this initiative is very much on restoring consumer confidence in the wake of a series of food scares.

Partly underlying this lack of effort in consumer education has been the mistaken assumption that consumers' rising health awareness or nutritional consciousness equates to nutraceuticals awareness. Indeed, while 90% of consumers surveyed by the American Dietetic Association said that nutrition was important to their health, the same survey found that 79% of consumers had never heard of nutraceuticals or functional foods and that the phrase had little meaning for them. Attempts to jump on the functional food bandwagon have further compounded this lack of consumer understanding by commoditizing key ingredients and fuelling consumer cynicism in key ingredients, such as fibre. Two issues are of particular importance in this context:

- *Unfocused fortification* of a very wide range of products with the latest ingredient fashion, without giving adequate consideration to the fit between the health benefit, target consumer lifestyle and perceptions, and the underlying product.
- *Overambitious claims* for products containing levels of functional ingredients far below effective levels, and containing high levels of other ingredient, such as fat, sugar and sodium, that are often considered nonbeneficial to health.

The breakfast cereal market clearly demonstrates the first point. In a market where between 90–100% of products are now fortified with a one-size-fits-all cocktail of essential vitamins and minerals, the issue of fortification has been reduced to a generic, non-differentiating characteristic of the product. In line with developments in dietary supplements, attempts are being made to focus on specific combinations of vitamins and minerals according to the core audience of the breakfast cereal product (for example extra calcium in products aimed at women and iron in products aimed at children). However, this is unlikely to repair the damage done.

Related to this is the issue of appropriate fortification and appropriate claims. The temptation exists to add vitamins and minerals to what are essentially high-fat, high-sugar junk food products with the aim of giving it a healthier positioning or to market a regular yoghurt as 'containing live bacteria', knowing that these cultures will not be viable (that is, do not survive in the human intestines). In many of these cases advertising authorities could be forgiven for considering these advertising claims as misleading. As a result, these types of initiative have to be managed extremely carefully. For example, while certain parents might accept a 'better-for-you' claim on a pack of children's vitamin-fortified crisps because it provides them with a Trojan horse for ensuring their children get enough vitamins and minerals, others are likely to feel misled by this health claim. This issue has strong parallels to the low and light issue. To achieve a similar taste and texture experience, the reduction in fat in many low fat products is matched by increases in sugar content. In balance, the total number of calories is often unchanged between the regular and the reduced fat version. It is vital, therefore, to identify what are the consumers' key concerns. If their key concern is that their children consume enough essential vitamins and minerals in whatever form, or to reduce their fat intake for cardiovascular reasons, rather than reduce calorie intake, then there is no problem. In all other cases, marketers risk a significant backlash against their product.

These issues are clearly illustrated by the experiences of MD Foods and SmithKline Beecham in the UK. Both companies, MD Foods with Gaio yoghurt and SmithKline Beecham with Ribena Juice and Fibre and Toothkind, were forced to change their claims after being criticized by the Advertising Standards Authority (ASA) about their health claims. It ruled that SmithKline Beecham's claim that its Ribena drinks could reduce hardening of artery walls was 'exaggerated'. Smithkline Beecham was in the news again in July 2000 with its Ribena Toothkind product. The ASA found SmithKline Beecham guilty of misleading advertising and ordered that the phrase 'does not encourage tooth decay' be dropped from advertising and packaging because it could not be substantiated. In the case of Gaio, the ASA said the Danish company could not provide sufficient proof to claim that its product reduced cholesterol because the evidence it presented was too scant, based as it was on clinical trials of just 30 people.

Although a change in marketing messages might not pose a major problem, the loss in consumer trust and credibility resulting from the publicity around these cases should not be underestimated. To halt the erosion of consumer confidence in the functional food concept, and prevent key functional ingredients from becoming commodities, it will be absolutely essential that claims are supported by more rigorous clinical research. In addition, it will be essential that products are marketed in an unambiguous way that aligns the health benefit perceived by the consumer with their perception of the underlying product. In the former case, the pharmaceutical industry has much to contribute. In addition, cooperation offers access to healthcare professionals, a highly underutilized channel for sale and promotion of nutraceuticals and diet-based therapies.

Holistic consumer marketing – focusing on consumer occasions

The pharmaceutical industry, however, has much to gain from consumer trend spotting and retail marketing expertise that the food industry has to offer. As discussed, the former has traditionally focused on producing products for well-defined medical conditions, such as cholesterol, diabetes and cancer, aimed at a captive audience of healthcare professionals and their patients. This fact puts these companies in a strong position for developing medical functional food products. However, the long-term research and development-based approach that this implies means that there is the danger that only the lowest common denominator products are produced and that more fashion-driven lifestyle opportunities are ignored.

In the fickle consumer marketplace of the 21st century, it is the more customized lifestyle products that are likely to demand the highest premium. Moreover, modern consumers are increasingly losing interest in one-dimensional products, which offer only one specific benefit, whether that is health, convenience or indulgence. Truly successful products manage to combine a number of these features into one attractive package that fits the wider lifestyles. On the one hand this implies the need for an in-depth understanding of consumers' wider needs, beyond just health. In addition, however, it implies the need for a much greater consideration for patterns of consumption across time, focusing on the consumer *occasions*, rather than merely looking at static consumer *groups*.

Blinded by the hype of consumer health awareness, it has been very easy for industry participants to fall into the trap of creating a caricature of the consumer as a 24-hour, 7-days a week health-obsessed being. Although segments of health fanatics exist, most consumers are individuals with good intentions, but with fluctuating levels of discipline, time and opportunity, not to mention changeable moods and different desires. Indeed, in an increasingly individualized, high-paced and pressurized society, where more people live on their own, both partners balance jobs and family and instant communication demands constant attention, consumers' health intentions often collide with a lack of time and the need for moments of escape, reward and comfort.

Food and drink products play an important role in providing escape, reward and comfort, both directly, through detectable tastes and, indirectly, by creating a special atmosphere around the eating experience. As consumers become more informed about health and dietary issues, they are accommodating these often conflicting needs in an increasingly calculating debits and credits approach to their lifestyle. This refers to the habit of many consumers to balance bad against good behaviour, discipline at certain times with unadulterated indulgence at others. Using this approach, visits to the gym, a period of abstaining from alcohol or a healthy lunch meal compensate for a night of drinking or a rewarding tub of 'Death by Chocolate' ice cream at the end of a busy day. This polarization between health and indulgence implies that, although the incorporation of nutraceutical aspects into indulgence products seemingly offers extra benefits to the consumer, these additions are actually likely to be perceived as distractions to the indulgence experience. Indeed, the psychology of pure indulgence implies that the inclusion of healthy elements might actually erode the indulgent positioning of the product in consumers' minds.

This would lead to the hypothesis that the strongest demand for nutraceuticals is likely to emerge in those occasions when consumers currently lack the time and opportunity to pursue a healthy lifestyle. The key to offering consumers higher levels of control over their health is therefore to provide them with new products that make it significantly easier for them to do so in a range of different situations. Although it is indeed easier than taking a separate dietary supplement, this significant improvement in convenience does not mean adding vitamins to breakfast cereal products. Instead, it implies a focus on fundamentally new products or product designs and widely expanded availability, particularly in convenience and impulse locations. Food manufacturers such as Kellogg's have recognized this issue in both the design of their Nutrigrain breakfast cereal bar and the fact that it is available through a range of convenience, impulse channels. The best example of this approach is Yakult.

Exploiting the opportunity – three strategies

Yakult, LCI and Actimel – healthy complements to the daily routine

Widely recognized as the pioneer of the nutraceuticals trend and one of the rare examples of a company that has been able to achieve commercial success in this area, Yakult Honsa launched its probiotic fermented milk drink in Japan in 1935. Each small, pink bottle is designed to provide a daily dose of the beneficial bacteria culture, Lactobacillus casei Shirota, which was isolated by Professor Shirota of Kyoto University. This bacteria culture is naturally present in the intestinal flora of humans and is thought to play a role in resistance against pathogenic germs.

For many years, the brand was available in Japan alone. Taiwan became its first overseas market in 1964, followed by a range of Far Eastern countries, Mexico, the USA and Australia. The first European office was established in the Netherlands in 1992, followed in 1994 by the establishment of a factory in the Dutch town of Almere. This enabled the company to deliver Yakult fresh to consumers in Germany, Belgium, France and the UK. Yakult has now developed a strong presence in many of the world's leading soft drinks markets and it is estimated that 23 million people consume the brand on a daily basis. Yakult's success stems from three key areas:

■ *Highly targeted positioning* – By targeting a specific consumption occasion – early morning or breakfast – the company has been able to carve out a distinct niche for its product. In its domestic Japanese market, it has achieved this goal with considerable success.

■ *Non-intrusive fit within the daily routine* – Ironically, the strength of the Yakult product is a positioning that has more in common with a dietary supplement than a food and drinks product. As a result, it is completely non-intrusive. Consumers do not have to change their food and drinks consumption habits in any way. In addition, because the product complements, but does not replace, the actual breakfast, Yakult does not need to maintain consumer interest through new flavours and varieties the way breakfast cereals manufacturers have to.

■ *High, ongoing investment in research* – Yakult invests a lot of time and money in their educational programmes, which include sponsoring of independent research into the benefis of probiotic products as well as presentations and free leaflets aimed at promoting understanding of gut health (rather than directly promoting the product).

■ *Unique marketing and distribution* – Yakult operates a highly sophisticated distribution network that employs 59,000 women in door-to-door sales teams in Japan. This team also peddles the drinks, some on motor scooters and others on push carts, through office buildings. Consumers can therefore purchase Yakult at the key consumption moment no matter where they are. This has enabled the company to maximize its sales in Japan, where daily throughput amounts to over 12 million servings.

However, in foreign markets, particularly in the West, Yakult has not been able to recreate this highly successful distribution process as a result of labour costs. Because it is no longer possible to place the brand close to the consumer during the key consumption moment, this has forced the company to reassess its approach to Yakult's positioning. With the scope for providing impulse purchase occasions markedly diminished, the focus has shifted towards a planned purchase positioning, with the retail multiples acting as a key distribution channel. As a result, Yakult has sharpened its position as an essential part of the breakfast routine and started to sell the product in seven-unit multi-packs.

With very similar positioning and strategies, two me-too products have since joined Yakult: Nestlé's LC1 and Danone's Actimel. Unlike Yakult, however, Nestlé has split its LC1 range into two distinct categories. While all LC1 products are marketed as 'a companion to good health that makes you look and feel good every day', the LC1 yoghurts and LC1 Go drinks are each designed to appeal to different consumer groups. While LC1 Go is aimed at 25–44 year-old male and female ABC1's, who have busy urban lives, LC1 yoghurts are aimed at people over 45 years of age, particularly women. Older people are said to be more comfortable with this format, rather than LC1 Go's little bottles. Another key benefit from this two-pronged approach is that Nestlé has been able to achieve a presence in both the milk and yoghurt sections of the supermarket. The LC1 Go drink is placed next to Yakult in the milk section, while LC1 yoghurts are placed next to Actimel with other yoghurts.

Most importantly, LC1 has been marketed as a product that promotes good health and no strong health claims are made on the packaging. However, one of Nestlé's websites claims that the bacteria culture included in LC1 is 'stronger than bulgaricus (found in yoghurt) and more powerful than casei shirota (in Yakult)'. This aggressive and slightly ambiguous statement would have encountered regulatory difficulties if placed on packaging, but on the unregulated Internet, Nestlé does not face this problem.

Novartis' Aviva Life Foods – replacing parts of the daily routine

Already one of the world's leading healthcare companies, Novartis, through its Consumer Health division, has made a major commitment to the nutraceuticals concept, with the recent launch of its Aviva Life Foods range of functional muesli, hot chocolate drinks, orange drinks, cereals bars and biscuits in the UK, Switzerland and Austria. Like Yakult, Nestlé and Danone, Novartis Consumer Health have taken the approach of designing a nutraceutical product that focuses on providing mainly preventive medical benefits by supporting a healthy daily routine, rather than addressing direct-result specific lifestyle issues. As a result, the products that are part of the range are designed to be taken as a daily dose. However, the key difference between the Aviva range and Yakult-type products is its intrusiveness. The Aviva products replace existing food products within the daily consumption pattern, putting Novartis in the much more complicated situation of having to match these alternatives in terms of taste experience and variety. As discussed earlier, it is unlikely that an outsider in the food and drinks industry will be able to achieve this. The joint venture with Quaker Oats might provide some support in this area, but it does not lessen the overall difficulty of managing this complex package of consumer needs – from variety to functional benefits.

On the positive side, Novartis Consumer Health has not underestimated the importance of focusing on those conditions about which consumers express concern. A group of the most important health concerns were identified through a series of studies in which consumers were asked to rate their interest in various issues. From this group three issues were chosen that would be most practical to address in food products. Consumers over 35 years of age were chosen as the key audience because this age group is the most susceptible to the three key issues that the range focuses on:

- *Bone benefits* – containing *Novacalcium.* a combination of milk calcium plus vitamin D_3, magnesium and zinc to aid the absorption of calcium. Dietary intake of Novacalcium in addition to load-bearing exercise has been shown to help to prevent bone loss. After the first 18 months of clinical trials, results suggest that the women who received the placebo had a considerable drop in bone mineral densities, as predicted by the natural rate of bone loss, while the group taking Aviva Bone Benefits maintained initial bone mineral density.

- *Heart benefits* – containing *NovaCol.* a blend of natural soya and oat extracts with antioxidant vitamins C and E. It is thought that NovaCol limits absorption of cholesterol when oat beta glucan combines with cholesterol-based components in bile. Novartis ran clinical trials on 120 patients and demonstrated significantly reduced cholesterol compared with the placebo.

- *Digestive benefits* – containing *NovaDigest.* a probiotic combination of soluble fibres, Benefiber and fructooligosaccharides which pass unaffected through the digestive system until reaching the colon, where they stimulate growth of beneficial bacteria at the expense of pathogens.

Like Yakult, Novartis had also not underestimated the importance of consumer education and rigorous clinical trials. Before launching the Aviva range (see Plate 16.1), Novartis Consumer Health carried out 160 independent studies worldwide to establish the effectiveness of Aviva ingredients, in close coordination with government advisers. Finally, in terms of marketing investment, Novartis recognized the role played by healthcare professionals in consumer education about health and diet and equal attention was therefore given to direct end-consumer marketing and campaigns directed at these opinion-leaders.

Red Bull energy drinks – targeting lifestyle occasions

Beyond the medical opportunities targeted by the previous examples, products such as the energy drink Red Bull (see Plate 16.2) have been very successful in developing highly fashionable nutraceutical brands around the lifestyle opportunities discussed earlier. A non-alcoholic drink, Red Bull is marketed under the slogan 'stimulates body and mind' and contains a number of active ingredients including *taurine* (claimed to act as a metabolic transmitter, to have a detoxifying effect and to strengthen cardiac contractility), *glucurono-lactone* (claimed to accelerate the elimination of harmful substances), *caffeine*, *B-complex vitamins* and *carbohydrates*. Red Bull was first introduced in the Austrian market after their current managing partner, Dietrich Mateschitz, came in contact with the energy drinks concept while on a business trip in Asia. Red Bull is now sold across Europe and much of the world with total sales in 1998 of about 300 million cans.

With a strong focus on consumer advertising and sports sponsorship, Red Bull's global marketing strategy reflects its aim of creating a fashionable brand with functional lifestyle benefits rather than hard medical or health benefits. Red Bull's marketing strategy therefore has much more in common with leading food and drinks brands such as Coca-Cola, than with most nutraceutical brands. In contrast to taking the more scientific, consumer education-based approach of brands such as Yakult, Red Bull focuses on targeting young people by creating an aspirational aura around the product, while leaving the exact functional benefits of the product intentionally vague.

In this sense, Red Bull, as well as the growing number of other products based around herbal active ingredients, is benefiting from the current consumer interest in herbal and new age ingredients. These high levels of consumer interest have meant that manufacturers are likely to benefit from a process of self-education by consumers, lessening the need for explicit claims for individual ingredients. Abdicating the issue for research and education in this way presents a number of inherent risks, however. Most herbal ingredients are highly complex chemical compounds, containing combinations of a wide range of different active ingredients for which the effects, both individually and in combination, are largely undocumented. As a result, the potential for unforeseen side effects in the future, and a consequent backlash against these products, is very high.

However, even without any side effects, it might be argued that in the absence of solid clinical evidence manufacturers are encouraging sensationalism to fill the consumer knowledge gap and publishing their own speculations as facts. The publicity surrounding the side effects of some of Red Bull's herbal ingredients provides a good illustration of this. Even if, as was the case with Red Bull, it is not based on any solid evidence, such publicity can still do considerable harm to the public perception of a product. Manufacturers are therefore advised to follow Yakult's example and start sponsoring independent research that provides solid counter-arguments for such rumours. Investment in independent clinical trials, feeding into consumer education, will therefore also be crucial to the development and maintenance of a solid competitive position in the lifestyle-driven nutraceuticals arena.

Conclusions – focus on complementary functionality

As the discussion in this chapter illustrates, the nutraceutical opportunity is far from clear. Although a wide range of potential application areas for the nutraceutical *concept* can be identified, from lifestyle issues such as presentation and well-being to the prevention and treatment of specific medical conditions, the majority of manufacturers have not been able to turn these into unambiguously successful nutraceutical *end-products*.

What seems to emerge from the experiences of the past years, however, is that *focus* is the key. There is no such thing as a generic 'nutraceutical opportunity' and, indeed, it is likely that the nutraceuticals market of the future will be composed of a multitude of niches. Vitamins and minerals are easily added to most existing food and drinks products, but to even begin to exploit the promise of incremental revenues that many feel the nutraceutical concept holds, it will be necessary to identify and target those opportunities where functionality is key. In all other cases, manufacturers will find themselves in the impossible situation of having to satisfy consumer demand on a number of different levels.

Why is the demanding consumer of the 21st century satisfied with breath fresheners that come in only one or two flavours? At the same time, why have fruit yoghurts to which probiotic benefits have been added not been as successful as Yakult? Why is Red Bull so successful? The reason is that for breath fresheners, Yakult and even Red Bull the specific functionality, whether this be medical or lifestyle oriented, is the key selling point of the product, rather than an extra benefit. In many of the recent initiatives, manufacturers have tried to satisfy everyone in a broadly defined consumer group and ended up not satisfying anyone. Instead, it is necessary to identify specific consumer segments that have such a high level of concern about a specific problem that a type of functionality that addresses that problem has absolute priority over any other product benefit.

Second, these success stories involve products that focus on delivering a functional benefit by supporting or complementing a consumption occasion, rather than trying to replace parts of it. They dovetail on the established consumption patterns. By being non-intrusive, these products therefore do not have to fight the battle for fickle consumer tastes. Although less apparent, this is even the case for a product such as Red Bull. An estimated 25–30% of Red Bull GmbH's 100 million litres 1999 sales is attributed to use as a vodka mixer.

The key is making sure the nutraceutical product is able to play on its strengths, its functionality, without getting into a multi-front marketing battle that is very difficult to win. The success of dietary supplements and quasi-supplements such as Yakult is testament to this fact. The real nutraceutical opportunity lies in developing complementary products that focus first and foremost on delivering a functional benefit – not food products with extra, secondary benefits.

17 Complementary and alternative medicines

PATRICIA TAN Interbrand

St John's wort is a herb commonly used to alleviate mild depression. In addition to depression, it is also said to relieve nerve pain, seasonal affective disorder and panic attacks. With a history and mythology that dates back almost 2000 years, St John's wort is widely used in Europe. In Germany, where the herb is listed in the *German Drug Codex*, approved as a medicine in the Commission E monographs and licensed as a standard medicinal tea infusion, doctors write three million prescriptions annually for the herbal remedy; it outsells Prozac by more than ten to one.[1]

St John's wort gained popularity in the USA in the early 1990s. Depression as a condition received widespread coverage when Prozac, an antidepressant by Eli Lilly, was released in 1987. Riding on a wave of popular interest, sales of St John's wort flourished. By 1998, American consumers were spending a projected US$ 400 million on the herb.[2]

How can the astronomical rise in popularity of this herbal remedy be explained? St John's wort and other herbal remedies are part of a broad range of therapeutic modalities loosely defined under the umbrella term 'complementary and alternative medicines'. In this chapter, the phrase 'alternative medicine' will be used to denote this spectrum of practices, each based on a healing philosophy quite different from the other, and quite distinct from conventional medicine. As the case of St John's wort demonstrates, consumers and some doctors regard certain alternative medicine products as viable alternatives to pharmaceutical drugs. Alternative medicine remedies capture market share and the trust of patients, however, in a manner very different to that of conventional medicine.

In Chapter 16 Hugo Ehrnreich addressed functional foods that aim to boost health benefits in general. Alternative medicine products and nutraceuticals clearly share much common ground, but this chapter will specifically address over-the-counter (OTC) alternative medicine therapeutic remedies, which present the consumer with an alternative to conventional medicine.

This chapter does not attempt to prove the efficacy or reliability of alternative medicine in general, or to fully explain any modality in particular. Instead, it focuses on what the different types of alternative medicine collectively have in common in the eyes of the general public that attracts their interest. How have these products shored up credibility and established a loyal and growing following? The answer lies in the different *public faces* that alternative medicine and conventional medicine present to the consumer. A close examination of the salient drivers of OTC alternative medicine products shows clearly that the values of alternative medicine are often presented as polar opposites to those of conventional medicine, and it is these values which have resonated with the public. The result is burgeoning sales.

Alternative medicine in the marketplace

In the USA, alternative medicine is defined as a practice that is not currently an accepted part of conventional medicine – that is, therapies which are not taught widely in medical schools, not generally used in hospitals and often not reimbursed by medical insurance. Nevertheless, its popularity is rising. In 1999, over 83 million Americans embraced alternative medicine.[3]

In Europe, several types of alternative medicine, such as herbal therapy, have gained much greater acceptance. In Germany, over 80% of all German physicians prescribe herbal remedies and approximately 40% of all these prescriptions are reimbursed by state medical insurance. And certain forms of alternative medicine, such as herbal therapy, are taught in medical schools as a matter of course.[4]

The alternative medicine industry commands an ever-increasing share of consumer spending on personal healthcare, to the tune of over US$ 27 billion a year in the USA.[5] Herbal therapy, in particular, is a real growth area. In recent years, sales of herbal products alone amounted to over US$ 1.5 billion in sales in the USA, and US$ 6 billion in the European Union.[6]

The majority of leading companies producing herbal remedies is located in Germany, France, Italy and Switzerland. The increasing popularity of such products has been recognized by most major pharmaceutical firms, resulting in a spate of acquisitions in the last decade (Table 17.1), as well as in collaborations between large pharmaceutical firms with smaller specialist firms to produce specific herbal lines.[7]

TABLE 17.1

Acquisitions of phytomedicine companies by multinational pharmaceutical firms

Multinational pharmaceutical companies	Phytomedicine/herbal remedy company (country of origin)
American Home Products	Dr Much (Germany)
Boehringer Ingelheim	Pharmaton (Switzerland) Quest (Canada)
Boots	Kanold (Germany)
Bausch and Lomb	Dr Mann (Germany)
Degussa	Asta Medica (Germany)
Fujisawa	Kinge (Germany)
Johnson & Johnson/Merck Sharp & Dohme	Woelm Pharma (Germany)
Pfizer	Mack (Germany)
Rhône-Poulenc Rorer	Natterrman (Germany)
Sanofi	Plantorgan (Germany)
Searle	Heumann (Germany)
SmithKline Beecham	Fink (Germany)
Solvay	Kali Chemie (Germany)

Source: Jörg Grünwald, *The European Phytomedicines Market: Figures, Trends, Analyses* [8]

Range of alternative medicines

This section will sketch the contours of this vast heterogeneous field to provide a backdrop to the following examination of alternative medicine's success. According to the National Center for Complementary and Alternative Medicine (NCCAM) associated with the US National Institute of Health (NIH), alternate therapy practices may be grouped within five major domains:

1. alternative medical systems
2. mind–body interventions
3. biologically based treatments
4. manipulative and body-based methods
5. energy therapies.

The OTC remedies examined in this chapter stem from several of these domains, such as homeopathic formulations (alternative medical systems) and herbal and vitamin pills (biologically based treatments). It is worth noting that consumers turn to non-conventional therapies for more than minor complaints. The American Cancer Society reported in July 2000 that 99.3% of 453 cancer patients surveyed had heard of some form of alternative therapy, and that 83.3% of those had used at least one form of those therapies, often in combination with the conventional therapy recommended by their doctors. Of these, 63% had used vitamin or herbal supplements. In the UK, Edzard Ernst from the University of Exeter has carried out similar research to find that 30% of cancer sufferers use some form of alternative medicine — a lower but still significant proportion.[9] These statistics are especially impressive in the light of the fact that most of these expenditures are personally borne by the consumers, and not by insurance.

Mainstreaming the alternative

Alternative medicine has broken the mould of obscurity and appeals to a broad spectrum of users today. The rising number of users has spurred the conventional medical community into action. In the USA, where alternative medicine does not enjoy official recognition as in Europe, the medical establishment has had to address this consumer trend. In 1992, the Office of Alternative Medicine (since 1999, NCCAM) was created within the auspices of the NIH to investigate and document the benefits and potential risks of various types of alternative medicine. After extensively questioning the efficacy of different modalities of alternative medicine in its journal, the American medical establishment went on record on 17 March 1999 to advocate the scientific study of alternative therapies out of a concern with the growing usage among patients.[10]

As conventional medical science turns its attention and research tools to alternative medicine, an analogous convergence to scientific precision can be observed in certain lines of alternative medicine remedies. Consumers are often persuaded that a remedy has been scientifically tested, or that the quality of the ingredients in a product reaches pharmaceutical standards.

The usefulness of scientific objectivity in instilling trust in consumers is thus not completely ignored by the alternative medicine community. Practitioners of herbal medicine, for example, organize to publish journals that follow the peer-review protocol of mainstream medical publications. *Herbal-Gram*, published by the American Botanical Council and the Herb Research Foundation, two non-profit organizations dedicated to educating the public on the use of herbs in the USA, is one such publication. The journal's advisory board includes medical researchers, ethnobotanists, medical herbalists, biochemists and physicians. For those forms of alternative medicine that welcome scientific investigation and regulation in order to raise the general standard of care, their differences with the medical community lie in the domain of timescale and feasibility.

Strict scientific standards for new drugs demand stringent testing and bio-medical explanations. But, as members of the European Herbal Practitioners Association argue, such prerequisites are impractical with respect to herbal remedies for two main reasons. First, herbs that have been in use for years are evidently safe, as long as they are handled knowledgeably. Research should focus on efficacy and dosage. Second, a complete investigation takes time and money. Requiring each herb to be investigated along the lines of a pharmaceutical drug would effectively put most herbal practitioners out of business. Instead, they advocate the notion of 'well-established medicinal use', and focus their calls for regulation on achieving consistency in service and products. Even seasoned herbalists acknowledge that the latter is notoriously difficult to regulate, as constituents and potency of herbs differ according to the grower, soil and harvest conditions, and method of extraction and storage. Reliable sources are thus extremely important.

Indeed, there is a much greater variation in the quality control and regulation of alternative medicine products compared to that of the pharmaceutical industry. European herbalists, for example, survey the American market with great caution. In the case of St John's wort, the herb is still poorly regulated in many markets despite its runaway sales success. In the USA and UK, St John's wort is available in different concentrations and forms: liquid alcohol extracts (the most commonly used in Germany), capsules of extracts or ground-up plants, teas, drinks and other 'functional foods'.[11] In Europe, a Working Party on Herbal Medicinal Products established by the European Agency for the Evaluation of Medicinal Products (EMEA) has already brought together representatives from industry, scientific societies and health professional and consumer organizations to determine test procedures, acceptance criteria and drug preparations for herbal medicinal products.[12] No such US regulation exists as yet. European herbalists are therefore concerned by the variable qualities of herbal products available for sale in the USA.[13]

Consumers' response to the lack of regulation in the USA, however, provides an important lesson for manufacturers. First, the difficulty faced by other practitioners in gaining official recognition appears to the consumer to be the result of a guild-like protectionistic mentality of the medical community. Since some forms of alternative medicine such as chiropracy are recognized and regulated and others not, the image of doctors guarding their economic and intellectual monopoly over health is further exacerbated. Many consumers would welcome regulation, internally or externally determined, as a welcome step in the right direction. Second, consumers tend to see no conflict in using both alternative medicine and conventional medicine. Instead, such an integrated perspective on health represents a synergistic partnership between old wisdom and modern technology. Third, the variable quality of products on sale does not deter them from using these remedies. Instead, they seek endorsements and recommendations of reliable brands.

Granted, alternative medicine is certainly a more ambiguous offering to the consumer, in contrast to the medical and pharmaceutical industries, bound as they are by rigorous testing. What are the main factors that convince consumers to try alternative medicine? What does alternative medicine offer consumers that conventional treatments cannot?

A consumer embraces alternative medicine because these alternative philosophies of health and well-being complement his or her belief system and outlooks on life. A 1998 study by JA Austin published in the *Journal of the American Medical Association* found that the majority of alternative medicine users are not dissatisfied with conventional medicine, but combine conventional and alternative therapies to formulate their own integrated healthcare. Austin concluded that those surveyed regarded 'these health care alternatives to be more congruent with their own values, beliefs, and philosophical orientations towards health and life'.[14]

Alternative medicine thus reaches consumers at an emotional level. As Tom Blackett observed in the first chapter of this book, 'at the heart of all brands lies a set of values'. The OTC alternative medicine industry is a cogent application of this theory, as well as a relevant catalyst for the discussion on whether, and, to what extent, emotional appeal can be employed in an industry as important as that of healthcare.

Back to the future: innovation versus tradition

How does the consumer compare pharmaceuticals and alternative medicine products? The pharmaceutical industry is characterized by intense research, often at the cutting edge of biomedical science. More than ever, the development of new drugs is intimately tied to basic discoveries involving the nature of disease or how the human body functions and reacts. Vast amounts of resources, time and expertise underlie the development of each new drug, a fact that justifies the patent system in allowing companies to recoup the initial investment of basic research. In contrast, many types of alternative medicine owe their existence to a distant past. Their reintroduction into modern use is

a sort of recycling of an earlier wisdom, occasionally repackaged with a
modern delivery system (pills, standardized extracts and so on). Traditional
medical systems currently in the marketplace include traditional Chinese
medicine, Ayurveda (the Indian 'science of life'), Native American, Aborig-
inal, African, Middle Eastern, Tibetan, Central and South American cultures.
By drawing upon a sense of ancient tradition, these types of alternative medicine appeal to consumers by representing a body of knowledge and practice
extending far beyond current scientific hypotheses.

Proponents of conventional medicine are not necessarily entirely at odds
with traditional medicine. Most doctors and scientists are well aware that
many modern drug therapies have their roots in traditional botanical remedies.
Aspirin, for example, was first derived from willow bark, penicillin from
mould, quinine from the cinchona bark, and several cancer drugs from the
rosy periwinkle. Taxol, an FDA approved cancer drug first available in the
USA in 1994, comes from the bark of the Pacific yew tree. Nevertheless, these
drugs are acknowledged and embraced by the medical establishment because
they have proved their efficacy in the same battery of tests to which any pharmaceutical drug must be subject. In most cases, their effects on the human
body can be physiologically and chemically explained. In other words, traditional medicines are regarded as a source material for modern science to
explain and verify through its own criteria of rational scientific explanation,
statistical significance and peer review. As stated in a *New England Journal
of Medicine* editorial:

> What most sets alternative medicine apart ... is that it has not been scientifically
> tested and its advocates largely deny the need for such testing. By testing, we
> mean the marshalling of rigorous evidence of safety and efficacy, as required by
> the Food and Drug Administration (FDA) for the approval of drugs and by the best
> peer-reviewed medical journals for the publication of research reports ... Alterna-
> tive medicine also distinguishes itself by an ideology that largely ignores biologic
> mechanisms, often disparages modern science, and relies on what are purported to
> be ancient practices and natural remedies ... fervently promoted despite not only
> the lack of good clinical evidence of effectiveness, but the presence of a rationale
> that violates fundamental scientific laws – surely a circumstance that requires
> more, rather than less, evidence.[15]

If this medical opinion considers alternative medicine to be anachronistic, the
general public regards the pharmaceutical industry and alternative medicine to
constitute the poles of human knowledge. The pharmaceutical industry represents a forward-looking, no-holds barred frontier mentality that probes further
and often with increasingly expensive technology into human biology at an

ever more microscopic or even molecular level. Alternative medicine, on the other hand, does not derive its legitimacy from scientific explanation, but from the very fact of its longevity.

In branding, a sense of a noble heritage can be a persuasive driver of sales. Notable examples in the bodycare and healthcare market that capitalize on a sense of nostalgia include the new SK-II brand of skincare products. The brand's history reads:

> For almost a generation, Japanese women have known a secret ... A Japanese monk visiting a sake brewery noticed that the brewery workers had extraordinarily soft and youthful hands. Even an elderly man with pronounced wrinkles on his face possessed the silky smooth hands of a young boy ... After a series of experiments a team of skincare scientists discovered the secret; a clear, nutrient-rich liquid that could be extracted during the yeast fermentation process. They named the liquid 'Pitera', which, over time, has become known as the 'Secret Key' to beautiful skin.

Herbal remedies and other alternative medicine therapies hold a similar mystique.

Furthermore, brands with well-managed histories are excellent candidates for brand extensions. In the same way that Coca-Cola now sells baseball caps, ginseng, once a rare and revered herb, has become ubiquitous, appearing in candies, face creams and sports drinks.

The healing arts versus the hard science of medicine

As already mentioned, the reliance on heritage as their primary assurance of efficacy does not preclude some types of alternative medicine to strive towards scientific objectivity. Other forms of alternative medicine, however, eschew the parameters of scientific proof. Rejecting the physiological principles of conventional medicine, they offer completely different healing philosophies. This is the case with many healing therapies based on theories of 'life force', such as many Chinese traditional and Ayurvedic treatments. Other holistic therapies, such as those based on the restoration of the innate harmony of the body, mind and spirit, resist the possibility of scientific examination because they lie outside accepted medical theory. Doctors and medical researchers are often frustrated by such responses to their calls for evidence-based clinical trials. Practitioners of those modalities stress the importance of tailoring treatment to each individual patient, rendering large, statistically significant experiments or double-blind trials impossible.

The complete redefinition of the body is not confined to traditional alternative medicine alone. Homeopathy is an unconventional Western system of healing, which has gained much prominence in Europe and the USA. Homeopathy is based on the principle of 'like cures like' – the symptoms of a disease are produced by substances in large doses, but cured by the same substances when administered in minute doses. Treatment thus consists of prescriptions of such greatly reduced concentration that the actual active ingredients would have absolutely negligible biochemical effects on the body. Practitioners of homeopathy argue that their remedies work differently from nutrients or drugs, and cannot be physiologically explained. In other words, modern science does not have the appropriate tools and techniques to evaluate the effects of homeopathy.

Scientists and doctors, trained to trust science, judge the completely different, but unverifiable, theories and practices of alternative medicine as profoundly inadequate. They are frustrated by what they perceive as a post-modernization of knowledge – a simultaneous scepticism and susceptibility to multiple claims of truth, such as the assertion that these systems evolved independently of and sometimes prior to the conventional biomedical approach. The irony is that the biomedical sciences have been one of the key fields in which old assumptions have been repeatedly broken over the last 25 years. In this way, biomedicine has contributed to the creation of a culture of change in which the public is more accustomed than ever to paradigm shifts in medicine, telecommunications, science and in their daily lives.

Natural versus new

Another factor behind alternative medicine's popularity is in the perception that these remedies are more natural than pharmaceutical drugs. Although many prescription and conventional OTC drugs are derived from natural sources such as botanicals, the extent to which they are processed and standardized removes all echoes of its origins. The ubiquitous forms of pharmaceuticals, coloured syrups, pills, capsules, skin patches and suppositories, all feel, look and taste synthetic. The recognizable form of many herbal remedies, such as teas and infusions, and the claim that these products are directly drawn from nature are attractive to consumers. After all, a brightly coloured pill capable of effecting significant physiological responses is for many people an impenetrable black box. Preparing and sipping a tea, no matter how unpalatable, is much less intimidating than popping such a tablet.

Consumers driven by this difference between alternative medicine and conventional medicine tend to equate nature with health, moving away from the increasing sophistication and complexity of the pharmaceutical industry. Moreover, many believe that active ingredients cannot always be fully isolated and reproduced in the proportions present in nature, making the consumption of herbal remedies au naturel especially beneficial. To a certain extent, herbalists concur:

> plant medicines invariably comprise a multiplicity of chemical components whose overall effect cannot simply be assumed by reference to perceived active constituents. In practice, apparently unimportant fractions of a plant may act in vivo to buffer or amplify the principal pharmacological characteristics of a plant.[16]

The propensity of these remedies to convey an impression of health as a direct result of their naturalness is largely a perceived rather than an actual reality; as already mentioned, herbal remedies in the form of infusions, teas or extracts vary greatly in potency. The claim that 'less artificial processing is better' is so popular that it even extends to the issue of preservatives or stabilizers, at the cost of possible degradation of effectiveness.

Much of this affinity for natural products stems from a popular backlash to the increasing syntheticization of modern life. Not only is 'choosing natural' an aesthetic and lifestyle choice, many consumers consider this a protective measure against the hazards of scientific progress, such as genetic modification, antibiotic abuse and drug side effects, which regularly hit the headlines with great furore.

Taken to an extreme, the naturalness of alternative medicine has also been proposed as a reason behind the pharmaceutical industry's reluctance to seriously consider natural remedies. In *The Melatonin Miracle*, for example, authors Regelson and Pierpaoli attribute pharmaceutical companies' reluctance to devote more resources to melatonin research to the difficulty of patenting a substance found in nature. Melatonin is a naturally occurring hormone produced by the pineal gland in the human body, and it has been widely marketed as a sleep regulator and alleviator of jet lag. Since companies cannot be assured of securing exclusive rights to melatonin, Regelson and Pierpaoli argue, the research necessary to have melatonin accepted as a pharmaceutical drug is economically unfeasible.

Regelson and Pierpaoli's point of view encapsulates the gap of understanding between members of the scientific community and practitioners of alternative medicine. The authors are respected scientists entrenched in the practice of researching patents. In contrast, alternative medicine organizations are lobbying not for alternative therapies products to be recognized as pharmaceutical drugs, but for a separate legislative niche within the framework of the current law for medicine.[17]

Channels: Rx, doctors or myself

Although Regelson and Pierpaoli's argument represents an extreme point of view, it highlights a popularly shared sentiment – that pharmaceutical firms are basically self-serving organizations driven by profit. The extent to which the revenues from new drugs must cover the extensive research and development necessary to bring a novel product to market is often lightly understood. The issue of the rising cost of new drugs, on the other hand, is a popular policy topic in contexts as diverse as development, social welfare or health insurance.

Furthermore, patients are becoming increasingly sceptical with not only the pharmaceutical industry, but also the medical community as a whole. In the USA, many health consumers believe that health maintenance organizations are more concerned with the bottom line than with their well-being. In the UK, the reputation of the National Health Service is repeatedly bruised by allegations of medical misdiagnoses, poor management and long waiting lists for treatment. These are all catalysts for public discontent. The increasing number of disillusioned doctors who leave the system bolsters patients' frustrations. Their faith in medical science is eroded further by the inexplicability of certain diseases and the medical community's reluctance to admit readily and honestly to the limits of their ability in the face of such problems.

All this has spurred many individuals to assume greater responsibility for their own well-being. In fact, the Austin Report showed that exclusive consumers of alternative medicine tended to be better educated in general,[18] suggesting that these individuals are ready to question the authority of their doctors, and are prepared to take their health into their own hands.

The trend for patients seeking other sources of health advice is facilitated by the ease of access to product information, products and services, a real point of departure from many patients' experiences of standard healthcare. In terms of obtaining pharmaceutical drugs, for example, the doctor is a necessary middleman for prescription medicines. Many patients also only learn of the array of conventional OTC remedies through their family physicians. These products are then purchased from clinics and pharmacies. A few are available in supermarkets and convenience stores.

Alternative medicine products, on the other hand, enjoy a greater and freer range of distribution channels. Mainstream vitamin brands such as Centrum (Whitehall Robins) and One-A-Day (Bayer) now have extensive herbal lines. As stated in the introduction to this chapter, multinational pharmaceutical firms have also bought smaller companies producing alternative medicine remedies. As a result, alternative medicine products need not be obtained directly from the relevant practitioner. They can be found wherever conventional OTC drugs and vitamins are sold.

Furthermore, alternative medicine remedies are often available where conventional drugs are not. Alternative medicine spills over into the food, sports and beauty industry, and can be found in health food stores, health clubs and beauty centres. Not only does its wide availability in these locations boost alternative medicine's image as 'natural' and 'safe', the multiplicity of channels moves alternative medicine beyond the context of illness. Alternative medicine's relevance to consumers is expanded through its associations with a multifaceted and textured image of individual health and well-being in general. As medical intervention is more clearly and rigidly defined through regulation, such stretching of the boundaries is more difficult for pharmaceuticals.

The different ways in which alternative medicine and conventional medicines reach the final consumer are reflected in the evolution of healthcare sites on the net. Two main trends are developing. Medical websites have realized that an exclusive focus on end-consumers is not financially viable, and many have shifted their attention towards attracting doctors, since they are the traditional medium through which people obtained their medicines. As Scott Gottlieb summarizes in *American Medical News*:

> What's unique about healthcare is that consumer opinion never really counted for much. Even with the advent of direct-to-consumer advertising, ubiquitous medical information, and the empowered patient, most clinical decisions are still made out of reach of patients.[19]

Gottlieb employed this observation to explain the advent of doctor-focused products such as ePocrates.com, and why conventional healthcare sites such as WebMD and MedUnite now vie for doctors' rather than patients' attention. His explanation also suggests the diminished role of the patient in conventional medicine.

On the other hand, interest in alternative medicine is growing exponentially: independent surveys from JD Powers show that approximately 30% of all Internet health searches are for alternative medicine. OnHealth, an alternative health website which categorizes its products and advice in themes such as 'Vitamins and Herbs' and 'Holistic Woman', clocked up 3.2 million unique users in December 1999 alone, a 593% increase as compared to the same month in the previous year. More tellingly, OnHealth, which enjoys fixed placement in the 'Alternative Medicine' category of Yahoo! Health and other popular portals, was nominated e-healthcare leader for the year 2000 by Media Metrix and PC Data. This increasing enthusiasm and interest reflects consumers' confidence and determination to view their health as a matter of their own decision making. Furthermore, this trend can be translated into purchasing patterns.

The top six online stores selling alternative medicine products also occupied the top six positions for one-stop health and wellness shopping and vitamin purchasing for the year 2000, according to gomez.com (Table 17.2). Even more telling is the performance of these companies in prescription drug sales. Four of these six consistently occupied top positions for these sales as well, suggesting that consumers see no conflict in integrating conventional medicine with alternative medicine in their own healthcare regimes. As a result, the pharmacies that embraced an integrated perspective on health performed well in the highly competitive and volatile world of e-commerce.

Some sources of conventional medical advice, such as the American Cancer Society, recognize the increasing popularity of alternative medicine and address this trend by encouraging patients to consult their doctors if they are contemplating using any particular modality. Consumers, however, tend not to discuss these issues with their physicians. Many do not see their physicians often enough to establish such a consultative relationship. Research in 1990 by Dr David Eisenberg from the Harvard School of Medicine found that more visits were paid to alternative care practitioners than to all regular primary care physicians combined. Many are also reluctant to bring up the issue of alternative medicine with their physicians as they anticipate a negative and dismissive response.[20] Patients are aware that, in spite of increasing interest in alternative medicine, many sections of the medical community remain dubious. This is apparent even in Germany, where some forms of alternative medicine have gained official recognition and federal support. Voices

TABLE 17.2

Comparison of sales of top six online stores

Company	Health and wellness (rank)			Prescription medicine (rank)		
	Alternative therapy	One stop	Vitamin	First time buyer	Advice seeker	Out of pocket
Drugemporium.com	6	3	6	1	2	1
Drugstore.com	2	1	2	4	5	2
More.com	4	6	1	6	3	6
Mothernature.com	1	4	3			
PlanetRx.com	5	2	5	2	1	5
Selfcare.com	3	5	4			

Source: www.gomez.com

of dissent, such as that of this German physician quoted in the American Medical Association's *Archives of Dermatology*, are common:

> When deliberating on the essence of alternative medicine we should simultane-
> ously reflect on the intellectual and moral basis of regular medicine ... (1) alter-
> native and regular medicine are speaking different languages; ... the paradigm of
> regular medicine is rational thinking [whereas] the paradigm of alternative medi-
> cine is irrational thinking; (5) the present popularity of alternative medicine can be
> explained by romanticism; ... (7) alternative medicine and evidence-based medi-
> cine are mutually exclusive; (8) the placebo effect is an important factor in regular
> medicine and the exclusive therapeutic principle of alternative medicine; ... The
> fact that alternative methods are presently an integral part of medicine as taught at
> German universities, as well as of the physician's fee schedule, represents a collec-
> tive aberration of mind that hopefully will last for only a short time.[21]

Finally, some individuals turn to alternative medicine products precisely because the ease of self-medication eliminates the need to visit a doctor for a prescription. This is a major contributor to the sales success of St John's wort in the USA. Most pharmaceutical antidepressants are prescription drugs. Many who self-medicate on St John's wort are reluctant to see a doctor to discuss their conditions before they can obtain a prescription. Self-diagnosis and self-medication have appealed to many. As a popular remedy for mild depression, the ready availability of the herb is a boon to those who are reluc-tant to visit their doctor for a condition that still carries a certain degree of social stigma.

In addition to the arm's length at which doctors are sometimes held, much family health is dispensed through one care provider in the family – a trip to the doctor is often preceded by a consultation with the mother or wife.[22] Women make up to 80% of healthcare decisions and 60% of the purchases for themselves and their families. The ease of self-medication and widespread availability of alternative therapy products ensure their place as stand-by remedies in the home medicine cabinet. A 1998 Cyberdialog study showed that women search the Web for health information at nearly twice the rate compared to men, both for acute situations as well as for information on general health maintenance. It has been suggested that women are more engaged in health issues because they are confronted with unique and varying sets of health concerns at each stage of life, ranging from puberty, fertility, pregnancy, infant care, family medicine, paediatrics, menopause and ageing. These issues certainly also affect men; even in this day and age, however, women's responsibilities for both themselves and their loved ones, as well as the significantly greater impact these life changes have on most women's lives, mean that they are more active information-gatherers than men. This significant fact for OTC drug sales, both conventional and alternative, is not lost on OTC retailers such as Selfcare.com, a leading online health and well-being store. Recognizing that women are generally the ones who buy non-prescription healthcare products for men and children as well as for themselves, the site is designed for gendered appeal even though the range of products for sale is not confined to products for women.

Word of mouth and recommendations

The discussion in this chapter so far has focused on the comparative strengths of alternative medicine over conventional medicines in the eyes of the consumer. Alternative medicine, however, benefits from a particular driver in boosting its credibility and popularity not typically enjoyed by conventional medicine.

By the very fact of their appearance on the market, conventional drugs are expected to work safely. While the public relies on the doctor's advice and regulatory endorsement for assurance of safety, such expectation is not as prevalent for alternative medicine across the board. Instead, alternative medicines, even where they are regulated, tend to gain a legitimacy and a following primarily via word of mouth and testimonials. Doctors constantly point out that individual case studies are no substitutes for controlled scientific trials, double-blind testing and peer reviews. This argument is true, but rational.

In contrast to the measured advice of the doctor, testimonials are often sincere and fervent. The NCCAM often receives individual testimonials about successful treatment or a particular healer, and those who approach the Center with ideas for alternative medical cures are often eager to have a research protocol formulated to test the method or cure. People recommend not for monetary gain or out of professional duty, but out of a genuine desire to share their experiences and to help others – this excitement appeals to the consumer at the emotional, rather than cerebral level.

Word of mouth is not only an effective way to catalyse interest and conviction in a product; it is also a potent influence that propagates itself organically. The marketing muscle of testimonials sustains a vibrant publishing industry around alternative medicine. Since the definition of a testimonial is that of individual experience, testimonials can be freely made in public. They are the mainstays of countless books, magazines and journals, and due to the lack of jargon, they make engaging reading.

This showcasing of new treatments is less widespread for conventional medicine.[23] Discussion of new drug therapies tends to take place in specialized medical and scientific journals that never reach the consumers. The

Lancet, the *Journal of the American Medical Association* and numerous other academic journals may be compared to the physician's trade journal. The extensive opaque medical jargon is also a barrier to public understanding, let alone public enthusiasm. Newspapers and general magazines recognize this difficulty, and need science and medical writers to decode thematically and linguistically medical jargon for the layman. In most cases, unfortunately, news about drugs only reaches the general public through the press in the case of failures, especially catastrophic ones.

The apotheosis of all these elements of alternative medicine's public image perhaps finds its form in the books written by doctors who have undergone a sort of Damascene conversion to embrace alternative medicine after successful careers of scientific scepticism in medicine. Their books bring together the vitality of personal testimonials, the popular appeal of alternative medicine and the authority of their medical qualifications. One of the most successful authors in this genre has been Dr Andrew Weil, a Harvard trained medical doctor turned persuasive advocate for holistic medicine. The success of Dr Weil, currently the Associate Director of the Division of Social Perspectives in Medicine at the College of Medicine at the University of Arizona, bears many of the hallmarks of alternative medicine's success today. Despite his training, Dr Weil has eschewed much Western medicine, regarding it as an interference to the body's natural systems for self-repair and healing. His book *Spontaneous Healing: How to Discover and Enhance your Body's Natural Ability to Maintain and Heal Itself*, punctuated with vivid accounts of extraordinary cases of drastic spontaneous healing, hit the *New York Times* best seller list upon its release.

Popular culture

If word of mouth and testimonials are important sales drivers, the strongest recommendations must surely come from personalities to whom consumers already aspire. Both the pharmaceutical and alternative medicine industries have a host of celebrity advocates who espouse the efficacy of their remedies. Bob Dole's endorsement of Viagra shortly after losing the Presidential elections was one of the first of its kind. 'Let the Dance Begin' still rings a bell in America years after the advertisement ran. Other examples include Nolan Ryan (Alleve), John Madden (Tinactin), Kim Alexis (Monistat), Joan Lunden (Clarityn) and Lance Armstrong (Bristol-Meyer Squibb cancer drugs). Although direct-to-consumer (DTC) marketing of pharmaceuticals is on the rise, alternative medicine endorsements gain a popular voice in more than paid advertisements such as Annie Potts' Herbal One-a-Day supplements.

They are woven into critiques of our everyday lives. The rocketing sale of melatonin for weary business travellers, for example, is often cited as a proof of a global economy with no respect for geography or time zones. They appear as emblems of popular culture, such as in Woody Allen's *Celebrity*, in which Kenneth Branagh's character purportedly 'loses the girl' when he does not have Echinacea on demand, suggesting the herb's status as *the* herbal product that Hollywood cannot live without. Few pharmaceuticals have enjoyed such cult status. Prozac and Viagra are notable exceptions.

Opportunities for branding in alternative medicine

This chapter on alternative medicine has attempted to examine how it has carved itself a niche in the healthcare market. As a category, it has employed many of the strongest elements of branding to differentiate its therapies from conventional medicine, distancing itself from the criticism of the medical and scientific community, and aligning itself with the evolving lifestyle changes of consumers. It is worth noting, however, that *within* the general category of alternative medicine products, branding is still fairly weak.

Most herbal remedies and supplements are ingredient focused. Herbal remedies, for example, tend to be marketed through their main active ingredients, such as ginseng, gingko biloba and evening primrose oil. Many alternative medicine products thus resemble their generic pharmaceutical counterparts rather than a new branded drug. Price, size and the attractiveness of the packaging, rather than the brand itself, are often the main differentiators of the products on offer.

The above observation most accurately reflects the state of the alternative medicine product market in the USA and Europe today. In regions where indigenous traditional medicine has as strong a claim on the local healthcare market as conventional medicine, branded remedies do offer unique propositions to consumers. This can be observed, for example, in many parts of Asia, where traditional medicine co-exists healthily with conventional medicine. Popular traditional remedies include Po Chai Pills for gastrointestinal complaints, Pi Par Kao for coughing and sore throats and Gan Mao Ling for influenza. Rather than offering single herbal extracts, these products are value added by boasting herbal mixtures formulated to treat specific ailments. In this way, they compete directly with products such as Pepto-Bismol, Robitussin and Thera-Med respectively. In fact, these products often sit side by side on the shelves of pharmacies. One of the most successful herbal mix products in terms of sales and strong branding is Tiger Balm.

Tiger Balm

Tiger Balm (Figure 17.1) is a topical analgesic marketed as an external OTC medication for a spectrum of minor pains such as headaches, rheumatism, arthritic pain, muscle sprains and strains. According to its promotional material, it also relieves insect bites and even flatulence. As a cure-all for so many common complaints, Tiger Balm is a staple in the medicine cabinet of most Asian homes, and has proved popular globally.

Manufactured by Haw Par Healthcare, Tiger Balm's geographical presence is impressive. It is produced in eight countries and sold in over 100 countries in all five continents. While capitalizing on its Asian heritage, it has also successfully broken cultural boundaries to become a truly international brand.

The brand's history is cleverly positioned. It does not claim to be an 'ancient Chinese medication', but a modern efficacious medication that draws upon the wisdom of Imperial Chinese sources. Its formulation is attributed to Aw Chu Kin, a herbalist from the Hakka province of China who emigrated to Rangoon in the late 19th century. Observing a need for a balm that was easy to store, transport and use, Aw brought his knowledge of Chinese herbal medicine to bear upon this local problem, and created Tiger Balm. The main active ingredients of Tiger Balm are menthol, camphor, cajuput, clove and cassia oils.

Tiger Balm has won international appeal by highlighting the universal elements of the brand. First, by sinking its roots in both China and Rangoon, the brand is not specifically Chinese, but generally Asian. This allows Tiger

Figure 17.1 Tiger Balm

Balm to be co-opted by almost every community in North and South East Asia as a 'local brand'. At the same time, it maintains sufficient exoticism to titillate the non-Asian market. Second, the altruistic beginnings of this medication are highlighted. The brand history stresses that Aw was motivated to treat his patients 'the best way he knew'. It was not he, but his commercially minded son, who aggressively marketed Tiger Balm worldwide after his father's death. The community-spirited origin of the brand contrasts starkly with the image of modern pharmaceutical firms. Third, the brand name and logo, which features a leaping tiger, is evocative of both Asia and general strength. The grace and tenacity of the tiger is a powerful image which is used repeatedly in advertisements and packaging.

At the same time, Haw Par Healthcare has complemented its brand development with the foresight to protect aggressively all aspects of the brand identity. In addition to owning the 'Tiger Balm' trade mark in every country in which it is marketed, the company has protected the image, name and reference to 'tiger' in both Class 3 and Class 5 in each country. This means that the Tiger Balm brand is insulated from competitors' attempts to capitalize on the vivid tiger symbol. In this way, the brand enjoys an unambiguous public persona.

The Tiger Balm brand successfully maintains a multifaceted persona by retaining its core values: it is a trusted remedy that enables users to get on with their lives unimpeded by pain. Significantly, Haw Par Healthcare has constantly updated and localized these values. Tiger Balm closely identifies itself with traditional Asian (not just Chinese) martial arts by sponsoring martial arts tournaments. It has reinterpreted the public-spirited beginnings of the product into a concept of ethical pharmaceuticals. Today, Tiger Balm is a major sponsor of tiger conservation projects in the UK (Woburn Safari Park), Singapore (The Night Safari), Australia (Melbourne Zoo) and the USA (the Global Tiger Campaign of the Endangered Species Project).

The popularity of Tiger Balm has gained a momentum of its own. The Internet, for example, is peppered with testimonials such as this:

> Tiger Balm IS the best stuff in the world. I was turned onto the stuff ten years ago and have since then become a 'tiger balm junkie.' I use it for muscle aches, headaches, sinuses, inflamed joints and for warm hands and feet. I buy a lot of the stuff because I am always giving it away to the people that I've turned on to it.

Personal recommendation is perhaps the strongest evidence of a successful brand.

At the same time, Tiger Balm has actively pursued extending the brand's image, availability and product line. From the martial arts arena, Tiger Balm is broadening its sportive image through endorsements by sports celebrities such as American football legend Joe Montana and tennis star Michael Chang. Chang proved a cogent choice for Tiger Balm. His pan-Asian appeal, coupled with his international success on the ATP tour, mirrored Tiger Balm's distinct, yet global, presence as an Asian brand. Television advertisements featuring Chang were aired in Hong Kong, Taiwan, Thailand, and Germany.[24]

Tiger Balm has simultaneously cultivated its multifaceted image through careful selection of distribution channels. As a ubiquitous everyday product, Tiger Balm is available in convenience stores and supermarkets. As a specialists sports aid, it is available in pro-shops, health clubs and sports stores. And finally, as an exotic momento from Asia, it is available in duty-free shops in Asia and on board several Asian airlines.

The huge value that can reside in a brand itself is well represented by the example of Tiger Balm. In addition to the original Tiger Balm, at least five other associated products have been developed successfully as brand extensions. Tiger Liniment, popular with the elderly, is a more liquid formulation for covering large surfaces. For the athletic user, there is Tiger Muscle Rub, a pre-exercise warm-up rub to prepare muscles for strenuous activity. Tiger Balm External Pain Relieving Medicated Plaster is a skin patch impregnated with Tiger Balm Formulation. It delivers more sustained relief while protecting clothing from any residue. The martial arts community favours Tiger Balm Red, an extra-strength formula befitting the tough strong image of its users. In contrast, Tiger Balm Soft, a gentler ointment, with a lighter fragrance and softer texture, is evidently aimed at the female consumer. When considering these brand extensions, it is important to note that these new products do not overly cannibalize the market share of the original product. Each of these appeals to a particular subsection of the Tiger Balm consumer market, and addresses a specific use. As an all-round topical analgesic, Tiger Balm Original is still the family favourite.

Conclusion

As mentioned in the introduction to this chapter, multinational pharmaceutical firms have already realized the growth potential of the alternative medicine industry, especially in the field of herbal medicines. Like pharmaceuticals in general, there is real opportunity for stronger branding. The feasibility of such success is demonstrated by brands such as Tiger Balm. The example of Tiger Balm, however, demonstrates that non-conventional remedies need not, and indeed should not, claim the status of pharmaceutical drugs.

Alternative medicine's greatest strength is that it focuses on health rather than on illness. Unlike conventional medicine, alternative medicine products address the concerns of both the 'worried well' and the 'genuinely sick'.[25] This enables alternative medicine users to be redefined as consumers rather than patients, as individuals actively making decisions about their personal lifestyles. This is a strong market position that should be exploited, most fruitfully by heeding the fact that alternative medicine products constitute a separate category of health products distinct from pharmaceuticals. The alternative perspectives on individual well-being as encapsulated by alternative medicine are the building blocks to strong elastic relationships with the health consumer.

Notes

1   Jane E. Brody 'Personal Health: About St John's Wort', *New York Times*, 10 September 1997.

2   Maryalice Yakutchik, 'On a Quest for Herbal Info, Who's Got the Answers?', *Nutrition Business Journal*, 16 November 1998.

3   Robert Bazell, NBC news, 20 December 1999.

4   Jörg Grünwald, 'The European Phytomedicines Market: Figures, Trends, Analyses', *HerbalGram*, 1995.

5   David M. Eisenberg, et al., 'Trends in Alternative Medicine Use in the United States, 1990–7', *Journal of the American Medical Association*, **280**(18), 11 November 1998.

6   Grünwald, 1995, source IMS 1994.

7   For example, Ciba daughter Zyma sells a special line called 'Valverde', produced by Swiss phytomedicines company Zeller AG. Grünwald, 1995.

8   The acquisition of Madaus (Germany) by Sandoz was also discussed but eventually rejected.

9   Edzard Ernst, *Cancer*, 15 August 1998.

10   See especially *Journal of the American Medical Association*, **280**(18), 11 November 1998.

11   Linda Ciampa, 'Herbal Antidepressant Use can Pose Problems', CNN.com, 25 July 2000.

12   Minutes of the Meeting of the European Medicines Evaluation Agency Working Party on Herbal Medicinal Products, 28–29 October 1999, 18 November 1999. EMEA/HMPWP/32/99.

13   In the USA, most alternative medicine products fall under the regulation of the 1994 Dietary Supplement Health and Education Act which defines 'dietary supplements' as a special category between foods and medicines which are 'safe within a broad range of intake', and safety problems within the supplements are relatively rare. There are no labelling guidelines.

     In Australia, the 1989 Therapeutic Goods Act and the 1990 Therapeutic Goods Regulations specifically exempt bulk liquids (herbal tinctures and extracts) from registration, if herbal practitioners dispense them. A registration for herbal products is also in force;

herbal products that are 'listed' must contain herbs known to be safe and data concerning traditional herbal use plays a major part in validating such products.

In Canada, the Standing Committee on Health has recommended a new category of products designated 'natural health products' (NHPs), proposing that NHPs be treated neither as foods nor pharmaceutical products but licensed as an intermediary category. An office of natural health products was created in 1999 to be responsible for the regulation of NHPs.

The Position Paper 'Alternative Licensing for Herbal Medicine-like Products in the European Union', March 1999, European Herbal Practitioners Association covers the different regulatory systems in the European Union prior to the October 1999 decisions of the EMEA Working Party on Herbal Medicinal Products.

14   JA Austin, 'Why Patients use Alternative Medicine: Results of a National Study', *Journal of the American Medical Association*, 279: 1548–53, 1998.

15   M. Angell and J. Kassirer, 'Alternative Medicine – The Risks of Untested and Unregulated Remedies', *New England Journal of Medicine*, 339: 839–41, 1998.

16   European Herbal Practitioners Association (EHPA)'s March 1999 Position Paper to the European Union.

17   'Should Herbal Medicine-like Products be Licensed as Medicines', *The British Medical Journal*, 310, 22 April 1995.

18   JA Austin, 'Why Patients use Alternative Medicine: Results of a National Study', *Journal of the American Medical Association*, 279: 1548–53, 1998.

19   S. Gottlieb, *American Medical News*, 10 July 2000.

20   www.oncology.com, 22 November 1999.

21   R. Happle 'The Essence of Alternative Medicine: A Dermatologist's View from Germany', *Archives of Dermatology*, 134: 1455–60, 1998.

22   www.oncology.com, 22 November 1999.

23   Notable exceptions do exist, such as Prozac.

24   'Top Singapore brands: Tiger Balm', *Singapore Trade News*, 4, 1999.

25   The distinction between these two groups and the medical profession's consternation with the growing numbers in the former, is borrowed from James Le Fanu MD, *The Rise and Fall of Modern Medicine* (Carroll and Graf, 2000).

VII

Conclusion

18 The future of branding in the pharmaceutical industry

TOM HARRISON Omnicom

One could make the argument that pharmaceutical marketers have not produced any brands that occupy a consistent and compelling mindshare over time as consumer marketers have done. There is no pharmaceutical equivalent to Coke, 'the number one cola' for decades; to BMW, 'the ultimate driving machine'; or to Burger King, 'the best place to get a big burger'.

This is not because marketers in the healthcare segment are any less sophisticated than in the consumer arena. Indeed, they utilize many of the same segment analytics, assess emotional and rational behavioural drivers and, overall, employ the same branding techniques as classic consumer marketers. The inherent nature of the healthcare arena is the main inhibitor to brands remaining significant competitors over time. That is, healthcare products enjoy a relatively short period of brand exclusivity before they lose patent protection and multiple, non-branded, lower cost generics are allowed to compete in their exact market space. This is the pharmaceutical marketers' ultimate and unchangeable dilemma. Branding, with all the emotional and core value appeal that can exist in the consumer market, is improbable, if not impossible, in the healthcare arena. As a result, branding has fundamentally meant life cycle optimization.

Until recently, the physician was the most powerful healthcare decision-maker, and all branded messages were targeted to him or her. The doctor wielded power over choice and decision making. So many changing market dynamics have substantially altered this classic picture: the role and impact of government and managed care, the increased influence of constituency groups and public health workers, and the fundamental responsiveness of the consumer. While the pendulum of power is slowly swinging back to the physician, the physician is just one important audience to whom the marketer needs to communicate a focused branded message.

Today the pharmaceutical marketer has the ability to target and market a whole new audience beyond the prescribing physician. We can now talk to the consumer – the end-user, the patient. With the emergence and impressively rapid growth in the direct-to-consumer (DTC) marketing arena – and its convergence with traditional, direct-to-physician marketing – and recognizing the awareness and power of selectivity now in the hands of the consumer, I would advance that there has been no time in the evolution of pharmaceutical marketing in which absolute branding is so crucial. Physicians must be selectively targeted and loyal franchises must be built with groups of consumers to create a branded strategic advantage. With such a short time to recapture the inordinate investments during the tortuous road from molecule in the test tube to brand on the pharmacy shelf, the healthcare marketer must be sophisticated and initiate the process of accelerated branding at the earliest possible stage of development.

No longer can we wait, as in the past, until the final clinical package is handed over to the marketing department to begin the branding cycle. Indeed today, the full commercial potential of the prospective product must be assessed concurrent with the establishment of the clinical studies required to gain regulatory approval of the new drug entity. The commercial team must be involved with the clinical development team. These teams together must envision the vision of the brand. They must be in total agreement as to the commercial potential of the brand, what the marketplace will look like and how it will behave when the new brand is approved, what specifically the competitive landscape will be, how physicians will be prescribing, what the consumers' needs will be, what specific rigorous clinical studies will need to be performed, and what type and number of patients will need to be accrued and followed throughout the clinical study phases. In short, it is at the earliest stages that the architectural marketing blueprint must be laid down and followed to build the ultimate brand, the potential blockbuster that, if branded and marketed successfully, will quickly be a significant corporate balance sheet asset.

There are two brand categories of healthcare products. One focuses on wellness, maintaining good health. These are the nutraceuticals, the functional foods that are taken by those consumers that have embraced Eastern strategies for healthcare. While I do not wish to focus on these products specifically, the Eastern appeal of preventive medicines is gaining momentum, is expected to grow dramatically, will impact prescription therapies and will seek a delicate balance with traditional medicines. Nutraceuticals have the appeal of health and wellness.

Western therapies, on the other hand, treat illness. This is not a subtle differentiation – Eastern wellness, Western illness – but one that must be considered as branded communications are directed to the consumer. Western medical orientation treats established illnesses as opposed to preventing illness. Both seek to maintain health. A legitimate place needs to be made in Western medicine for the nutraceuticals. Physicians today are just beginning to recognize and accept the trend towards Eastern modalities of wellness. While it is not what is taught in their medical training, the notion that non-FDA sanctioned substances may confer health and wellness is being somewhat reluctantly embraced by physicians today.

Patients want to be healthy or returned to good health. Physicians want to confer good health. They want to restore health with the most appropriate, specifically targeted and safest medical product available.

Four years ago the unmistakable boom of the first baby boomers turning 50 was heard, and since then another boomer turns 50 every eight seconds. What the recent surge of DTC advertising and promotions has revealed to us about this one group is their overwhelming interest in self-care, preventive therapies and palliative treatments for themselves, their parents and their children. They remain aggressive consumers of information.

Patients have become strong advocates of their own healthcare. They do their own research, whether by traditional means or the Internet – facilitated websites specific to particular conditions or disease status. Patients actively discuss medications with their doctors who have lost, at the hands of managed care, much of the power they once enjoyed. Time will tell whether this power will return fully, but today physicians and their patients discuss healthcare and treatment options, and if a patient asks for a particular treatment, he or she will most likely have it prescribed if it is deemed clinically appropriate or equivalent to a more routinely prescribed alternative. So, in essence, more power has been conferred on the patient than at any point in history to help to arrive at patient acceptable yet physician appropriate treatments.

Once the physician has prescribed a particular brand for a particular patient, it is then up to the physician and now, more often, the pharmaceutical manufacturer to ensure compliance. This is accomplished through permission-based traditional or Web-enabled one-to-one relationship building between the pharmaceutical company and both the prescribing physician and the patient. At no point in our history have value-based relationships been so important to the growth of pharmaceutical brands. Companies must support the rational decision to prescribe a specific brand, manage information for the patient about that brand and the particular indication it treats, help to manage potential untoward effects of the brand and build customer equity and loyalty towards the manufacturer.

So, branding efforts are begun earlier in the products' lifecycle, at the clinical development stage, and branding strategies directed to the physician and his patients must be designed to establish both market and mindshare.

Branding strategies to rapidly build share incorporate a fluid spectrum of integrated tactical elements including traditional advertising and promotions; more non-traditional, well-poised public relations channels; evolving direct marketing channels; and Internet-enabled, permission-based, original content communications to consumers and physicians. Thus brand communications will not necessarily be on our terms, but will be available to our audience when they want to receive them. The Internet will become a much more powerful vehicle for branding and communications. Increasingly, physicians and patients will seek content from Web sources. Content is king, but original content will win out over repurposed traditional information.

The blending of all channels will create effective branding that will aggressively capture mindshare and withstand the on-demand rigours of this marketplace. Branded communication will need to be on call – available when our audience wants it, consistently channel to channel, and, as always, peer-reviewed to meet the most stringent clinical scrutiny.

On the whole, more will be invested to create a brand that will compete over the short period of brand exclusivity. And, more capital return will be realized because the integration of efficient and effective branding strategies will focus on more appropriate, more productive and more highly targeted physician and patient populations.

This chapter has not specifically mentioned global branding. The concepts herein are relevant both locally and globally. It is evident that the industry is moving towards more global branding – more uniform and consistent messaging worldwide. While consistency for branding is significantly important, just as important is the recognition of local market sensitivities that might dictate variance of message. Brand experts must understand the subtle differentiation between markets, rationalize them and weave them into the global brand communications. Perhaps a somewhat better term for this sensitive, worldwide branding is 'glocalization' – globalization that recognizes and embraces local subtleties.

Appendix

Interbrand's Billion Dollar Brands

Rank 2000 (1999)		Brand	Country	Brand Value 2000 ($m)	Brand Value 1999 ($m)	% change
1	(1)	Coca-Cola	USA	72.5	83.8	−13
2	(2)	Microsoft	USA	70.2	56.7	24
3	(3)	IBM	USA	53.2	43.8	21
4	(7)	Intel	USA	39.0	30.0	30
5	(11)	Nokia	Finland	38.5	20.7	86
6	(4)	General Electric	USA	38.1	33.5	14
7	(5)	Ford	USA	36.4	33.2	10
8	(6)	Disney	USA	33.6	32.3	4
9	(8)	McDonald's	USA	27.9	26.2	6
10	(9)	AT&T	USA	25.5	24.2	6
11	(10)	Marlboro	USA	22.1	21.0	5
12	(12)	Mercedes	Germany	21.1	17.8	19
13	(14)	Hewlett-Packard	USA	20.6	17.1	20
14	(−)	Cisco Systems	USA	20.1	*	*
15	(20)	Toyota	Japan	18.8	12.3	53
16	(25)	Citibank	USA	18.8	**	**
17	(15)	Gillette	USA	17.4	15.9	9
18	(18)	Sony	Japan	16.4	14.2	15
19	(19)	American Express	USA	16.1	12.5	28
20	(24)	Honda	Japan	15.2	11.1	37
21	(−)	Compaq	USA	14.6	*	*
22	(13)	Nescafé	Switzerland	13.7	**	**
23	(22)	BMW	Germany	13.0	11.3	15
24	(16)	Kodak	USA	11.8	14.8	−20
25	(21)	Heinz	USA	11.7	11.8	−1
26	(27)	Budweiser	USA	10.7	8.5	26
27	(23)	Xerox	USA	9.7	11.2	−14

Rank 2000 (1999)		Brand	Country	Brand Value 2000 ($m)	Brand Value 1999 ($m)	% change
28	(26)	Dell	USA	9.5	9.0	5
29	(29)	Gap	USA	9.3	7.9	18
30	(28)	Nike	USA	8.0	8.2	−2
31	(31)	Volkswagen	Germany	7.8	6.6	19
32	(17)	Ericsson	Sweden	7.8	14.8	−47
33	(30)	Kellogg's	USA	7.4	7.1	4
34	(37)	Louis Vuitton	France	6.9	4.1	69
35	(32)	Pepsi-Cola	USA	6.6	5.9	12
36	(36)	Apple	USA	6.6	4.3	54
37	(−)	MTV	USA	6.4	*	*
38	(53)	Yahoo!	USA	6.3	1.8	258
39	(−)	SAP	Germany	6.1	*	*
40	(43)	IKEA	Sweden	6.0	**	**
41	(−)	Duracell	USA	5.9	*	*
42	(−)	Philips	Netherlands	5.5	*	*
43	(−)	Samsung	S. Korea	5.2	*	*
44	(−)	Gucci	Italy	5.1	*	*
45	(33)	Kleenex	USA	5.1	4.6	12
46	(−)	Reuters	UK	4.9	*	*
47	(35)	AOL	USA	4.5	4.3	5
48	(57)	Amazon.com	USA	4.5	1.4	233
49	(39)	Motorola	USA	4.4	3.6	22
50	(41)	Colgate	USA	4.4	3.6	24
51	(34)	Wrigley's	USA	4.3	4.4	−2
52	(44)	Chanel	France	4.1	3.1	32
53	(40)	adidas	Germany	3.8	3.6	5
54	(−)	Panasonic	Japan	3.7	*	*
55	(50)	Rolex	Switzerland	3.6	2.4	47
56	(42)	Hertz	USA	3.4	3.5	−3
57	(46)	Bacardi	Cuba	3.2	2.9	10
58	(45)	BP	UK	3.1	3.0	3
59	(48)	Moët & Chandon	France	2.8	2.8	0
60	(49)	Shell	UK	2.8	2.7	4
61	(47)	Burger King	UK	2.7	2.8	−4
62	(51)	Smirnoff	UK	2.4	2.3	6
63	(38)	Barbie	USA	2.3	**	**
64	(52)	Heineken	Netherlands	2.2	2.2	2
65	(−)	Wall Street Journal	USA	2.2	*	*
66	(54)	Ralph Lauren/Polo	USA	1.8	1.6	11
67	(55)	Johnnie Walker	UK	1.5	1.6	−6
68	(58)	Hilton	UK/USA	1.5	1.3	12
69	(−)	Jack Daniels	USA	1.5	*	*

Rank 2000 (1999)		Brand	Country	Brand Value 2000 ($m)	Brand Value 1999 ($m)	% change
70	(–)	Armani	Italy	1.5	*	*
71	(56)	Pampers	USA	1.4	1.4	–2
72	(–)	Starbucks	USA	1.3	*	*
73	(59)	Guinness	UK	1.2	1.3	–3
74	(–)	Financial Times	UK	1.1	*	*
75	(–)	Benetton	Italy	1.0	*	*

Source: Interbrand/Citibank

* New entry
** Not comparable to 1999 valuation due to improved data availability

Big Brand Groups

Rank 2000	Brand	Country	Brand Value 2000 ($m)	Brand Value 1999 ($m)	% change
1	P&G	USA	48.4	49.2	–2
2	Nestlé	Switzerland	40.3	38.8	4
3	Unilever	UK	37.1	33.9	9
4	Diageo	UK	14.6	13.7	6
5	Colgate Palmolive	USA	13.6	11.3	20

Source: Interbrand/Citibank

Index